Klaus W. Bender

Moneymakers

Klaus W. Bender

Moneymakers

The Secret World of Banknote Printing

WILEY-VCH

WILEY-VCH Verlag GmbH & Co. KGaA

The original edition in German *Geldmacher* was published by
Wiley-VCH Verlag GmbH & Co. KGaA
in 2004.

1st translated edition 2006,
revised and updated.

1. edition 2006

Library of Congress Card No.:
applied for

British Library Cataloguing-in-Publication Data
A catalogue record for this book is available from the British Library.

Bibliographic information published by Die Deutsche Bibliothek
Die Deutsche Bibliothek lists this publication in the Deutsche Nationalbibliografie; detailed bibliographic data is available in the Internet at
<http://dnb.ddb.de>.

Printed in the Federal Republic of Germany

Printed on acid-free paper

Composition DTP-Studio Michael Bechtold, Mörlenbach
Printing and Binding Ebner & Spiegel GmbH, Ulm
Cover Design init GmbH, Bielefeld

ISBN-13 978-3-527-50236-3
ISBN-10 3-527-50236-X

To S*A*M*I

The money that we possess is the instrument of liberty, that wich we lack and strive to obtain is the instrument of slavery.

Jean-Jacques Rousseau, *The Confessions of Jean-Jacques Rousseau*, Book I (translated by W. Conyngham Mallory)

Emporer: There is no money. Well then, get it now!

J. W. Goethe, *Faust II*, Act I, The Emperor´s Palace (translated by George Madison Priest)

Contents

Moneymakers, Klaus W. Bender

ISBN: 3-527-50236-X

Moneymakers II

Money Losers

Money Jitters

Preface

We have banknotes, these precious pieces of paper, in our hands daily. Paper money invented by the Chinese! One thousand years later, the American colonists were the first ones in the Western world to systematically use it, even financing their revolution by issuing huge amounts of dollar bills. Modern life would, in fact, be unthinkable without it. Nevertheless, the general public is kept quite in the dark about how banknotes are made or who makes them. The world market for banknote printing – the special printing machines and the security inks, as well as the fully automated machinery for high-precision banknote inspection or the highly secure shredding machines for used notes – is dominated by European companies. Private banknote printing itself is completely controlled by a handful of European high-tech companies. All this is almost unknown to the general public. Such secrecy is regularly justified as being a consequence of the intense security surrounding the production of this very special product. It is, however, also the result of the highly politicized structure of the market in which central banks, as well as state and private banknote printers, operate. The situation is not dissimilar to that reigning in the armaments industry. In an open society, however, this obsession with secrecy is out of place, since banknote printing involves the massive use – and often waste – of public funds.

Take, for example, the almighty U.S. dollar, the epitome of America's economic might and world influence. The Fed's own printing works today churn out almost 9 billion dollar notes a year. The two printing plants operated by the Bureau of Engraving and Printing are considered models of efficiency. Yet their undisputed success is built on European high-security printing technology. The greenback would even look pale without its European high-security inks. In banknote security and the fight against

Moneymakers, Klaus W. Bender

ISBN: 3-527-50236-X

counterfeiting, however, America pursues a policy distinctly different from Europe's approach. The cost in terms of counterfeited notes has been high for the dollar, as illustrated by the appearance of the so-called superdollar. This is a counterfeit 100-dollar note of such high quality that the laity cannot distinguish it from a genuine 100-dollar bill. The mystery of who is making these perfect counterfeits has not yet been resolved. The American government is blaming the Stone Age, communist regime in North Korea for being the author of the supernote and conducting economic warfare against the United States. However, this book reveals for the first time that these supernotes might well be printed at a top-secret printing works run by the CIA, located not far north of Washington D.C.

Moneymakers, by offering a detailed view of the banknote industry and its modus operandi, removes the industry's carefully imposed shroud of secrecy. The only previous attempt to reveal this story was published in 1983 by an American author. However, the entire edition of that book was bought up – straight from the printing presses – by two prominent representatives of the industry to prevent the public from getting an inside view of the business. That book is impossible to find today. Now the curtain is lifting on this secretive industry.

The institutional culture of secrecy surrounding the high-security printing industry has served, as would be expected, to mask business arrangements hardly in the public interest and practices of sometimes rather questionable ethical standards. In fact, firms holding monopolies on materials can practically hold central banks –and through them, the public – for ransom. Here new research reveals for the first time the full story of Gualtiero Giori and his »Giori System.« This mechanical engineer of Italian-Swiss origin has developed a system of multicolor intaglio sheet-fed printing presses that revolutionized the world of banknote printing. With the help of the German machinery firm Koenig & Bauer, Giori convinced central banks to build expensive but frequently superfluous printing works. Moreover, additional new material shows how Giori cleverly managed to thwart a Japanese attempt to copy his machines, successfully preserving his control of the world market for banknote printing machinery. Of course, some private banknote printers, fearing the loss of important customers, tried with many dirty tricks to stop the advance of Giori's machines. This book tells the story of one private British banknote printer who, fearing the loss of his Egyptian customer, informed the Egyptian secret service that the machinery they were about to order from Giori would be »of Jewish origin.«

Yet, in the embattled world of high-security printing, the »license to print money« and the sometimes gigantic profits pocketed are not a foolproof guaranty for success. There is, for example, the story of the Swiss inks maker Albert Amon. Sailing in the wake of his close friend Giori and his new machinery, Amon developed a new line of high-security inks, which in the end gave him almost total control of this very special market on a global scale. One brand of Amon's security inks, a color-shifting ink called »optically variable ink,« sells for up to 1,950 dollars per kilo. Despite such exorbitant pricing, the two sons of Albert Amon, who took over from their father in the nineties, managed to get their family company into very serious economic trouble. And there is the private British banknote printer and papermaker De La Rue, which for decades ruled the world market for banknotes. However, a sequence of management mistakes committed by rapidly changing CEOs has reduced this once proud company to a shadow of its former self. Not even efforts to strike secret deals in order to fix prices or divide markets could avert that fate. It was this British company which, after the fall of the Berlin Wall, convinced Poland to destroy a complete issue of brand new banknotes worth 35 million Deutschmarks (20 million dolars) in printing costs by claiming that the banknotes printed by their German competitor were »no good." De La Rue then reprinted other new bills for Poland but soon lost the contract – because of too many misprints.

There is also the story of the German private banknote printer Giesecke & Devrient, which was almost completely destroyed during the Second World War. Under its charismatic and aggressive owner, Siegfried Otto, it became the only fully vertically integrated, high-security printing company in the world, including everything from paper to printing, to banknote inspection systems and shredders for used banknotes. However, Otto's cupidity and that of his two sons, who because of their own greed were disinherited by their father, threw his company into a deep crisis that still affects it. Furthermore, for the first time the story is told of how the Bundesdruckerei, the highly respected German federal banknote printing works, at that time probably the most modern printing plant in the world, was brought to the brink of bankruptcy during its privatization by noisy posturing, lack of vision, and rapaciousness. Rapaciousness also spelled doom for the Ciccone brothers and their Ciccone Calcogràfica in Argentina. They dreamt of becoming the first high-security printing company in the Southern Hemisphere – and of the continuous high profits to be made in banknote printing. The firm's highly leveraged expansion into high-security printing, however, drove it into the arms of a gang of international mafiosi. In two sting operations, which smell of the Belgian and French secret services and could have been taken right from the script of a Hollywood film, the brothers printed »genuine fake banknotes« for Zaire and Bahrain. The company in the end had to seek protection from its creditors under Chapter 11.

It was said in the beginning that today the high-security printing industry is a European industry. It may not be so for much longer. The writing is on the wall. It is the common European currency, the euro, which has forced upon the private high-security printing industry a process of profound change, the end result of which is completely open.

For the first time this book relates the politically as well as technically painful paths towards a true common currency. This book describes the extremely cumbersome decision-making process in Europe even when it comes to such an important issue as the common European currency. Since everybody wanted to share the advantages of a common currency but not relinquish any of his national prerogatives, the whole endeavor turned sour. This book describes for the first time how the involvement of too many paper suppliers and printing works – public as well as private – pushed up the production cost at the same time as lowering the quality of the new Euro notes, because not all of the state printing works involved in the printing of the euro notes were technically up to the job. This is the main reason for the steady increase in counterfeit euro notes. In Europe, in fact, phony euro bills by now have replaced fake dollar notes as the most counterfeited currency. And it explains how the introduction of the new currency has served as an excuse for the dominant state-owned high-security printing works to build up huge capacities. Now these capacities are underutilized, and the highly subsidized state printing works have started to look to the world market for banknote printing for additional orders to fill their capacities. The private high-security printers depend on this world market. The euro was supposed to further competitiveness and efficiency in Europe, not to kill the industry. If nothing is done soon to reign in the state printing works with their dumping prices, the very future of the private high-security printers as a European industry is at stake.

Money Magic

1
From ›obelos‹ to ›e-cash‹

Fresh cash – paper money. What can be more exciting and invigorating than a handful of crisp, new banknotes that have never been folded? Maybe not for some, like Howard Hughes, the mystery-shrouded American oil magnate. He suffered from chrometophobia, the fear of money, a clinically documented disorder. How ironic can destiny be. We run our fingertips with relish over the engraved rills and ridges of a banknote, hear the creaseless bill crackle dryly when pressed between our fingertips, and savor its scent of fresh printer's ink. In the modern world, with its division of labor, life without money is inconceivable. We use money as a measuring unit in pricing a transaction, offer it as a medium of payment in settling a debt, and make it a store of value for our savings. This is the stuff that makes dreams come true. Yet when and how exactly did it come to pass that we began to prefer this abstract »money« – the »third good« – to the concrete value of a real good in a trade? The answer is hidden in the dawn of civilization. The most exotic of media were employed during the slow transition from simple barter to free trade: bricks of pressed tea leaves in Tibet and southern Siberia, stone slabs with drilled holes on the island of Yap, cakes of salt, axes, cooper rings, glass beads, cowry shells in Africa, and many, many more. Rarity, stability of material value, and sometimes also the simple matter of durability determined the selection.

The priests of antiquity probably were the first to ponder the invention of the abstract good »money.« They wanted tribute of lasting value, payments that could be compared with one another, for their sacral services, such as fertility rites and oracles. The idea of money germinated comparatively early, in Mesopotamia in the fourth millennium before our modern time measurement. The Sumerians set fixed quantities of metal – gold, silver, also copper at times – because they grew tired of measuring,

Moneymakers, Klaus W. Bender

ISBN: 3-527-50236-X

weighing, and examining every item separately, again and again. That was the first near-money. But Pheidon, the tyrant of Argos according to Greek chronicles, first took the step to the minting of coins in northern Peloponnesus at the transition between the eighth and seventh centuries before the Christian era. He had two aims in mind: fostering trade and strengthening his own authority. This was the dawning of the right to strike coinage. Judges of that time received for their verdicts a wage of roasting skewers, *obelos*[I], from which derived their claim to a certain number of cuts of meat from the sacrificed animal. Pheidon had the clumsy obelos collected and replaced with coins, which the people called *obolos* in a slight linguistic shift. The next higher coin was then called *drachma*, which originally signified a »handful of roasting skewers.« Our Latin-derived concept of »obolus« comes from the »obolos.« Hence the creation of money as a quasi-religious act! Other sources, of course, cite a later moment of birth and another cradle. According to them, the Lydian king, Alyattes (ca. 619-560 B.C.) caused the first true coins to be minted in western central Anatolia. Hardly coincidental, it was also Alyattes who built the first permanently installed vending shops in history. He used electrum for his coinage, a naturally occurring alloy of gold and silver. The gold and silver content of these coins fluctuated widely, hindering their acceptance. For this reason his son, Croesus (560–546 B.C.), whose riches remain proverbial to this day, caused the first gold and silver coins to be minted. He guaranteed their content of precious metal. That is, however, what was passed on by Greek historian Herodotus. The Greek also let on that he was not much impressed by Alyattes' »new economy.« The religious link to coins – substitutes for cuts of meat from a sacrificial animal – was long preserved. In ancient Rome the coins in the temple of Juno Moneta, located today on the Capitoline Hill, were minted by priests.

We have the Chinese to thank for paper money. They also invented paper in the first century of our Christian era. The first historically documented paper money appeared during the first Tang Dynasty (618–907 A.D.), a flourishing political and economic period in China. It was certificates of deposit, namely receipts for precious metals held in custody for someone else. These receipts were executed by private persons and widely accepted as a medium of payment in trade. Emperor Hien-Tsung (808-821 A.D.) declared the issuance of these deposit certificates to be the privilege of his fiscal authority. The copper for his coin minting had supposedly become scarce. Possibly he was also looking for a new source of revenue, for the bearer of the emperor's deposit certificates had to pay interest. In return he could tender the certificates everywhere in the realm to imperial authorities as a credit toward payments. They were even accepted in meeting tax liabilities. This was the first government paper money in history. Regular issues of monetary notes then began with the Sung Dynasty (960-1279 A.D.). People spoke of »flying money.« Traders loved it. Foreign trade experienced an unexpected upswing. A specimen of this oldest surviving monetary paper note in the world is preserved in the money museum of the Deutsche Bundesbank in Frankfurt. It is a piece of blue-black colored paper, with dimensions of 34 by 22 centimeters, made from the pulp of the bark of the mulberry tree. The inscription shows it to be a »state banknote of the Ming Empire« worth 1,000 *cash*, as the monetary unit was called, and issued by the new Mongol rulers during the »era of the horrible war« (1368-1398). A whole bundle of these notes fell into the hands of the international expeditionary corps at the storming of Peking during the Boxer Rebellion. This occurred when a grenade shattered a statue of Buddha and the monetary notes concealed in its base spilled out.

In the description of his travels, the Venetian Marco Polo (1254–1324) was the first to report this invention of the Chinese. The first banks were developing in Italy at exactly that time.[2] Bills of trade and promissory notes were being executed in swelling numbers. They offered better protection against loss of assets in the extremely dangerous travel by land and water in those times, for in the event of a mishap or a robbery, gold and silver coins were lost. But promissory notes could not be cashed by unauthorized persons. These slips of paper with handwriting on them made their way to the farthest corners of the known world. They still were not banknotes. The dominance of coins would not change for centuries, despite the many forgeries and the deliberate manipulation and devaluation of gold and silver coinage. One still had to wait for Johannes Gutenberg and his invention of moveable type with reusable letters for printing before the Western world would make its acquaintance with the advantages of paper money.[3] The spread of paper money was rather sluggish even thereafter. An important stage on the way to the banknote was the founding of Amsterdam's Wisselbank in 1609. It issued interest-bearing certificates against deposits and introduced a clearing system for drafts. Customer receipts for precious metals deposited and stored with the bank came later. When endorsed, they could be used in lieu of cash for the settlement of payments without money.[4] The mission and goal of this bank for bills of exchange was to promote payments traffic without cash. It is no wonder that the Dutch then played a leading role in foreign trade. The Wisselbank, however, was not permitted to extend credit. It was the English who took this step. King Charles I (1600–1649) – he was later to be beheaded for this – had his subjects' silver inventories that were stored in the Tower of London confiscated. He needed money again at that time to finance his Scottish wars. London's powerful goldsmiths thereafter took over the job of safeguarding, in their own storage vaults, the precious metal of their frightened clientele. That was more secure. On demand, they made out deposit certificates, »goldsmith notes,« for these deliveries. These were negotiable and could even be cashed in fractions of their face value.

Europe's first true banknote was issued in Sweden in 1661. People there were lugging around as pocket money copper plates weighing as much as 20 kilograms. At the suggestion of Johan Palmstruch of Riga, the Stockholms Banco issued banknotes denominated in silver or copper thaler. The bank, initially private and later government-run, soon became insolvent as a result of its excessive lending. This progression was to repeat itself with a certain regularity during the coming century. The right to issue paper money at that time still belonged to the banks, however. There was neither supervision of their issuing activities nor did they bother to coordinate the discrepancies in maturities of short-term (precious metal) deposits with mostly long-term lending. Therefore, insolvency was inevitable. The breakthrough for paper money in the form of banknotes came in 1694 with the founding of the Bank of England – the mother of all central banks – by a private investors' consortium. It was formed in response to yet another royal plundering of the Tower of London, this time organized by William III of Orange (1650–1702), who then occupied the British throne. He had been running short of money for his military campaign against the French. The private Bank of England was allowed to issue banknotes and extend credit, but it was obliged to maintain a certain coverage ratio to its own deposits of precious metal.[5] The »Bank of England notes,« issued against customer deposits and allowed to circulate freely, supplanted the goldsmith notes. Paper money had finally established itself. The crown was compensated with generous loans for the privilege granted the private Bank of England. Wars and the necessity to finance them were henceforth to be *the* driving force behind the triumphal march of paper money.

Paper money experienced its first, albeit short-lived, flowering on the continent at the beginning of the 18th century, thanks to the imagination and persuasiveness of, of all things, a professional gambler from Scotland in the service of the French. John Law of Lauriston (1671-1729) was a notorious philanderer, a card player with a phenomenal memory, and a financial genius all in one. Sentenced to death by a London court for manslaughter in a deadly duel but rescued with the help of influential friends abroad, Law surfaced in France when it was paralyzed by an economic crisis. Louis XIV, the sun king, had left behind for his subjects not only considerable territorial gains and monumental structures upon his death in 1715 but also a gigantic national debt. It corresponded to 25 times the yearly tax revenues. Not even a minimal interest payment on the debentures was possible. In a memorandum to the crown, the Scotsman recommended an expansive fiscal policy to resuscitate the economy. The volume of (paper) money should no longer be constrained by coverage with precious metals. Instead, the national assets, such as natural resources, population, and technology, should be invoked as the basis for measuring the volume of banknotes. This was supposed to serve as investment capital to develop France's overseas colonies, especially Louisiana in America. This would soon revive government financing and the economy in the mother country, Law promised the crown. With »national resources« as a yardstick there was no limit to imagination. Paper money could practically be issued at will. The Scot received a hearing with the regent, the prince of Orleans. Law took over all the outstanding national debt and promised to pay back the nearly worthless paper at its nominal value in precious metal when it fell due. All he asked in return was permission to found a private bank and the privilege of issuing his own banknotes. Even the share capital of this bank, Law & Co., could be subscribed partly with payment in government paper. His bank then indeed granted credit in great volume, divorced from its deposits of precious metals. This was the moment of the birth of money creation, of wealth based on paper. Goethe, also highly adept in economic matters, erected a literary monument to Law's monetary theory in his *Faust II.* The invention of paper money was presented there as a continuation of alchemy – the attempted conversion of lead into gold – by other means, and the process of money formation was subtly insinuated as masquerade.[6]

The Scot had promised the regent to make all citizens rich, and he also bequeathed to modern times the appropriate term of »millionaire.« His concept was so successful at the start that the court, in its perpetual shortage of money, hurriedly nationalized Law & Co., renaming it Banque Générale. It was exactly this initial success that fired up speculation with the bank stock issued by Law. The unavoidable collapse followed in train. The experiment of an imaginative Scotsman with his paper money failed because of the exaggerated profit expectations from the business with the overseas colonies and the indifference of his borrowers – including the many political enemies Law had made at the court – toward productive investments. Capital flowing in from England and Holland – »hot money,« one would say today – contributed substantially to the crash. Banque Générale went bankrupt in 1720 after three turbulent years. Law had to flee and died penniless in Venice a few years later. The French currency of that time was called *écu,* by the way. It's understandable that this name struck the experts as rather inappropriate for the European common currency three hundred years later. Also, because of that turbulence the topics of paper money and monetary stability have remained inseparably linked. The substantive erosion of the value of coinage had already enraged the Greek philosopher Diogenes in the third century before Christ. Coined money is a »dice game of politicians,« he fumed. The erosion of value through public mismanagement also marred the introduction of paper money, for both absolute rulers and democratically elected politicians have treated the »government's pledge of value,« which was necessary to make paper money a generally accepted payment medium, with downright carelessness in the sweep of centuries. Paper money was to shed its value even more quickly than money coined of gold and silver. The scandal with Law and his bank, by the way, had devastating consequences for Europe, dragging half the continent down in tow. France's economy would not recover from the shock until many years later, when the French Revolution broke out and the new rulers of the country nationalized church property as a way of meeting the tremendous costs of the revolution and its wars. Therefore, interest-bearing payment drafts, called *assignats,* were issued in great volumes in anticipation of the proceeds expected from the sale of the confiscated church assets. Creditors had to accept this paper in lieu of cash. The idea perhaps was not ethical but it was financially sound, since the assignats were backed by assets, the clerical lands. The French economy slowly started to recover after decades of stagnation and destitution. But this recovery was brief. Mismanagement and corruption reduced the proceeds from the sale of nationalized property far below expectations, devaluating the assignat. In addition large quantities of counterfeited assignats, printed by the royalist émigrés in Great Britain with the expressed blessings of William Pitt´s government and brought to the continent as contraband, were flooding France. After a few years the assignats were not even worth the paper they were printed on. The last bit of confidence in paper money was destroyed. The lasting preference of Frenchmen for gold as a store of value has been attributed to those bad experiences with Law's paper money and with the assignat.

The decisive chapters in the history of paper money were actually written in the New World, in the »land of unbounded possibilities,« where even a »tobacco-leaf currency« had circulated widely since the first third of the 17th century.[7] The tax burden imposed by the British colonial rulers rose steadily there. The scarcer precious metals – and therefore money – became in America, the more strident became the demands for independence from Great Britain. Even playing cards cut into pieces served at times as a substitute for money. Benjamin Franklin, whose portrait today adorns the 100-dollar note, had already called for more freedom for the colonies in the printing of paper money in an essay in 1729. Franklin was a printer by trade, which might also explain his interest in paper money.[8] London's repeated refusal to consider these demands and the issue of paper money by banks on their own authority in the insolent colonies then contributed to the outbreak of the American Revolution in 1775. Independence was won, but monetary stability was frittered away. The massive issuance of paper money by the Continental Congress to finance the revolutionary army – diluted by the massive printing of counterfeit money by the beleaguered colonial rulers – ended in hyperinflation. Between June 1775 and November 1779, it authorized no fewer than 42 dollar issues for a grand total of 241.6 million dollars, an incomprehensible amount in those days.[9] The loss of value of the *continental*, the currency of the breakaway states – even became a saying: »not worth a continental,« it was said in derision.

It took a long while before the independent United States of America struggled back to monetary stability. Decades of uncontrolled issuance followed. There were paper monetary notes from thousands of local – sometimes tiny – banks, and a rising tide of counterfeits of these simple notes. »Wildcat banks« were what ordinary people called those banks that carelessly printed banknotes and cared little about their backing by precious metals. Their headquarters were concealed so that only a wildcat could find them, the citizens complained. But one could only exchange the paper money for gold or silver at those main offices. The government was divided on the matter of whether the central government would have to take over the issuance of banknotes and guarantee their value. A bitter dispute about this raged among politicians during the first half of the 19th century. The flood of dollar notes, genuine and phony, backed by gold and silver or not, was enabling the immigrants flooding into the United States from Europe to purchase property, making possible the settlement of a vast, nearly empty country. Not until 1863 did Congress suspend the – often fictitious – convertibility of all these circulating banknotes and ordain with the National Banking Act the introduction of uniform national banknotes, entrusting their issuance exclusively to the Treasury Department. This was the moment the greenback was born. It was named after the dominant green color on the reverse side of the dollar notes.

All this did little good for the idea of the banknote. Its range remained limited, at least in Europe. Initially that was quite in line with the interests of the issuing banks. They, of course, had to pay out the equivalent value of a tendered note in precious metal on demand. »I promise to pay the bearer on demand ...,« is printed even today on British banknotes, although one cannot envisage anymore a disbursement of pieces of gold in exchange for the proffered paper note. The fear of counterfeiting was already great in those days and the production of banknotes was expensive. Smaller denominations of notes would have a destabilizing effect in the event of a crisis because of their greater proliferation, it was feared. The banks avoided the issuance of notes with low face values. Banknotes remained the privilege of commerce and the more prosperous classes of society. The Bank of England was even forbidden by its by-laws until 1793 to issue banknotes with face values of less than 20 pounds sterling, a considerable amount at that time. In rural France people still got along largely without paper money through the end of the 19th century, paying with coinage instead. The Banque de France didn't issue its first banknote of less than 500 francs – the annual wage of a worker at that time – until 1847. And in the German Empire the issue of a Reichsbank note that was less than 100 marks did not occur until 1876. A Reichsbank director still could complain at the beginning of the 20th century that the wary German people have to be forced to make use of paper money.

Paper money by then had long since established itself even in Europe, for, after the Napoleonic wars, more and more countries had taken the production of paper money into their own hands, declaring their paper monetary notes alone to be »legal tender« – while the precious metal backing was reduced in stages and then entirely abandoned. Henceforth, every citizen – and the government – would have to accept paper bills in redemption of debt, although the citizen was not obliged to use them for other payments. Even the obligation to accept the legal tender, both coins and notes, is not really compulsory, however. The legal department of the European Central Bank cites an example of a justifiable refusal: if the creditor had unilaterally announced certain payment terms before the contract was made, if he and the prospective customer had previously agreed upon compensation other than cash payment (check, EC debit card, money transfer), or if the payment offered would violate recognized principles of reason and fairness. The airline ticket to a tropical vacation paradise cannot be paid with the contents of the piggy bank, however well fed with coins it might have been. In any event, recurring bursts of inflation have weighed heavily upon the reputation of paper money. For example, Germany was literally inundated with worthless emergency banknotes during the period of hyperinflation after the First World War. In the most extreme form these ended up printed on one side and posted in notebook binders. The final break with the era of gold backing came in 1971, when U.S. President Richard Nixon, in order to avoid a devaluation of the dollar, dispensed with the obligation to exchange dollar balances for gold. By that time, this obligation had still only existed toward central banks anyway. The last hurdle on the way to the printing of *fiat money* was cleared. Paper money merely offers the authorities a still cheaper way to cheat the people than had already been the case with coinage, railed liberal national economist and Noble laureate Friedrich A. von Hayek in his later essays. The best thing is to abandon it again, he said.[10]

The Chinese, the inventors of paper money, had briefly toyed with this thought in the 13th century. Counterfeits were appearing too frequently. »Anyone who turns in a counterfeiter to the authorities will receive a reward and the confiscated assets of the perpetrator« was printed right on the cash notes mentioned. Thus, the Chinese also simultaneously came up with the punitive sentence. It is quoted on banknotes in watered-down form to this day. But the genie was out of the bottle. Trade and development had become too easy with (paper) money. No one would like to do without it anymore, not even Karl Marx and his disciples. Vladimir I. Lenin, the father of the socialist revolution in Russia, had to »postpone« the planned abolition of money. It was supposed to be officially abolished when Soviet citizens were so richly supplied with all the goods for their daily needs that they no longer needed money as a medium of exchange. That socialistic paradise never became reality. Not even a utopian revolutionary like Mao Tse-tung could envisage a life without banknotes. When his soldiers finally reached their refuge in the loess caves of Yunnan at the end of their casualty-strewn Long March straight across China, the printing of their own renminbi people's currency was among the first administrative measures of the newly proclaimed socialist state of workers and peasants. Since there was no paper, they helped themselves to linen cloth. Cut into small rectangular pieces, this cloth was printed on one side as revolutionary money. The paper money collection of the Hypovereinsbank in Munich owns several of these linen-cloth banknotes.[11] The only serious attempt to do without this »symbol of capitalist exploitation« is passed on from the »Stone-Age communism« of Pol Pot. When the Khmer Rouge took power in Cambodia in 1975, as eye-witnesses reported, they broke open the vault of the central bank, threw bundles of banknotes out the windows, and reveled in the sight of freshly printed notes sailing on the wind through the streets. Even they later came to their senses. Yet before these communists got around to issuing their own banknotes, the neighbor from communist Vietnam put an end to their bloody regime.

The value of banknotes is not just measured in numbers. Banknotes are the calling cards of governments, even the bearers of subtle political messages.[12] Business travelers and tourists size up the unfamiliar paper money in their hands upon arrival abroad, unconsciously getting their first impression of the unknown that awaits them. In many countries banknotes have become the symbol of national identification and an integration factor. The greatest artistic, aesthetic, and technical care is lavished on their preparation for this reason as well. The Finish state bank, Suomen Pankki, for example, chose an aspect of the monument the Finns had erected in the center of Helsinki to Alexander II, the Russian czar, for their 20 Finn mark note in 1897.[13] It was a hidden message to Nicholas II, the czar then reigning in St. Petersburg, not to interfere with the autonomy granted by Alexander in 1809 to the (Russian) grand duchy of Finland. Kaiser Wilhelm II was less subtle in these matters. He not only adorned his 1908 banknote issue in the 100-mark denomination with a wary-looking Germania under a German oak, her hand menacingly on the hilt of a sword; on this note he also had a formation of battle ships martially steaming through the seas of the world to serve notice that the German empire would advance to become the world's second-largest sea power.[14]

Banknotes as symbols of the issuing countries are also regularly examined by the central banks for authenticity and physical condition, on average three times a year. This procedure occurs fully automatically at least in the European common currency sphere and guarantees a uniformly good condition of euro banknotes in all twelve member countries – or at least it is supposed to. Even the health of banknotes, their hygienic condition, is tested continually and in strict secrecy in laboratories. Out of concern about carcinogenic substances, for example, the central banks had the usual animal gelatin for the surface coating of banknotes replaced with synthetic products. This prolonged the longevity of the banknote – and raised the bacterial contamination of paper money. Nevertheless, the spread of AIDS viruses with banknotes belongs in the realm of fables. Also China's concern in early 2003 that the deadly SARS virus could be spread by banknotes could more easily be explained by the general hysteria than with laboratory findings.[15] Nevertheless, the Bank of China systematically sequestered all surrendered banknotes for 24 hours, the assumed life span of the SARS virus, before putting them back into circulation. Naturally, bacteria and viruses can also be transmitted by a banknote, but that is more likely to happen from contact with a door knob that has just been handled by an acutely diseased person. The hygiene test conducted by a Bristol institute in 1999 did reveal that 99 percent of the used notes it had been furnished by the Bank of England showed traces of cocaine. Lest anyone get the notion that the absurd price spikes of the IT-bubble may have been the crazed handiwork of habitual coke sniffers in the City, the Bank of England intervened. It was not so much the cocaine dusting but rather that a few of the very dirty notes would have contaminated the sorting machines, it was said in a hastily drafted press release from the Old Lady of Threadneedle Street, as the Bank of England is called with good-natured irony.[16] By high summer of 2002 this »machine contamination« had apparently spread to Germany. A test conducted by the Institute of Biomedical and Pharmaceutical Research in Nuremberg showed that nine of ten euro notes it examined exhibited cocaine residue.[17]

Even if a banknote were »contaminated,« one ought to think twice about destroying it. When a famous courtesan of the court of Louis XIV tried to display her wealth by devouring a promissory note worth 500,000 francs at a party one evening, the courtiers worried only for the financial health of her benefactor. But when the French chanson singer Serge Gainsbourg torched a 500-franc note before running television cameras in 1984 to protest what he regarded as excessive taxation of his income, an outcry reverberated through the republic: Sacrilege! A hail of charges ensued. Gainsbourg went unpunished. The law that prescribed punishment for such willful destruction had just been repealed by court edict. The fractious bard would not have gotten off so easily in the United States of America. The deliberate destruction of a greenback there amounts to an insult to the national pride. The Deutsche Bundesbank is more tolerant. The loss of an asset by willful destruction of a Deutschmark note would be punishment enough for the perpetrator, it said laconically when asked. Nothing of this pragmatic stance has changed under the aegis of the European Central Bank.

Ideologues haven't succeeded in putting the coup de grace to cash. Yet the issue of the future of money, particularly the banknote, has not gone away. What has been commonplace for centuries needn't apply forever. Experts in many central banks and research institutes brood over the question of what volume of paper money might still be needed in coming years. The threat comes from two directions: from counterfeiters and from alternative payment instruments. Ever more sophisticated and cheaper devices for high-tech reproduction – PCs, scanners, and color printers – are available to those who would copy money. These can be mixed and matched to suit individual requirements. With them the forgers can make, as needed, copies of notes of a quality that would have been inconceivable twenty years ago. The future of the banknote as a payment medium rises and falls with the unshakable trust of the citizen in the security of his banknotes. The greater the exertion to heighten security against copying, the higher the production costs of the banknote. The manufacture of money consumes money – the money of the taxpayer. It is obviously more and more important to make paper notes with the greatest security, but at acceptable costs.

Recommended again and again as an approach to cost suppression has been the replacement of banknotes of paper with those of plastic polymers. Haiti made a beginning with plastic notes in 1974. These were produced by American Banknote, which has since dropped out of the ranks of banknote printers. It was a glorious flop. The printer's ink rubbed off completely in a matter of a few weeks in the humid tropical climate. The notes had to be pulled from circulation. Another twenty years elapsed before Australia switched completely to plastic, this time a polymer substrate, for its banknotes. Since then nearly a dozen countries in the torrid zones have at least experimented with issuing such a polymer note. Those countries include Brazil, Brunei, Indonesia, Mexico, Papua-New Guinea, Romania, Taiwan, and Thailand. Even socialist Vietnam is currently converting all its banknotes to polymer notes. The conversions were often done with help from the Australians, who wanted to export the polymer substrate in order to defray the extra cost of its production costs with the additional demand. Polymer notes cost considerably more to make. But they also have a substantially longer longevity than paper money, making them cheaper in the end. At least that's what is said by their proponents, principally the petrochemical industry that serves as the supplier. The opponents of plastic money counter that for security reasons a plastic banknote cannot be kept in circulation as long as the material would otherwise allow and would be necessary also to amortize its cost. The destruction of the huge mountain of plastic banknotes that are no longer suitable for circulation each year would also become an environmental problem. Naturally, it is especially the manufacturers of secure paper who are leading the charge against plastic notes – and they double as the leading private printers of banknotes. For purely aesthetic reasons, in any event, plastic notes are a nightmare. They feel like recycled Aldi discount grocery bags, an observation made not just by the business magazine *Wirtschaftswoche.*[18]

The second threat to the banknotes arises from the alternative instruments of payment. The more harmless challengers appear in the form of economic alternatives rooted in local civic pride. All around the world, in Australia, Brazil, England, France, Germany, Japan, and the United States, thousands of organs are sprouting that promote their own »local money« by taking clever advantage of legal loopholes. Services there are redeemed in coupons under a fixed system of valuation. Local tradesmen accept the coupons as a payment medium. This is supposed to stem the outflow of money, stimulating the local economy and spawning jobs. Legal tender is not supposed to be abolished, but merely complemented.

A more serious challenge that is hard to measure is posed by the electronic age and »e-cash,« electronic money or »e-money,« e-commerce, and Internet banking. There is no shortage of forecasts of the end of the banknote. At a Washington conference in the mid-1990s a representative of the Federal Reserve Bank of Cleveland had already predicted that money would one day be replaced by electronically actuated account movements, much as precious metal backing once was by paper money. The speaker even foresaw the possibility that e-money created by private entities could one day compete with the coins and banknotes issued by the governments.[19] It was reminiscent of the debate two hundred years ago in America over the role of government in emitting paper money. In historical retrospect money has steadily lost its physical substance, something also confirmed by the Deutsche Bundesbank in an extensive study on the subject.[20] Cash transactions now make up only 5 percent of the whole payments traffic in Germany.[21] Why, then, have paper money, if there can be access to the balance of a bank account in real time, if e-commerce instantly makes possible price comparison and purchase and if the plastic card or Internet banking enable the payment of any purchase without problems? Compared with more than 2 trillion dollars – a 2 with 12 zeroes – in virtual accounting money that darts daily around the planet by cable or satellite, the 200 billion pieces of issued banknotes do not seem very impressive today, regardless of how large their denomination. Banking and commerce are no friends of cash. They would only too gladly dispense with it because the handling of money costs them a lot of money. Sorting, checking, and counting – this work has to be done daily. The accrued cost amounts to tens of billions of euros in the Euro-zone alone. Yet, in their initial euphoria, the purveyors of Internet services underestimated the problems of payment. Electronic payment has to be »user-friendly« and, especially important for the customer, it has to be safe from abuse. The damage done by fraud within Internet banking and electronic payment systems far exceeds the losses from forged banknotes. These issues have defied a technical solution thus far. The moment one can pay without pulling a crispy banknote out of a wallet still seems to lie in the distant future. Money is just as much a social contract as it is an object or a technology, warned another speaker at that same conference. Its utility in a given form depends entirely upon the general acceptance of that form.[22] And this form is still the banknote of paper.

Banknotes have cogent arguments on their side. They are incomparably cheap in daily use because there are no service charges attached – at least none that the customer notices, even if they are heaped upon him in the opaque pricing of the product he obtains. They offer him a high degree of security because no computer hacker can eavesdrop on the transaction and clean out his account. They can be used (nearly) as often as one cares to. And they are absolutely anonymous because banknotes leave no trace – much to the chagrin of the internal revenue agency. Surveys in Europe and overseas unanimously confirm that the citizenry clings stubbornly to its payment habits with paper money. Widespread fears of potential abuse, plus ignorance and indifference, as well as the cost of additional safeguards for the connection between the card and the net, have so far obstructed the breakthrough to electronic money. The Bundesbank study mentioned here did indeed show that only 67 percent of the turnover in German retailing was still paid in cash in 2002, compared with 79 percent in 1994, while in that same period the share of purchases made with card-based instruments rose from 6 to 29.5 percent. Yet, this growth was attributable to the »pay-now« debit card, which is now equipped with the personal identification number (PIN) just as the EC card. In 2001 more than 1.2 billion transactions worth nearly 90 billion euros were settled with such debit cards, meaning that the number and value of transactions with debit cards had doubled in just four years. The »pay-later« credit card, on the other hand, had a much harder time because of the tedious examination of credit-worthiness, awkward settlement, and high additional costs for overdraft interest. Compared with the debit card, it rolled up only one-third the turnover value, accomplishing that only thanks to its popularity in flight and hotel bookings. The share for the »pay-in-advance« cash card, onto which the user has to transfer an amount from his account, is now so small that it plays no role in the statistics.

The question is not whether there will still be paper money in the future but rather what future role banknotes will play in modern life and what reputation they will then have, concluded Thomas A. Ferguson, director of the Bureau of Engraving and Printing, in his presentation.[23] The sensuous feel of cold cash in the hand will sustain the banknote for a long time to come, believes Ferguson, whose government printing plant after all prints the world's reserve currency, the dollar. It will take a while before electronic money replaces the banknote and central banks start issuing virtual e-money instead of crisp banknotes.

2
Why the market for banknote printing is special

We know a great deal about money in theory and practice. We know who manages it, why its buying power and exchange rates rise and fall. Yet about those who make the banknotes we know next to nothing. There is no other industrial product in the world that everyone handles so much and so often. Nor is there any other branch of industry that is so hermetically sequestered from public view. And no other is so shrouded in mystery as the printing of banknotes. The manufacturers, governmental or private players, take great pains to hold their cards close to the vest. This obsession with secrecy seems anachronistic in the age of the Internet. For the printing of notes is not just a sophisticated technological production process. The industry is also in the throes of a profound restructuring process. And after all, this involves the use of taxpayer money because it is the citizen who pays for the printing of banknotes.

The printing of banknotes and the closely associated manufacture of secure paper form the core of this high-security branch of industry. Yet there is much more to secure printing. There are checks, securities, passports, personal identifications, driver's licenses, tax forms, stamps, lottery chances, tickets to big events, and airline tickets. And in recent years there are also the magnetic strips and chips in the plastic cards for controlled access, payments traffic, cellular telephones, and health insurance services. In the broader sense, the suppliers also belong to this industry. They provide the special cylinder molds for the making of secure paper, the printing machines for securities, the serial numbering machines, and electronic testing devices. The list goes on with pre-print products, special ink colors, pigments, security threads, holograms, foil strips, and other – sometimes highly secret – security features. None of these machines and supporting materials, whether new or used, can be had legal-

Moneymakers, Klaus W. Bender

ISBN: 3-527-50236-X

ly in free trade. And the sale of a used intaglio printing machine is routinely reported to the international police authority Interpol in Lyon. This is a production process for which, apart from the highest discretion, the greatest accuracy is also required. No other industrial product brings together such an array of complex materials in the production process while simultaneously demanding such incredibly tight tolerances, observed the printing trade magazine *Print Week* with a whiff of self praise. The printing of banknotes is high technology. Only a small, exclusive branch of industry offers this. Here, everyone knows everyone else personally, including the customers – one's own and those of the competitors. Regularly – and many would now say too frequently – the representatives of the central banks, the security authorities, and their more or less independent advisers meet to exchange views, strictly by personal invitation and always at gorgeous, selected locations in posh, chosen hotels.[I] They are acutely conscious of their craft and their products and see themselves as confidants of the governments. The competition is hard, often bitter. Yet they remain in constant contact with one another, help one another out with printing capacity in all secrecy, and are sometimes ready to forgo a bidding war – not exactly to the customers' advantage.

Secret and farcical

Those who delve into the inner workings of this security branch can expect to find both the secret and the farcical. That was shown some years ago at a meeting in the fine Roman hostelry, Grand Hotel Excelsior. An Italian cognoscente of the branch very privately related the fascinating story of the Swiss-Italian Gualtiero Giori. Rino, as everyone knew him, developed the printing machines for the multicolor intaglio or engraved printing, which printed with such precision and therefore offered such effective protection against forgery that no high-security printer in the world could operate any longer without them. »Intaglio« (from *intagliare*: engrave) as a technique for working metal plates goes back to the Milan armories of the Renaissance, which used such plates to decorate their ceremonial armor. This process was taken over as engraving or etching in the painting and printing arts. Gualtiero Giori, as the insider told it, revolutionized with this technique the multicolor printing of banknotes and securities. Yet Signor Giori was not only an ingenious designer but also a brilliant salesman. He had a de facto worldwide monopoly on the market for machines that print securities. At De La Rue plc. (DLR), the English high-security printer in London, he sealed a deal in which he would be paid a license fee of 2 percent of net income for every single note printed on his machines. De La Rue was then the largest private printer of banknotes in the world. At the end of the 1980s it was producing more than 5 billion notes a year, providing a tidy little sum to Gualtiero Giori.

This story fit the prevailing notion of banknote printers, with their legendary profits, as people with »a license to print money.« A verification of the licence fee-story, of course, would be sought in vain in the secretive world of secure printing. Yet an article based on this scant information then found its way into the newspaper with the effect that the author of this book subsequently received an invitation to chat with Gualtiero Giori, for whom a luxurious suite had been reserved in the aforementioned hotel for many a year. Signor Giori, an imposing presence in his elegant, gray double-knit of the finest cloth, was athletically trim and sun-tanned, a man with a striking face and not an ounce of extra fat around the midsection. He wanted just one thing from his guest: the name of the informant. When the author did not reveal this despite persistent questioning, Giori after a pregnant pause remarked almost as though he were talking to himself: »That could only have been my son!« The visitor was back in the hotel corridor within a few minutes, sent off rather ungraciously with the comment that »the published assertion, of course, has no basis in fact.« Long afterward, a confidant of Signor Giori confirmed that the quoted license fee did very well exist. The episode took place some years ago. Gualtiero Giori died in 1992. His son, Roberto, has since sold the company built by the father. Yet the episode still left an impression. To begin with, it made clear that the public knows nothing about the manufacturers of banknotes or the way the notes are made. Second, it was apparent that secure printers react sensitively to every attempt to dope out the secrets of their branch and make them more transparent.

Those who seek information on secure printers in libraries and newspaper archives will find scarcely anything. There is a wealth of glossy volumes with colorful pictures of banknotes. Their expensive format arouses the suspicion that their financial backing – and editorial »guidance« – comes from a central bank. But there is little of substance about the secure printers themselves. Such a thick curtain of silence is spread over hardly any branch of industry other than the manufacturing of banknotes and everything associated with them, bragged the publication distributed to a restricted audience in 1977 for the 125th anniversary of the founding of Giesecke & Devrient GmbH (G&D) of Munich.[2] The Munich people know what they are talking about. This tradition-steeped family company is one of the oldest private printers of banknotes in the world and is today the biggest high-security printer of them all. Even the few exchange-traded companies that produce for this branch as suppliers, such companies as the printing press manufacturer Koenig & Bauer AG of Würzburg, systematically omit from their annual reports any statements on their business in the segment of the printing of securities. Publicity is undesired. There is no public advertising for their products. At the start of the 1980s an American journalist tried for the first time to take a peek behind the scenes of this branch of industry.[3] As historic literature, his book practically cannot be found, even in the largest libraries: Gualtiero Giori and his friend, Albert Amon, an entrepreneur of the printing ink industry, bought up the edition in all haste in order to keep it out of circulation. Eyewitnesses later saw the pile of books in the cellar of Le Mont, Giori's technical center above Lausanne.

Attempts to engage representatives of the industry in conversation while doing research for this book were systematically deflected. Questions submitted in writing or asked on the telephone went mostly unanswered. Central banks would say nothing. Lawyers banned contacts on orders from the companies. Press officers and their promotional agents speculated about the motives of the author asking questions. Who´s paying you? was more than once their rejoinder. Companies resorted to evasion, entered into international cabals of secrecy, and delays occurred wherever possible. In a nutshell: They reacted only under the pressure of facts, when there was no other way out. The festive publication of Giesecke & Devrient called for »absolute professional discretion by *all* persons knowledgeable of the making of printed monetary instruments.« That is justified by the safeguarding of one's own production process and the fiduciary relationship to the customers. Professional discretion and imposed secrecy are also commonplace in other industries. In the contractual arrangements of the high-security printers, however, they are set forth in particular detail. They extend far down through the company hierarchy and still apply to persons for many years after they leave the companies. Whoever breaches these agreements has to expect sanctions that can be painful. This aspect was repeatedly cited by those refusing to be interviewed. Those who did speak would only do so »off the record,« so that they would not be quoted by name. However, as long as it was about their competitor – in the broadest sense – many interview partners then turned out to be downright forthcoming.

Monetary sovereignty, meaning the exclusive right to issue money, whether as coinage or banknotes, underpins every state. The right to strike coinage is vested in the finance minister and serves as a welcome additional source of revenue for the budget. The production and issuance of paper money, however, is entrusted exclusively to the respective central banks with only very few exceptions, such as Hong Kong and Singapore. In all the larger countries today, the central bank allows its banknotes to be produced in the government printing office under its control and keeps an Argus eye out for any incursion on its influence. In the early days of paper money, during the 19th century and into the first half of the 20th century, this wasn't yet the case. A few private printers of banknotes dominated the world market in those days and they dictated the prices. Those countries that could afford to have their own government printing establishment for banknotes could be counted on two hands. This changed completely after the Second World War. Technical innovations in the design of printing machinery, which will later be treated in detail, then caused the smaller countries to discover the printing of banknotes as a »sovereign task.« Measured by the number of individual banknotes produced, the government printing offices easily have the upper hand today, while the private printers, or commercial printing works, have receded in significance. This is one of the causes of their tense relationships with one another.

The production of banknotes is industrial production »sui generis« (unique), asserted Banca d'Italia. For this reason fiduciary printing (from the Latin *fiducia:* trust), as the printing of banknotes is also called, merits special protection in the production process. With that, the Italians are reciting the credo of many central bankers for whom not just the issuance but also the manufacture of the banknotes is assumed to be a sovereign task. They derive from this the consequence that the production of notes has to be reserved for their government printer and that commercial printing establishments cannot be trusted with the manufacture of such a sensitive product. A publication on the subject of printing banknotes could awaken greed and anxiety in the public, worried a senior representative of the European Central Bank in the course of research for this book. Indeed, the idea that the citizen should blindly trust an arbitrary notation of value printed upon a rectangular piece of paper that is no longer guaranteed coverage by precious metal can hardly be understood rationally and probably reflects only the force of habit – or deeply rooted faith. Nothing captures the inexplicable, indeed irrational phenomenon of modern paper money better than the term coined for it by economists in the English-speaking world, namely the term *fiat money*, as mentioned before. It amounts to the creation of »value« out of nothing – scarcely by coincidence reminiscent of the creation myth of *fiat lux!* – let there be light. Money has value because it is universally accepted, once scoffed German author and émigré Kurt Tucholsky, and it is universally accepted because it has value. Abuses of any type would indeed diminish confidence in the banknote – instantly and permanently. But the assertion that the printing of banknotes is and must remain a sovereign task of government is not rendered more persuasive by this. Only the issuance of banknotes is a sovereign function. For their production, where what counts are quality and cost, this doesn't apply. An analogy is offered by the armaments industry. Private industry is allowed to produce weapons; only the state, with its monopoly on violence, may put them to use.

It is not without cause that the high-security printing branch is so named. In the general public, the extreme requirements for security are known best in the transportation of banknotes. A special transport can move banknotes by the millions. Depending upon the denomination here, an amount in the billions of euros rolling along the highways is easily conceivable. No wonder the timing of deliveries from every banknote printing plant is a tightly guarded secret – even internally. Nor is it any wonder that this valuable cargo is escorted by special, heavily armed guard detachments. But the requirements for security and secrecy are also extraordinary in the production and storage of banknotes. The production plants are designed with special security criteria and sometimes resemble true fortresses. The strict observance of security regulations is under sharp surveillance by the plant's own control and security service. Personnel coming in contact with banknotes, especially those ready for delivery, are hand-picked. In Germany a clean police clearance is a requirement for employment in this production sector. Russians and Indians once quartered their entire workforce in sequestered living areas – and sometimes still do today. In many a printing plant the worker has to strip and don overalls without pockets before commencing his work. The printing room is off limits to visitors, even representatives of central banks. The exception to this rule is the printing plant of the Bureau of Engraving and Printing in Washington. A second one in Fort Worth, Texas, is off limits, however. At the printing works of the Bundesdruckerei or Giesecke & Devrient in Germany the printing area can still be viewed, but only with written permission from the Bundesbank. And even then the machines may be covered with cloths. The guest is not supposed to learn the country for which the current printing order is being executed. Controls are standard at the entrances to the printing and packing rooms, where every person who goes in or out is recorded. If a particularly secret characteristic material is being made or processed, absolutely no one is allowed to enter or leave the space affected. Every movement in the printing room of a modern banknote printing plant today is, of course, recorded by video camera. And the film is kept for a long period, sometimes years. In some printing plants there are surprising controls. None of those present in the printing rooms are allowed to stir from their work stations when an acoustical signal is sounded and they are then searched by security guards. Visitors may be randomly controlled at the plant gate of, for example, the paper factory of Louisenthal. A record is kept of every step in production, be it printing or paper making; every aspect of the work is tallied anew and measured. Printing blanks, cut sheets of paper, misprints, simply everything is meticulously documented. This record must be turned over to the relevant committee of the customer, the central bank, when the printing order is completed. In particular, all misprints without exception have to be turned over to the customer for destruction. The paper may only be delivered in a specially prescribed form, namely as a so-called ream of 500 sheets with the edges exposed so that the number of sheets can be checked. Only unusable paper upon which nothing has been printed may be destroyed at the scene, a procedure that must also be documented. If a defective machine has to be repaired, especially during the final surveillance of finished banknotes or in the packing plant, the »four-eyes« principle of security is used, despite uninterrupted surveillance of all work by video cameras. Two employees, one of them from the internal security detachment, together open the machines with two separate keys. Thanks to today's transparent plastic coverings, these machines are hermetically sealed. It is without a doubt an industry with exacting security requirements.

The desire of the producers, printers and their suppliers, and of their customers for secrecy in the business of banknotes is, of course, also associated with the unusual structure of this branch of industry. The production of banknotes is a market without a market price. In the printing of banknotes as in the procurement of paper and supporting materials such as security features and secure colored inks, there are public contracts. If a state printing plant is involved, the contracts have to be put out for bidding. But the number of bidders – like the number of purchasers – is very limited. As one central banker put it, negotiation takes place in a bilateral quasi-monopoly. There is also a nearly irreconcilable contradiction between the often enormously cost-intensive development work and the subsequent compulsion to allow only a few potential contractors to bid. Apart from the printing of banknotes alone, suppression of costs through mass production is impossible. For example, if a process or a security feature developed for banknotes could also be used to protect products such as branded merchandise, it would automatically become worthless for note printing. To combat counterfeiting, exclusivity is absolutely compulsory. This exclusivity of the product on offer has to be compensated with a price premium, which must be negotiated between the supplier and the customer. Yet to what extent can this still be justified if there happens to be, for example, just one single supplier of a certain production material in the whole world? Where does the abuse of market dominance begin? Moreover, why should a private printer haggle tenaciously over an advantageous price with a supplier of secure printing inks or a special security characteristic if he can pass on these extra costs to the customer without any problem, raising his own compensation in this way? Perhaps there would even be a nice special commission in this for him from the material supplier for not energetically bargaining the price down. The danger of market and price cartels cannot be overlooked. Officially competing suppliers can easily structure their bids so that there is something for everyone.

In the so-called Third World especially, it is often comparatively poorly paid officials who decide on the awarding of multimillions in contracts for the printing of banknotes. The attempt to exert improper influence on the decision needn't proceed from the supplier. It is hardly probable that one could raise the actual requirement of a country for banks notes with illegal gratuities, but one certainly can influence the selection of suppliers. Everyone in this branch on both sides of the Atlantic knows the problem. No one has reason to point the finger at another. The cost of bribery to German industry was quite legitimately entered under the line item »N.A.«- which means in English the catch-all phrase `useful expences´ - and was even eligible for tax deductions until a few years ago if the charges were taken abroad. The Swiss customarily treated bribery with similar nonchalance – so long as it involved foreign countries. The Organization for Economic Cooperation and Development (OECD) in Paris has for years sought greater transparency in public procurement. It declared war on corruption. An international convention was adopted in 1997 and has now come into force. Even before it widely took effect, Germany in 1998 was among the first countries to incorporate this convention into its national laws. Pragmatic Britain took its time. For the reality has changed but little. In many countries a bidder hardly needs to come forward if he is unprepared to match the demands for baksheesh. The industry knows how to help itself. It has detoured to countries, such as the Arab Emirates, which haven't signed the OECD convention. These countries are often tax oases as well, meaning that one can kill two birds with one stone.

A market, but no market price

The market for printing banknotes has a somewhat confusing structure. The overwhelming majority of banknotes are produced by state printing plants that are merely subordinated departments of the central banks. Such a government printing establishment – Italy offers an example – needn't worry about its cost structure. There are also a few state printing plants that have been privatized pro forma but whose share capital is still mostly or wholly held by the central bank – for example, Austria. One can assume here too that the central bank as the owner naturally shoulders the costs – buildings, security, personnel. The smallest group in terms of numbers and market share is the private printers. They all operate on the principles of the private marketplace and are all profit-oriented but depend in quite different degrees upon the market. Some print mostly the national currency – and with attractive prices – under contract from the central bank. Examples are Orell Füssli of Switzerland and Enschedé of the Netherlands. A second group is permitted to share in the well remunerated printing of the national currency but works mainly for the export trade, such as Giesecke & Devrient. And finally, there are still those private printers that are excluded from printing the national currency, at least to date, for example De La Rue in Britain and Francoise Charles Oberthur Fiduciaire in France. But something is stirring here, as shall be explained later.

Official data on the volumes or value of the world market in banknotes are unavailable. The British consulting firm Secura Monde International Ltd. (SMI) of Kingsclere in Berkshire estimates that a total of 180 or 190 billion units (individual banknotes) are in circulation for a current world population of at least 6 billion. The printing volume is pegged by SMI in the range of 85 to 95 billion units a year. Most of that is required to replace notes taken out of circulation. Both estimates seem too low. Walter Schlebusch, who is responsible for the whole division of banknotes and paper as an executive of Giesecke & Devrient, estimates a global circulation of well above 200 billion banknotes and a printing volume of more than 90 billion units, with 80 billion of them printed by the state printing plants.[4] At least 45 billion of those units are produce by just four countries, namely the United States in two government printing plants, Russia with its two, India with four, and China with six. With their annual 20 billion individual banknotes, the Chinese are the world's leader. Sometimes, however, these notes are only half as large as the face of a cigarette pack. In building up their gigantic capacity in which three paper factories are also included, the Chinese once even leveled a mountain and forcibly resettled a village – including the top soil for its farmers. The idea that the Chinese with their huge production capacity especially in banknote paper one day might turn to the export market does worry quite a few in the industry. The extremely taciturn Indians follow in second place with a yearly requirement estimated at 16 billion units. This is likely to rise sharply in coming years with the sustained modernization of the country and the new policy of the »clean banknote.« Apart from the share of the state printing plants – whether government-owned or privatized in name only – one comes up with a volume of 10 billion units a year for the free market in banknotes. Subtracting the share of printing that is only allocated and not put to bid, one comes up with the *available market in banknotes.* Only this is open to private printers. Its current volume ought to be somewhat more than 8 billion units a year.

The requirement for banknotes depends upon the degree of economic development and the climatic conditions. A rule of thumb in the industry holds that the population in the temperate zone has to be multiplied by ten in order to calculate a country's approximate yearly requirement for banknotes. The replacement need is higher in humid regions. High-security printing costs a lot of money. The necessary investments far exceed those of a commercial printing establishment. The printing machinery and the extensive security installations, especially for the construction of security vaults, swallow a great deal of money. Depending upon the cost of the property, little can be done for less than 80 million euros. For this one can procure a line of printing machines that can produce as many as a billion units a year, depending upon the number of shifts worked. And this often coincides with a national requirement for banknotes of fewer then a hundred million units a year. Despite that, 64 of the 191 members of the United Nations currently afford themselves the luxury of a state printing plant for banknotes. The others have their notes produced abroad. And for security reasons, it better not be with a next-door neighbor, if at all possible. Most of these countries contract the work out to one of the private printers authorized by their central banks. The central banks keep a list of potential suppliers, screened according to stringent criteria, because the state printing plants will work for foreign countries only in exceptional cases. It sometimes happens that a government has to include a private printer in the production of its banknotes because its own state printing plant – sometimes for reasons that are hard to fathom – isn't able to deliver on time. Such printing orders, called *overspill* in professional jargon, naturally occur only irregularly. But they can then amount to a volume of several billion individual notes. Around 20 countries are regularly forced to let such overspill contracts. Overspills are supposed to be put out for bid. Under time pressure, however, they are often contracted without bidding. In this case the contracts are especially well paid and are commensurately coveted.

Estimates of the contracting value in the business with banknotes are sketchy because of the highly diverse cost structures of the individual providers. One can assume, however, that the dominant state printing plants produce more expensively than the private printers. Yet a deafening silence is maintained by the central banks and their state printing plants on their actual costs. A report by SMI for the venture-capital firm Apax in the summer of 2000 still quantified the global contracting value at about 6 billion euros a year. That's a highball number. The estimate is based on figures for a specific period in which the fear of bottlenecks in the cash supply at the turn of the millennium, the Y2K effect, shifted note printing into high gear. The Bureau of Engraving and Printing, for example, printed 11.3 billion dollar notes in 1999 instead of its customary number of just under 9 billion. And the printing of the large first issue of euro notes had also just started. In the wake of the euro's introduction, the global requirement for banknotes has normalized again in the meantime. The global volume of sales in 2004 is likely to have been around 4 billion euros (see Table I).

Note printing is a tight market. That's what makes the business so difficult. On one hand, the possibilities of differentiating the product are limited; banknotes are comparatively homogeneous. On the other hand, the rise in demand, although continual, has slowed markedly. Population growth, economic expansion, and inflation are the three main factors that determine the demand for banknotes. Growth today amounts to only 2 or 3 percent a year. It used to be 5 percent. This current pace is slower than the growth of the world's population. In the industrialized countries, which loom large in the statistics, the additional demand resulting from population growth, which is weak there, and from economic activity is disproportionately low. This demand is also offset partly by alternative payment media, such as credit and debit cards and electronic cash. Things look different in the countries of the so-called Third World. Not only is population growing strongly there, but also the monetization of the economy, the transition from barter to a money economy, is in full swing. This process still is also mostly associated with higher inflation.

Table I: Estimated sales volumes of the world market for banknotes (2002)

Bureau of Engraving and Printing (BEP) 7 billion units at the average price of 43 dollars per 1,000 notes	301
Printers of euro notes, government and private 4.8 billion units at 100 dollars per 1,000 notes	480
»Free market« for private printers without euro share 10 billion units at 62 dollars per 1,000 notes	620
Other government printers outside euro zone 74 billion units at 38 dollars per 1,000 notes	2,812
Total world market for printed banknotes Estimated printing volume 95.8 billion banknotes	4,213

The printing market is subject to considerable fluctuation. In the year 2004, for example, BEP printed 8.7 billion banknotes and the euro printers 1.6 billion.

The private printers love this mix of population growth, monetization and inflation. It bestows a steadily climbing requirement for banknotes, because the technical conditions for electronic payment are still missing in the emerging countries, with certain exceptions. But this does not mean that the printers of banknotes would fire up inflation in the countries with which they do business. The responsibility for monetary policy lies exclusively with the respective government and its central bank; the printers of banknotes deliver only a product.

Essentially only three private printers still divide up the available global market. They are all located in Europe: the British De La Rue, the German Giesecke & Devrient, and the French Francois Charles Oberthur Fiduciaire. Together they have a market share of around 90 percent, although there are considerable gaps between them. The Dutch Enschedé and the Swiss Orell Füssli, both known as private printers of outstandingly secure and technically excellent banknotes for their national banks, carry little weight on the free market. Those others in the circle of non-government banknote printers from Europe or the two Americas, which have tried their luck in this so prestigious and difficult market, have failed in past years because of the technical requirements or because of their own business ineptitude. Astonishingly, that applies to the tradition-rich American banknote printers. Without exception, they have had to beat a retreat from banknote printing.

The securities printer must be of the »most honest, upright, reputable character,« a Swiss trade magazine proclaimed half a century ago.[5] Much has changed in the world since then, but people have become scarcely more considerate and deferential in their choice of weapons. In the struggle for market share no quarter is given. Every trick to drive the competition away from a desirable printing contract seems allowed, even punches below the belt. The collection of newspaper reports on a competitor's scandal with tax and billing practices was more than once sent to his clientele of national banks by another private printer. A manufacturer of secure paper in the United States caused first-class counterfeits of 100-Deutschmark notes to be fabricated in his research laboratory in order to persuade a Turkish customer that even the German secure paper for the Deutschmark with its partly exposed security window threads wasn't really safe from forgery. Or, at the IMF and World Bank meeting in Hong Kong in 1997, the central bank governors found in their mail drops an extensive report on the embarrassing printing mistake of a private printer.

In such an environment it is easy to imagine that occasional marketing assistance is rendered with the help of a friendly intelligence agency. After all, close ties are traditionally maintained with these agencies. It is not just cooperation in the fight against counterfeiters. Every secret service in this world must now and then forge or counterfeit something for itself: passports, identifications, and banknotes. This skill isn't taught in any of the world's technical colleges, only in the high-security printing establishments can the government agents learn this skill. The Bundesnachrichtendienst, Germany's national intelligence agency in Berlin, previously Pullach, and the federal printing plant, the Bundesdruckerei, would have a few items in stock, not to mention the traditionally close relationship of the private printer De La Rue to the Foreign Office and Her Majesty's Secret Service.

Despite the ever tougher competition, the production of banknotes remains a lucrative business for the private printers. Payment as a rule is made in hard money – not in the colorful bills that one has just printed for some potentate. Discipline in remittance is high. Yet in the countries of the so-called Third World there is often a shortage of negotiable currency. Unfortunately, these are the best customers of the private printers. But who's going to take a deadbeat central bank to court? The battle for the available market rages usually among the three private printers mentioned. In a pinch, though, this trio closes ranks in the field against the state printing plants, especially when the state printers calculate their costs at the margin because they want to embark on a fishing expedition with their excess capacity.

No private printer of banknotes would publicly name the countries for which he prints. Even the once common company insignia of the printer, which was even required by law in some countries such as Great Britain and was hidden somewhere on the note, has largely fallen out of fashion. Central banks would go »absolutely wild« over disclosures of business relationships, is how the private printers like to explain their anonymity. There are other reasons. Globalization has long since caught up with elite high-security printing, too. A market transparency and competition once unknown now prevail among private printers. The loyalty of the central banking customers has declined noticeably. Much to the distress of the private printers of banknotes, they easily switch suppliers today from issue to issue. Even central banks – some at least – are increasingly concerned with cost suppression and attempt to keep their inventories of banknotes as low as possible. Thus the order volumes they commission are falling steadily and the time intervals between orders are becoming shorter and shorter. Details betray this change. The printing plates, in principle the property of the customers, used to stay with the printer in secure storage in his vault. If a national bank called for the return of its plates because it wanted to change printers, it could happen that a valuable printing plate would »accidentally« brake into pieces during transport. Today, many national banks insist upon immediate return of the printing plates just to hold open the option of switching printers. The once revered banknote is losing its mythical aura and degenerating into a simple trading commodity, complain many in the industry. The pendulum is swinging from one extreme to another.

The fat years of high-security printing are over. More than a quarter century of economic expansion and spreading prosperity in large parts of the world, if not everywhere, have stimulated the demand for banknotes and securities of every type. The whole branch, including machinery manufacturers, materials suppliers, or security printers, has profited from this. The first cautious warning signals were given at the end of the 1980s, when this branch began to complain about excessive capacity and falling prices. The opening of Europe's East ushered in another boom. But that, too, was soon history. Then began the displacement of physical securities by electronic trading, the diminishing importance of bank checks, traveler's checks, and traditional postage stamps, and the replacement of airline tickets with Internet bookings.

Secure printing – and the manufacture of secure paper – represent »mature industries.« For all of that, they are still a long way from becoming a smokestack industry, an industrial fossil, even if many newcomers to the scene might not think so. Paper manufacturing and the printing of banknotes remain an attractive business with stable sales and comparatively high earning power. The increasingly tough battle against counterfeiters raises the demand for ever more costly security features. Just after the turn of the millennium this even caused the average price of banknotes to rise again. In view of excess capacity in its core business, the industry also started to move into complementary fields. The process of restructuring is easier for those diversified into several different types of business. The private printers are trying to position themselves as systems providers, for one thing. With a policy of a complete package from one provider – from security characteristics tailored to the customer to note printing and special machinery for processing and destroying banknotes – the customer is supposed to become bonded to the provider. Central bankers do not like that, however. It makes them dependent. Moreover, the private printers have discovered the processing of banknotes under contract to industry outsiders as a business niche. Maintaining the highest security standards in their work is a matter of routine for them. As »cash handling« they offer the centers with high daily throughput of cash – commercial banks, big department stores, supermarket chains, gaming casinos, transportation systems, security transport firms – the counting, sorting and wrapping of money. This service offer extends as far as »direct cash recycling« in which they can return banknotes to circulation through automatic teller machines after a check of their condition and authenticity without having to undergo first the compulsory test formerly done by the central bank.[6] Only banknotes no longer suitable for circulation – or counterfeits – have to be turned over to the central bank by law, since it alone has the right to destroy banknotes in exchange for a credit.

Since the rise in circulation of banknotes has been flattening for years in the industrialized countries as the plastic card gains in importance, it became apparent to private printers that they should be taking an ever stronger interest in the technology behind cards and their deployment in various walks of life. The card business, however, is technologically demanding and a drain on financial strength. In their starting phases the cards were used in banking operations only to assist with authentication. Today the card stands on its own as a payment tool. The telephone cash card with its magnetic strip was the next step from authentication. It was replaced by the chip card, which has also found use in cellular telephony as the SIM card. In the meantime, private printers also offer processor cards with their own computing capability, so-called smart cards, some even with digital signature. The storage capacity of the smart cards is nearly unlimited and their employment possibilities are correspondingly varied. These stretch from access control, especially in municipal mass transit, to the driver's license and the health-care or citizen's card. Only data privacy protection stands in the way of their spread in many countries.

European high-security printing today is regarded as leading the world. The graphic design, technical security safeguards, and quality of multicolored printing of notes serve as the model for most of the banknotes issued in the world. It was naturally assumed that the introduction of the euro would be used as a unique chance to present Europe's high-security printers – and the common currency itself – as modern, capable, and forward looking. There is an extensive report in the last part of this book on the troublesome birth of the euro notes. The verdict can be disclosed in advance: the historic chance was thrown away. The wish to involve all participating countries in the euro's production turned into a heavy burden. The traditional rivalry between state printers and private printers additionally complicated the project. Unprecedented in the history of paper money, the parceling out of the euro printing to multiple paper suppliers and note printers raised the security risk in production and drove the costs unnecessarily skyward. Diverse production equipment and uneven levels of craftsmanship of the participants ensured lapses in quality. This diminished the security of the euro notes against counterfeiting, although they were supposed to be the world's most secure banknotes.

An historic opportunity was blown. The new common currency could even endanger the existence of the private banknote industry. In the run-up to euro printing the state printing plants greatly increased their production capacity, financed with tax revenues. There is no demand for this capacity today. It is to be feared that the highly subsidized state printers will go looking for printing contracts in the export markets from which the private printers live.

In coming years excess capacity and technological transition will exact thoroughgoing structural changes of this branch, both the private printers and the state printers. Survival will be determined not only by business foresight, capital backing, and strength in research and development because political influence is much too strong. The time has come to take a deeper look at the main players in this industrial branch and their often quite fickle fate.

Moneymakers I

3
How Signor Giori was able to carve out a worldwide monopoly with his printing presses

»Perfect gem of mechanical engineering.« »Porsche of printing presses.« Secure printers were given to such rhapsody when speaking of the securities printing machines of Gualtiero Giori. His name stands for development, delivery, and servicing of special machinery for printing banknotes and securities. He revolutionized the printing of banknotes nearly single-handedly. More than 90 percent of all banknotes printed in this world are produced on machines that bear his name. This phenomenal success is the result of an extraordinary printing technology – and of a very special marketing talent.

Gualtiero Giori did not invent the technology of multicolor intaglio printing and simultaneous background printing of banknotes and securities all by himself. But with imagination, determination, and keen business sense, this equally gifted engineer made those processes the industrial standard, enabling them to prevail. Born in Milan, he had secure printing in his blood. He learned the trade from the bottom up in the securities printing establishment his grandfather, Dino Coen, had founded in Milan in 1876. This was shortly after the 1870 conquest of the Papal State that resulted in the complete unification of Italy. It was a time of political and economic ascendancy in the *bel paese.* Stocks, bonds, and checks were needed in proliferating numbers, and Officine Grafiche Coen e Compagnia, »C e C« for short, printed those with high quality. Not until 1939 did this printer receive its first order for banknotes. By then the family company was led by his sons Augusto and Renato and had been renamed Calcografia & Cartevalori (English: Copperplate Engraving & Securities). This was a precaution, since Fascism also prevailed in Italy. That first printing order, moreover, came from the government of General Francisco Franco of Spain.

Moneymakers, Klaus W. Bender

ISBN: 3-527-50236-X

Right after his victory in the civil war and his proclamation of the republic, *el Caudillo* in 1936 entrusted the first order for the printing of his country's banknotes to the land of his German allies. It went to the secure printer Giesecke & Devrient in Leipzig. Altogether, Giesecke & Devrient printed around 300 million peseta notes between 1936 and 1939 for Franco's Spain. It was the biggest order the Leipzig plant had ever landed, as the commemorative publication for the company's 150th anniversary proudly noted. There were no hitches, as several follow-up orders showed. Yet in mid-1939, shortly before the German attack on Poland, Franco changed printers. Political caution advised somewhat less dependency upon Hitler's Germany, at least in the sensitive field of note printing. Even a supplier from Fascist Italy still offered advantages that were not just geographic. The twenty-six-year-old Gualtiero, one of Renato's two sons and the technical director of the secure printing plant, was entrusted with filling this order. It was his first contact with Giesecke & Devrient and it was still indirect. The printing was done in Milan with machines from the Frenchman Serge Beaune. Father Renato had secured the general distribution of these machines in Italy, but the Beaune machinery it purchased was only for the use of the printing house. One needn't nurture one's own competition.

Gualtiero's family had to flee at the outbreak of war. His father had already immigrated to Argentina; the rest of the family crossed the border into Switzerland. Gualtiero, who changed the family name from Coen by assuming the maiden name of his mother, Giori, remained behind. He intended to save the printing plant and its valuable machinery from the Germans – who seized control of the operation – and from the bombs of the Allies. Gualtiero succeeded in doing this with a great deal of courage and cunning. Several times he escaped by a hair from an SS detachment and had to live in the underground. When father Renato returned briefly to Italy after the end of the war, he sold his interest in the printing firm.

The meeting in Alexandria

Lucrative and prestigious as it was, the business with banknotes was in the hands of just a few private printers at the end of the Second World War. These were: the British high-security printer Thomas De La Rue & Co., Waterlow & Sons, and Harrisons & Sons; as well as the American competitors, led by American Banknote with its British subsidiary, Bradbury; Wilkinson; U.S. Banknote; and British American Banknote. The British controlled the printing market for banknotes and securities in southern Europe and in Africa and Asia. These were generally countries of the collapsing British colonial empire. The American competition – which had never been included in the printing of their own dollar notes – had the upper hand in the highly inflationary countries of Central and South America as well as in Nationalist China and the Philippines. Their printing machines were mostly their own designs. The printing of banknotes on flat-bed plates was time consuming. Background as well as intaglio printing were monochromatic and required a separate throughput for each color.

Gualtiero Giori had been toying with the idea of developing a high-performance multicolor intaglio printing machine that was nevertheless highly precise. It would have to be able to print several colors in a single press run. He wanted to sell these machines not so much to the handful of private printers but rather to those many countries that lacked their own printing plants for banknotes. Serge Beaune, whose machinery Gualtiero Giori already knew from the plant in Milan, had developed the basic concept for multicolor intaglio printing. The Frenchman was a capable engineer and inventor, but a less capable businessman. Gualtiero bought up Beaune's patents and began further development of the intaglio machine with the help of a team of Italian designers and mechanics. Giori's first multicolor steelplate engraving machine, called »Piloto,« was built in 1947 by the Mino machinery factory in the Piedmont industrial city of Alexandria. Giori's father had good connections to Chief of State Juan Perón. Thus, the Argentine state printing plant Casa de Moneda in Buenos Aires bought the prototype. Gualtiero moved to Argentina, regarded then as the »country of the future« in the Southern Hemisphere. His Italian team accompanied him but the machinery production remained in Alexandria. Italy's industry had suffered comparatively little from the war and Italian mechanical engineering enjoyed a strong reputation. With his references from Casa de Moneda, the adroit Italian quickly succeeded in selling a half dozen of his Piloto presses to Latin American countries, among them Brazil, Chile, and Columbia. They used them to produce over the years some of the prettiest polychromatic banknotes in the world. Yet in the United States of America and Europe, where the international leaders of securities printing were located, the breakthrough took its time. The multicolor technology of the Piloto was too complicated and the printing machines were too vulnerable to breakdowns.

When Giori finally sought to present his machine to the curious European branch professionals at the headquarters of Mino the start of the 1950s, the demonstration of the machines was repeatedly interrupted by technical problems. Among Giori's guests was a German, Siegfried Otto, the sole managing director of Giesecke & Devrient in Munich. Otto desired to print banknotes and monetary securities that would offer the highest possible protection against forging and counterfeiting. Even before Germany regained its sovereignty, Otto had suggested in a memorandum to the leadership of Bank deutscher Länder, the precursor of the Deutsche Bundesbank, that German banknotes had to be printed in Germany again. That still worried the U.S., British, and French printers for the three Western zones of occupation. Giesecke & Devrient had been permitted to print for the Reichsbank in only very few exceptional cases. If its securities printing plant was to stand a chance in the post-war period, Otto had to offer quality that no other country possessed. His printing plant operated at that time with a copperplate engraving press, which he had bought used from the Swedish state banknote printer and paper manufacturer, Tumba Bruk. Such a printing press was a rarity in Germany at that time, but it was technologically outmoded nevertheless. Giori's machine offered multicolored intaglio printing from a single printing plate and steelplate engraving of high precision and accuracy. Taken together, that meant an enormous improvement in printing performance and printing quality. But it was also clear to Otto that the sensitive mechanisms of the securities printing machine required a manufacturing quality that a maker of standard machinery could not possibly offer. And Giori's machine was one of many in Mino's production program. Otto therefore offered to put Giori in contact with the machinery factory Koenig & Bauer, which had long years of experience in this segment of machinery. Even at the time it was founded a hundred years before, Giesecke & Devrient had obtained its first heavy special press for copperplate engraving from Würzburg and still maintained cordial relations with that company.

The ›Italian connection‹

Koenig & Bauer is unquestionably the oldest maker of printing machinery in the world. Group sales of 1.4 billion euros also make this thoroughbred printing machinery manufacturer for newspaper and jobber printing the world's third-biggest purveyor of printing systems and peripheral equipment. In the self-confident German mechanical engineering industry, the tradition-steeped company ranks as one of the finest. The company is still controlled by the founding family with its majority of the share capital. The company was officially launched in London in 1817 by Friedrich Gottlob Koenig and his friend, Andreas Friedrich Bauer. This occurred after the two engineers had already worked together in England for years, a period during which the duo developed the world's first cylinder printing press. On the continent, in the courts of Berlin, Vienna, and St. Petersburg, there was a lack of interest in this invention that was to revolutionize newspaper printing – too great was the rulers' fear of the printed word. Therefore, the first fast cylinder press from the two German engineers went to the *London Times*. The unparalleled printing performance of this machine in those times enabled the London newspaper to raise its daily press run considerably. It created the conditions that first made the *Times* a mass-circulation journal and then a newspaper of worldwide significance. The *Times* came to be called »Thunderer,« thanks to its formidable political influence. At the invitation of the Bavarian king the engineers returned to the fragmented German states of 1817. They went to Würzburg on the navigable Main River, which permitted economic transport of the heavy castings for the printing presses.

Six years after the end of the Second World War, there was nothing of the old sparkle left to be glimpsed in Würzburg. The city lay in ruins, divided Germany at its economic bottom. The main plant had been a bombing target, the engineering blueprints incinerated. A single printing press was sold initially in 1951 to a local newspaper, the *Darmstädter Echo*. Hans Bolza, the senior boss of the firm, was struggling to revive his foreign business. He traveled regularly to South America, once an important market for the newspaper and securities printing machines of Koenig & Bauer. On his way, he stopped off in Madrid, where he negotiated with an old customer, the state Fábrica Nacional de Moneda y Timbre (FNMT), the delivery of a heavy machine especially for the printing of banknotes.[1]

The IRIS four-color relief printing machine he offered had been put on the market by Koenig & Bauer in 1923 and was technologically somewhat behind the times. Nevertheless, Bolza entertained the hope of signing a contract with the Spaniards on his return trip. When he knocked on the door again in Madrid, his business partners revealed to him that in the meantime they had had a visit from an Italian designer of printing machinery named Gualtiero Giori. This young engineer had imparted exciting information to them about his plans for the multicolor printing of banknotes. They said the situation had radically changed and that FNMT had to rethink everything. Bolza also learned that this greenhorn had flown in with his own airplane and had summoned the FNMT representatives to him at the airport. The man from Würzburg had already heard of this person. His own chief engineer, Hanns Fritz, had been in Alexandria for the luckless machinery demonstration. Fritz had also written a report, which like so many others had gone unread. Now Bolza was interested – and upset.

The first meeting took place in Munich. It was arranged by Siegfried Otto. The rapport between Hans Bolza and the considerably younger Gualtiero Giori immediately clicked into place, as Bolza's adopted son, Hans B. Bolza-Schünemann, recalled many years later. A minor detail was to play a mighty role here. Bolza's ancestors had come from Lake Como in northern Italy. Bolza had always cultivated this family bonding to the South and spoke, among other languages, fluent Italian. This was to become the basis for a close relationship between two towering entrepreneurial personalities.[2] In March 1952 Gualtiero Giori and Hans Bolza sealed a preliminary agreement that culminated six years later in a long-term contract of cooperation. This meant the coup de grace for the already ailing company, Mino. It went into bankruptcy.

At the moment Bolza put his signature on the preliminary agreement with Giori, Koenig & Bauer already had more than 130 years of experience in building machinery and had amassed an invaluable store of technical knowledge. Seen in this light, greenhorn Giori walked away with richly embroidered terms. The Würzburg company not only had to deliver at fixed prices, calculated at that time in Deutschmarks per kilogram of machinery weight.[3] It also had to surrender the distribution completely, including that for the domestic German market. Moreover, it had to make a commitment to surrender to Giori free of charge all future patent applications for these securities printing machines. Yet Bolza was not naïve; the cooperation also offered him advantages. The war wounds were still fresh. Not everyone abroad was again willing to buy a German machine. Now Koenig & Bauer was able to build several complete series a year of machinery for securities printing, which Giori ordered in advance on his own account. In the highly cyclical business with rotation presses for commercial printing, this secured a sustained use of base operating capacity. Würzburg did not have to worry about advertising, sales, and exchange rates. Giori's payments formula was also comfortable. Under the contract, 30 percent was due upon order, 50 percent upon delivery, and the remaining 20 percent upon purchase of the machines. But Giori made the first payment only when he had a buyer for the machine.

It was a respite for the Würzburg company that Giori was contractually bound to it as the exclusive manufacturer. After all, the share of these special printing machines contributed as much as 30 percent of the group sales of Koenig & Bauer AG in peak years. With respectable amounts of cash, disbursed informally and within hours if need be, Giori also rendered assistance to the Würzburg company in its protracted financial pinch. Giori also purchased registered shares of Koenig & Bauer on the market in the course of several capital increases. This was a welcome price support in the still weak German capital market, making Gualtiero Giori an important strategic investor in Koenig & Bauer in the course of time. There was no reciprocal participation in the share capital of Giori's company in Lausanne.

Developer, supplier and service provider in one

Giori's choice of a partner proved correct in every respect. It was the expertise and capability of the Würzburg company that assured the technical success of the new sheet-fed printing presses. But it was the marketing genius of the multilingual and glib Gualtiero Giori that made a commercial triumph out of it. Giori was already thinking globally when the term of art still wasn't included in every formal address. Politically, his business was highly sensitive. Therefore, on the advice of his friend Albert Amon, he transferred the headquarters of »Organization Giori,« through which he distributed his machines exclusively, to Lausanne. The Swiss cantons offered not only attractive tax rates, anonymous bank accounts, and, as mentioned before, a generous attitude toward »useful outlays.« Switzerland was also a neutral country from which one could do business perfectly with West and East in times of rising heat in the Cold War. Giori set up shop in one of the discreet patrician mansions on Lausanne's Rue de la Paix. It was simultaneously the administrative headquarters of Amon's ink factory, SICPA, about which a great deal will still be reported. From there Organization Giori took control over not only the distribution of the Koebau-Giori machines from the printing through the final packing of banknotes but also the training of printing personnel. Additionally, Organization Giori also offered complete pre-printing services, from the designing of the banknote or security, including their embellishment with security characteristics, through the making of originals, to the manufacture of a printing plate. And Giori undertook the erection of turnkey printing plants for securities as well as their technical operating direction during a transition period.

An extensive research and development department was set up in the Lausanne suburb of Sévelin. The demonstration center was installed in neighboring Le Mont. Giori had a complete working model of a printing bay for securities built there, equipped with all the large machines he offered for printing, processing, and final packaging, including the complete infrastructure required by a printing plant. In both of these protected centers, hermetically sealed with the most modern security systems, customers could monitor the designing of banknotes or the hand engraving of the portraits they bear. They could practice note printing on original machines and follow the training of their employees. Just the staging of the printing hall tour in Le Mont, accompanied by music and lighting effects of the *son et lumière* genre, sticks with each visitor as an unforgettable experience. Automatically opening blinds reveal the sight of a gallery of 50-metric-ton printing machines as long as 11 meters. In the secretive world of the printing of banknote and securities, into the working of which no one was permitted insight and in which technical knowledge was jealously guarded, Gualtiero Giori's service offer looked like a revolution. It was this complete service, this »Giori system,« that was to usher in the success.

A year after the signing of the contract, Giori and Koebau put on the market the world's first multicolor steelplate sheet-fed printing press. With an etched or hand-engraved metal printing plate one could in one printing step now produce a multicolored printed image that heightened relief and could be felt with a touch of the finger. To do this, the printing roll is pressed on the paper with a force estimated at 80 metric tons, until then technically impossible. The ink in the engraved depressions of the printing plate is transferred to the paper in this way.[4] Intaglio printing is a volume printing process in which the pressure of the rolling cylinder determines the amount of ink applied. Only one side is printed. The note has to be turned over and run through the machine again for the intaglio printing of the other side. A printing machine that accomplished these two steps simultaneously soon complemented this program. It permitted for the first time the simultaneous multicolor printing of extremely subtle background tones on both sides of the note. These consisted of identically matched, interlacing guilloche patterns. A perfect transparency of pattern could then be printed, with the complete image becoming visible only when held up to the light. More than twenty years were to transpire before this security feature, now universally acknowledged, was incorporated into the printing of banknotes. Yet in short order a line of machinery was taking shape, going from background to intaglio printing and a two-color numbering letterpress, or *numerota,* to the final packaging, all perfectly attuned in one swoop. That was also new in the world of security printing.

Just to gain a hearing among the cautious central banks, Giori urgently needed one or two projects of reference. The Dutch private printer Enschedé – which printed the Dutch guilder notes – and Munich's Giesecke & Devrient helped. They took the first two intaglio sheet-fed printing machines. Introduced in Vienna, the prototype of the simultaneous machine was then purchased by the Oesterreischische Nationalbank (OeNB). The door to the central banks had been opened. Although Würzburg kept for itself the construction of the intaglio and numerota letterpresses, the building of the simultaneous printing machines was assigned to Maschinenfabrik Mödling, near Vienna. This was explained with lower production costs, although there was also a political motive. Koenig & Bauer was involved in difficult negotiations with the government in Vienna over the return of the Mödling factory. It had actually belonged to the Würzburg company for forty years but was confiscated at the end of the war as an »enemy asset.« So Koenig & Bauer had to buy its plant for a second time. In the course of time the Super-Simultan, Super-Numerota, and Cutpak, a cutting and packaging machine, and parts of the intaglio printing machine were built in Mödling, which was strictly a production base. All of the designs came from the home base in Würzburg.

The comparatively slow standard series was a great commercial success from today's vantage point. It was manufactured for twenty years. Not until the 1970s was it replaced in phases by the »Super« series with its higher performance. The new equipment owed its product designation to the super-large sheets of paper on which it prints. The new format posed great challenges for printing technology, because these large sheets of paper were extremely sensitive to humidity and were inclined to deform on the edges in trapezoid shape under the intense cylinder pressure. Both problems can render notes useless. In a masterful achievement of precision, however, even such distortions were offset from the start by the placement of watermarks in the paper and by the design of the printing plates. Toward the end of the 1980s a machine for intaglio printing in super-format with fully electronic control marked a preliminary culmination of this development. It received the nickname Orlof, in deference to Ivan Orlof, an engineer of the czarist period, and to the high-security concern Moskovskaya Pechatnaya Fabrika Gosnaka (Gosnak). This company, with its two printing hubs in Moscow and Perm, was to advance over the years to the second-largest purchaser of Koebau-Giori machines.[5] Thanks to a special printing process, the Orlof intaglio printing machine offered an even clearer printed image, a considerable conservation of ink – and especially a further, impressive increase in printing performance. The standard machines had a »technical printing performance« of 3,000 small-format sheets of 32 unit notes an hour, which could not be reached under the conditions of industrial production. The last generation of today's electronically automated Orlof intaglio printing machines, by contrast, is offered with a maximum technical performance of 12,000 super-sheets an hour, with as many as 60 unit notes per sheet. How many sheets of banknotes a particular printing plant actually can achieve then depends upon many parameters – the composition of the note, technical knowledge of the personnel, union rules. The mechanical drawings of the first printing machines still came entirely from Giori. Subsequent development shifted successively to Würzburg, especially that which involved the increase in printing performance. But the obligation to sign over all patents remained. Albrecht Germann, who worked for forty years as an engineer at Koenig & Bauer and who was responsible for sheet rotation presses in the end, wrote 145 patent applications alone for the benefit of Giori.

Rino and Sig

The meeting between the former armor officer of the German Wehrmacht, Siegfried Otto, and Gualtiero Giori in Alexandria also marked the beginning of an enduring, decade-long partnership between these two men, whose biographies could hardly have been more different. Rino and Sig, as they called themselves, were both obsessed with their work and were each marked by robust ego. This made for a cooperation rich with tensions and full of theatrical outbursts of anger, and with no less theatrical reconciliations. Otto was due a favor or two for having arranged the meeting between Giori and Bolza. The deal promised success and he wanted to be part of that. He proposed to Giori to test the Italian's printing machines under industrial conditions in his securities printing plant. The result was an »agreement on technical cooperation and development,« which could be prolonged automatically. Otto received the concession that he alone would be permitted to print with Giori's special printing machinery in Germany. He also succeeded in negotiating a juicy rebate on Koebau-Giori machines required for his own use. There was even a price discount – admittedly more modest – on deliveries made to third parties for which Otto served as intermediary. Giori, however, was definitely not interested in letting Otto handle deliveries; Giori regarded that matter as his pre-eminent domain. Conflicts were built in. The exclusivity clause was questionable under cartel law and collided with the interests of the Bundesbank. Therefore, it had to go sooner or later. At the end of the 1950s, when the Bundesbank actually divided the initial printing of Deutschmark banknotes fifty-fifty between the federal printing plant and the private Giesecke & Devrient, the necessity arose to equip both contractors with identical machinery. Otto was smart enough not to insist on fulfillment of his exclusivity clause. On the other hand, the more favorable price for the purchase of printing machines then became an advantage for Munich in international competition, demonstrating once again the business foresight of Siegfried Otto.

As far as technological exchange was concerned, the ever mistrustful Giori was a vigilant partner in dealing with his friend. Although Würzburg was less than a three-hour drive by car from Munich, Giori insisted in principle that all information must flow through Lausanne. There was good reason for this. Siegfried Otto had been looking into the lucrative equipment business too openly. And with the founding in 1958 of Security Printing AG of Glarus, Switzerland, about which more will be said, he made a concrete move in this direction – provoking one of those temperamental reactions from Lausanne that often characterized the manner in which the two company bosses dealt with one another. Not until it became clear that Otto would not remain engaged in the equipment business with printing machines for the duration did Giori permit direct contact between the private printer in Munich and the machinery manufacturer in Würzburg. But he continued to insist that he be informed in every instance. His chief engineer, Gazzola, is still remembered in Würzburg as a difficult partner during that period.

But Giori himself occasionally had to rely upon Otto's help in the equipment business. Giori's problems with Egypt are still a topic of conversation today when old Lausanne employees meet. The Egyptians had customarily had their banknotes printed in England. In step with the growing tensions with London over the 1956 Suez crisis, however, they decided to build their own note-printing plant. It was supposed to take shape symbolically on the road spur from Cairo to the pyramids of Giza, and Organization Giori was supposed to be commissioned for the plant's erection. Giori's representative in Egypt was Walter Scharff, an emigrant from Germany who owned a printing plant in the Egyptian port city of Alexandria. De La Rue was angered by the threatened loss of its traditional customer. It was the time of the government of the leftist-nationalist General Gamal Abdel Nasser and the growing tensions with Israel, which later led to the Six-Day War. The British therefore caused Nasser's government to be discreetly informed that it, of all entities, was about to affiliate itself with »Jewish business interests« in a matter of such importance for its national security. The reaction lived up to expectations. The Egyptians sought pretexts for a retreat, and Giori was threatened with the loss of this important contract.

In his dilemma, Giori asked his Munich business partner to take over the erection of the banknote printing plant. Otto, the former German Wehrmacht officer, was from the Egyptian standpoint above all suspicion, and perhaps even welcome in Egypt in light of Nasser's known partiality toward German (armaments) engineers. The Egyptian central bank made a contract with Giesecke & Devrient in 1960 for the erection of a high-security printing plant with a starting capacity of 80 million banknote units. Munich also took on the training of personnel, the designs of the first series of Egyptian banknotes and the technical direction of the printing plant during the start-up phase. The operating debut, however, was delayed for several years by tardy construction work. This in turn caused problems with the machinery suppliers and the banks. Otto dispatched a young employee, Manfred Beck, to Egypt as project director. Beck was twenty-nine years old and had had no experience abroad. Yet two years later, as the Six-Day War was brewing, he was able to report the start of banknote production and in 1969 was finally able to turn the printing plant over to Egyptian leadership. Since then Egypt has met its own requirement for banknotes – around a billion units a year most recently – solely from the production of this printing plant, where capacity was subsequently augmented. The English competition was driven from the field, and Giesecke & Devrient was even able after a time to win over the Egyptians as a new customer for its Louisenthal paper factory. Portals, the traditional supplier, seemed to have drawn the short straw. But that joy didn't last long. When the federal German printing plant began to print banknotes for Israel and took delivery of paper from Louisenthal, the British foreign secret service gave the Egyptian colleagues a friendly tip and Louisenthal lost its customer again. And that's the way things still stand today.

Cairo was not a precedent for the cooperation, or even for Otto's solo venture in the equipment business. Giori was zealously trying to hold his covetous friend at arm's length here. That was demonstrated in short thereafter in Burma, where Giesecke & Devrient had signed a contract to set up and supply technical direction for the »Wazi Project Directorate.« This was a high-security complex consisting of a banknote printing plant, security paper factory, and minting, with the military in charge. It was actually an East German aid project led by the VEB Polygraph state *kombinat* of Freiberg, Saxony. The comrades from the GDR, however, took their cue somewhat too literally from their masters in Moscow. As good communist atheists they fanned out to the villages and attempted to incite the population in devout Burma against its own Buddhist monks. General Ne Win, the government chief who was given to choleric reactions, had the GDR men thrown out of the country literally overnight, although their job in Wazi was still not even close to completion. The project was turned over to Giesecke & Devrient upon intermediation by the federal West German state-owned Deutsche Industrieanlagen AG (DIAG), which included the machine tool-making company Fritz Werner that was helping to build the armaments industry in Burma. In the »competition of systems« of that period and in the general currying of favor with that »non-aligned« country of Southeast Asia, the Munich company had the expressed blessing from the Bonn government for its engagement. There was trouble, nevertheless. Giori had previously sold the printing machines for Wazi to the ousted supplier from communist East Germany for hard currency. Missing was only a second intaglio printing press, since the Burmese wanted two-sided intaglio printing for their banknotes. When Otto broached the matter of the purchase of this intaglio machine to his partner, Giori was determined to dissuade him from it. The discussion became quite heated, people in Lausanne recall. But Otto finally received his machine. It made Burma an especially profitable foreign engagement of Giesecke & Devrient, but at the same time a controversial one in view of the contemporary geopolitical climate.

Every triangle is perfect

The Koebau-Giori printing presses slowly conquered the printing market for banknotes and securities. But Giori had never been able to land one of most important banknote printers as a customer: the U.S. government's Bureau of Engraving and Printing. Those who met the strict requirements the Bureau imposed on printing machinery could indeed print for anyone, the experts would say. In the mid-1950s the Bureau had retooled from flat-bed plates to rotation sheet-fed printing. For its banknote printing plant in Washington – its only one at that time – it had solicited tenders for printing presses. Giori bid with his standard series, but the award for 10 intaglio printing presses went to De La Rue. The dollar notes of that time were still printed on both sides in steelplate engraving but only in the traditional colors of green and black. The Bureau had no use at all for complex multicolor intaglio printing machines. The disappointment was great in Lausanne and Würzburg and the loss of face smarted. The printing machines built for De La Rue by various manufacturers were not particularly successful. The last intaglio printing press, this one built by Rolls Royce and considered an answer to the Koebau-Giori intaglio, had been a commercial flop. But De La Rue was a corporation with a globe-girdling presence and could make life difficult for Giori. The experience with Egypt reinforced Giori's desire to improve relations with the competitor. In the early 1950s De La Rue had once made him an offer of cooperation. It would have involved the sale of his technology to the British. He declined for that reason. Now Giori approached De La Rue, offering the firm a participation in his Organization Giori. The number of customers is limited, the costs of development and marketing high, he said to De La Rue. So why don't we get together? After protracted negotiations, the British agreed in 1965. Organization Giori embarked on a joint venture. While the stake holdings were equal, the operating control was still in Giori's hands. He became »chief executive« and chairman of the supervisory board of the joint venture named DLR Giori S.A. The unusual concentration of power was supposed to ensure that he remained the boss. In the eyes of many beholders it was a marriage of convenience »against nature.« The private printer wanted to produce as many banknotes as possible for others, while the supplier of printing machinery wanted to take precisely those customers away from him. The alliance contradicted the logic of the marketplace. Yet Giori's close friendship with Peter Orchard, later the chief executive officer of De La Rue, was a guarantee that the interests of both parties were protected. In fact, De La Rue for many years expressed satisfaction with the gushing dividends and refrained from interfering with Giori's operating control. Koenig & Bauer had agreed to the entry of the British partner under the condition that De La Rue would only be entering into the existing contractual arrangement. Koenig & Bauer categorically rejected the British request to become involved in the manufacture of the printing machinery, although they had energetically pressed this point in Giori's company during a remarkable plant tour in Würzburg. But the anticipated expansion of the business made additional investment necessary at Würzburg. Its financial position was still quite weak. So Giori and De La Rue agreed that they would each purchase 12.55 percent stake holdings in Koenig & Bauer separately from the contract.[6] The printing presses subsequently left the plant with the amended title »Koebau-Giori-DeLaRue.« Yet nothing betrayed Giori's satisfaction with his coup – and his predilection for grand gestures – so much as the new company logotype. It was an equilateral triangle containing the Latin inscription *omne trinum perfectum est* – every triangle is perfect – and the corporate names of the three partners. It was displayed on all future machines.

This invocation of harmony, however, did not hold Giori back from the pursuit of his own business interests. Whenever and wherever in the world his partner De La Rue landed a printing contract for banknotes, Giori traveled there and dutifully suggested that the country in question could also take the printing of its banknotes into its own hands. Actually, there was a taboo list compiled with De La Rue and listing mostly former British colonies in which Giori was not supposed to offer any machines. But what could he do if there was a »pressing desire« of a customer for his machinery? He was especially partial to the newly independent countries of Africa and Asia. »If you want to be somebody in the circle of independent countries, you have to print your own banknotes,« was his simple but impressive message.

Now the ›greenback‹ too

The new partner also blazed the trail to America for Giori's machines because De La Rue withdrew from machinery manufacturing. At the start of the1960s, during the Kennedy years, Giori had also laid out his concept in Washington for the printing of multicolored dollar notes. This was rejected by the U.S. Congress, which is responsible for this matter, however. As a result, Lausanne and Würzburg undertook at great expense the development of an intaglio printing machine specifically for U.S. requirements. When the Fed and the Bureau again called for tenders for printing machines in the mid-1960s, Giori bid with this special development, a »Mono-Intaglio.« His competitor was now American Banknote. Renowned at that time, this American securities printer entered the bidding with a »Magna« intaglio machine developed by Ivando Gazzola, who once had been Giori's chief engineer. The dependency upon Würzburg had always been a thorn in the side of this ambitious designer. He turned his back on Giori when his own plans for developing a wholly new process for intaglio printing came to naught amid the inclusion of De La Rue. He went to Bradbury Wilkinson, a subsidiary of ABN.

Giori raged at this »betrayal« and had private detectives put Gazzola under surveillance. Their reports confirmed that Gazzola was working on a machine for intaglio printing. The U.S. solicitation required a machinery test in the printing plant of the Bureau in Washington. A standard machinery crew had to print a prescribed amount of banknotes in an appointed time. Germann, who directed the on-site machinery demonstration for Koebau-Giori, recalled that his own two Mono-Intaglios had long met the requirement, while adjustments were still being made on Gazzola's four Magna machines. Despite that, the Bureau bought all the Magnas presented, but also eight Mono-Intaglios from Koebau-Giori. The Magna machines did not work properly. American Banknote had had them built by American Can Company. This company had otherwise supplied only the food processing industry and lacked any experience in the construction of complex securities printing machinery. The purchase of the Magna by the Bureau became the subject of a highly embarrassing hearing before a Senate committee at the end of the 1970s. The incumbent director of the Bureau had to vacate his office.

The breakthrough had been made. Koebau-Giori, of course, had import difficulties for a while because of the Buy American Act. Since the 1970s the government in Washington had sought with this legislation to combat its mounting balance-of-payments problems. For public procurement contracts it prescribed among other things that a comparable U.S. product would still be considered competitive if it were 10 percent more expensive than the imported good. The 10 percent price premium, of course, would be calculated from the CIF price of the imported product. This price included merchandise, freight, insurance, and even import duty. The U.S. product could therefore cost considerably more but would win the auction just the same.[7] The designation of imported product could be avoided if at least 30 percent of the value of the good came from U.S. production. Koebau made the tedious conversions of metric values to inches and tried to build U.S. electrical circuits or motors into the machines. This lowered the performance. In the end Washington lost. The Bureau accepted not only the metric industrial standards of the Würzburg company; Koebau-Giori was also recognized with the status of »sole source supplier.« The Buy America Act was circumvented. The efforts of Giori and Würzburg were richly rewarded. While the exact number of machines delivered may not be published at the behest of the customers, central banks, one can still assume that around 80 major machines have been obtained from Würzburg since the start of the supplier relationship. Only the Indians and Russia's Gosnak were more avid buyers, namely with about 90 machines each. At the turn of the millennium the Bureau then bought a whole line of multicolor steelplate engraving machines and Super simultaneous machines for multicolor background printing for the first time for both its printing centers. For industry insiders this was the first sure sign that the days of the green-black monotony were numbered. Progress in copying technology left no other choice.

Pay and say nothing

Giori had taken on an ambitious mission, the success of which was in no way assured. The handful of private printers pulled hardly any weight when it came to delivery potential. The central banks had to be his target. But a need for their own banknote printing plants was not always there. Giori was only too well aware of this, as a small episode from the start-up phase illustrates. In his search for a company emblem for Organization Giori, the Italian had decided upon the winged horse Pegasus. In Greek mythology Pegasus issued forth from the severed head of the deadly Medusa. But when the Italian graphic artist Florenzo Bessi-Masino, an internationally recognized expert in lira banknote design, presented his sketch, Giori was shocked by what in his opinion were excessively large wings, recalls Paul Wernli, who was for years responsible for procurement of materials at DLR Giori and for coordination with Koenig & Bauer. With those wings he would fall like Icarus to the derision of the industry, Giori complained. The outcome was an energetic company logo in fine graphic taste, which departed sharply from the stiff portrait head à la George IV of a De La Rue and from the menacing bird of prey of Giesecke & Devrient. Giori's anxiety was alleviated.

Giori's market was actually a typical buyers' market in which the customer had the last word. The cunning Italian made it a seller's market. He exploited the traditional jealousies between central banks, which were concerned about their independence, and the politicians. He knew how to play on national or personal vanities and dangled the economic advantages – lowering of printing costs and conservation of hard currency – that would attend note printing in the home country. In talks with the customers Giori knew how to strike all the chords of his eloquent and formidable persuasiveness. The imposing, nearly intimidating presence of this worldly, polyglot Italian contributed considerably to his success here. He was the modern version of a baroque prince. When he visited with his last wife – he was married five times – and his granddaughter China, he naturally traveled in the private jet – with eighteen suitcases. Reports of visitors to his luxurious villa, richly studded with antiques, in Lonay, near Lausanne, sounded like a tale from *Thousand and One Nights.*[8] His full score was perfectly orchestrated. In the end it was mostly Giori who determined what the customer would order, or what he would have to order. The central banks were at his mercy. They were traversing uncharted terrain. They lacked the experience. Naturally they wanted their own note printing plant, even if that warred with all economic reason. How many countries have such a great demand for banknotes that this justifies the procurement of their own line of printing machinery that can produce a billion notes? And naturally the savings waved before them frequently proved to be a fata morgana. Even when a printing plant was running, expensive materials still always had to be imported and the small series left hardly any room for cost savings.

No customer was too small for Giori. This later caused him occasional difficulties. In 1973, for example, with the help of a member of the Italian royal family who was living in Geneva exile he succeeded in selling the machinery for setting up a complete banknote printing plant to Bank Markazi Iran, the Iranian government bank. In the course of a decade the two standard lines of machinery were delivered. But the plant was still under construction when Shah Reza Pahlaevi was toppled by the mullahs in 1979. Still in their packing crates, the valuable machines stood around in a warehouse. The new rulers in Iran were internationally isolated. They needed the note printer more than ever and insisted upon contract fulfillment. This was politically sensitive because the tensions between Washington and the Islamic fundamentalists in Teheran were at their peak – and the U.S. Bureau of Engraving and Printing was Giori's best customer. Giori found an excuse. He signed over the equipping of the banknote printer and the training of its personnel to Kassemchitta Asavachinda, the technical director of Thailand's government printing plant, who had also been helpful to Giori in other delicate missions. The mullahs were so satisfied that they even ordered another two Super printing machine lines in 1987.

About the time the Iranians put their signature to the contract with Giori, a delegation from North Korea was also in Lausanne for talks. As usual De La Rue Giori had put up this delegation's members at the best address in town. What had been intended as a brief visit, however, developed into a long sojourn. The emissaries from austere North Korea liked it so much on the banks of Lake Geneva that they didn't want to leave even after months elapsed. With requests for unusually detailed information and tough price negotiations they prolonged their stay more and more. When finally their suits no longer fit them – the Western cuisine became them – and Giori also had to provide them new attire at his cost, the gentlemen were shifted to new quarters in a modest and reasonable hostelry. Presented with great determination, the North Korean demand for unusually long-term financing was indeed an obstacle. Pyongyang had no hard currency and all the Western banks approached refused to open a letter of credit for the purchase. A return to North Korea with empty hands could no longer be ruled out, and the members of the delegation began to worry about their future. Finally Giori found in Zurich a special private bank that granted a credit with a ten-year redemption, but with interest that was far above the prevailing market rate. Pyongyang received its coveted banknote printing plant, including the standard line with complete printing plate preparation. It was set up by German and Italian mechanics next to a barracks on the edge of Pyongyang. But the Zurich lender never received his money. After just two installments, Pyongyang ceased payments to the »capitalist exploiter.«

Gualtiero Giori's printing machines sold like hotcakes on both sides of the Iron Curtain. After the collapse of the Soviet empire deliveries even rose. For example, the now independent Ukraine with its 52 million people snapped up four complete printing lines. They were installed in a rocket factory converted into a high-security printing plant. The expensive machines are probably still rusting away in the giant halls because only one line runs regularly. The rulers of Kazakhstan, with 17 million people, and Uzbekistan, population 24 million, also believed they owed themselves a banknote printing plant for their freshly won independence. Printing capacity that would have comfortably sufficed to cover the banknote requirement of Germany was installed in both those countries. This equipment even had to be flown in by Russian Antonov 124 wide-body transport planes in several flights because the sensitive machines could not have withstood the deep freeze in transit by train or trucks. The Uzbeks also had Giesecke & Devrient install a factory for banknote paper for 100 million dollars. Its capacity would have sufficed to cover the needs of a population of 300 million. To finance this, by the way, part of the Uzbek gold hoard was sold in Zurich. Shortly thereafter Tashkent declared its insolvency to the IMF.

Giori's pricing policy was as imaginative as his sales strategy. This remained, to put it cautiously, his invisible capital. Lausanne calculates the »manufacturing cost plus 100 percent,« customers would complain. There was more than just a grain of truth in this. And it probably had to do with the fact that this involved public money. For new machines there was a repurchase clause with a time limit, the sense of which observers did not immediately grasp. And there were price discounts. They worked out sometimes lower, sometimes higher, and were pegged to the financial clout of the customer. Differences in the technical specifications of a machine were always good for an explanation of the price difference. Every customer had to undertake a written obligation to keep his purchasing price a secret. Many complained but few resisted openly. Frans Lesilolo, then boss of the Indonesian high-security printing facility of Perum Peruri Percetakan Uang Ri in Jakarta, once refused to sign the secrecy clause. That caused a scene, but had no consequences. The South Koreans have even tried to mobilize other customers against the price policy. But the men from the Land of the Morning Calm overlooked the fact that more than 90 percent of all machines from DLR Giori were sold to government printing plants. Among these customers a high delivery price was not necessarily regarded as disadvantageous. Lesilolo, moreover, felt the selling pressure from Lausanne when the Patraikos, bound for Perum Peruri in 1996, sank in the Strait of Malacca with a new »Super-Sumultan« and two processing machines on board. The machines with the equivalent of 10 million euros were recovered but Lausanne wanted to scrap everything in order to make a new delivery. The insurer refused to pay and called upon Rolf Westphal, the veteran technical director for banknote printing at Giesecke & Devrient, as an expert. He actually succeeded in saving substantial parts of the shipment. Lausanne was not amused.

Known for his perfect manners and charm, Giori could also be nasty – preferably toward his own partners. The venomous letters that he composed to De La Rue whenever he felt constrained by the British, or to Otto, whenever he believed he had been duped, became famous in the company. Giori even took his British partner to court – then only to waive magnanimously the payment of damages to him. Not even Koenig & Bauer was immune to his displeasure. When the Würzburg firm once wanted to negotiate the easing of a fixed price clause, Gualtiero Giori angrily swept from the table with his arm the statistics they had brought along. In the end he relented, but the ranting and raving henceforth belonged to the negotiating ritual between Lausanne and Würzburg.

Mistrustfulness wasn't alien to Giori. In business he relied on a small group of friends, such as the Sacerdoti family, which had become the owner of his grandfather's printing establishment in Milan and which repaired used, returned printing machines in their Ormag machinery factory under contract to Giori. In his own company Giori – here the true Italian – relied on »famiglia,« his numerous cousins and nephews. Giorgio Coen, responsible for all Latin America, took on a special role under him. Coen had survived the German occupation as a half-orphan hidden in a Carmelite monastery at Monza. He later immigrated to Argentina and actually wanted to become an architect. In the branch the now retired Giorgio enjoyed a reputation as one of those natural talents, who could promptly sell an Eskimo two refrigerators – the second as a reserve for a power outage. Coen, for example, had sold the central bank of Venezuela two complete lines of printing machines for its planned money center in Caracas. That was far beyond the actual need. But when the construction dragged on over seven years, Coen also sold the Venezuelans the machine versions that had been modernized in the interim – although the original printing machinery, long since delivered and still in its crates, was watig in perfect condition in a warehouse. It was also Coen who, for the crowning finale of his career, was able to talk the Portuguese into building their own banknote printing facility – something that Lisbon had rejected for many years. Giorgio Coen failed only once: in Baghdad. Iraq had long had its printing done abroad with De La Rue. After the imposition of the trade embargo Iraq had to print its »Saddam« banknotes itself. Since it possessed no special machinery for the printing of banknotes, this was done on an old Compacta printing press from Koenig & Bauer. It was for commercial offset printing and used normal paper. Saddam Hussein's half-brother and then ambassador to the UN in Geneva, Barzan Ibrahim Hassan al Takriti, had personally pressed Coen to deliver a line of printing machines. And Bazan, the feared ex-boss of the secret service, was not known for taking any backtalk. The purchase was supposed to be settled under the UN aid program »Oil for Food.« Coen traveled to Baghdad repeatedly on invitation and trampled on the mosaic picture of George Bush Sr. in the lobby of Hotel Rashid. But he was not allowed to sell the Iraqis his printing machines in the end. The UN embargo imposed on Iraq after the first Gulf War allowed no other option. One might assume that in such a difficult case an especially juicy commission would have been due. Roberto, the son of Gualtiero Giori, who was already dead by this time, did not want to take no for an answer. He tried on his own in a private jet to fly in at least electronic accessories for the antiquated Iraqi printing machines. The CIA got wind of this. And Roberto came within a hair's breadth of landing in a Jordanian prison instead of in Baghdad.

Komori-sans admiration

Imitation is the highest form of admiration, goes a Japanese saying. Where this sort of compliment can lead was painfully experienced by not just a few Western suppliers in the early days of the Japanese economic miracle. DLR Giori also paid its dues. Japan is a country with an uncommonly high requirement for banknotes. That is explained partly by the cult of cleanliness, which the Japanese also follow with their banknotes. In what other country of the world would it be conceivable, for example, that children's piano lessons would have to be paid with immaculate, newly printed banknotes presented to the *sensei,* or master, in an equally immaculate envelope? The Bank of Japan has made this behavior of the citizenry its own. Every banknote that shows even the slightest soiling or damage is immediately recalled in Japan. For this reason the average circulating life of banknotes in Japan is shorter than in Europe. And this is the reason why 3 billion yen notes are printed a year in today's four printing centers of the Government Printing Office – Hakone, Odawara, Shizuoka, and Takenogawa. An interesting market, but also a difficult one.

At the start of the 1960s, counterfeit 1,000-yen banknotes turned up in great profusion in Japan. They were of such high quality that the finance ministry and Bank of Japan decided to issue a totally new 1,000-yen note. The most modern printing technology was supposed to be used in order to heighten the security against copying the new banknotes. There was a local supplier of securities printing machinery, Komori k.k. of Tokyo. This well established machinery plant is actually a specialist for commercial printing machinery and regards itself today, by its own claim, as the largest supplier of offset printing machines in the world. In the second half of the 1950s Komori began to take an interest in securities printing, the most demanding segment of machinery manufacturing. Yet this machinery manufacturer had problems with the complex technology. Therefore, the finance ministry, the authority which then presided over the Government Printing Office, gave the order to Lausanne for delivery of 36 standard machines for background, intaglio, and two-color numbering letterpresses. It was at the time the largest single order that Signor Giori had ever booked and the first from the Land of the Rising Sun. It was also to be Giori's last order from there.

Initially inquiries came from Japan about technological improvements that were supposedly needed. Then Koebau assembly technicians at the state printing plant brought back word of a room they were not permitted to enter. It concealed a simultaneous background printing machine that had been disassembled into parts. Soon afterwards a letter from Tokyo arrived at the headquarters. In it the Japanese finance ministry announced that unfortunately no further Koebau-Giori presses could be procured after the delivery contract was met. Komori would take over the manufacture of securities printing machines for the Government Printing Office. The fact was, though, that the Japanese in the years of their incipient economic miracle lived in fear that they could one day wake up without the foreign currency with which to pay for their life-sustaining imports of raw materials. Giori's machines were too expensive for them. So the Government Printing Office made available to the local competitor in short order a Koebau-Giori machine, which the development engineers of Komori were permitted to take apart completely and sketch down to the last screw.

Koenig & Bauer was assigned the delicate task of launching a suit against the Japanese government, also in the name of Organization Giori. The world-famous German machinery maker would pull more political weight than a Swiss machinery dealer, it was hoped. But the complaint took time. Japan was far away, and the Japanese market was hard to penetrate because of the linguistic and cultural hurdles. So Signor Giori reacted as many another Western entrepreneur had reacted before him. He offered the government printer his original blueprints for the standard series of intaglio and simultaneous printing machines. They didn't exactly contain the very latest technological innovations. And he agreed that they could be shared with Komori on condition that the competitor would pledge not to export his machinery. No foreign customer should be permitted to buy these machines from Japanese production. A memorandum to this effect was indeed adopted under political pressure. In time the Koebau-Giori machines were completely replaced by Komori products, and the Tokyo producer was quite officially promoted to »exclusive supplier of the Government Printing Office.« But the export market remained closed to Komori.

The private truce lasted at least a decade and a half. In this period the Japanese were also informed about the development of the Super line. Then the technical director of the Japanese state printer retired and Komori concluded that sufficient grass had grown over the matter. Komori Currency Technology UK Branch was founded in England in the 1980s. It was a development center for securities printing machinery with a small production line attached. For its foreign distribution Komori got together with a large trading company, Marubeni, as is the custom in Japan. Together they founded MC-Komori Currency Press. De La Rue unintentionally supplied the necessary experts. That company had just taken over note printer Bradbury Wilkinson, which had been in distress, and had shut down Bradbury's banknote printing. For this reason highly qualified experts were sent packing and gladly entered Komori's service.

The danger wasn't long in coming. The securities printing presses in Super format from Komori might have had fewer color capabilities, their intaglio printing might have been less impressive, and perhaps they required more working stages for background printing. But they were much cheaper than the machines of the competitor from Lausanne. This time DLR Giori cranked up a suit in Japan against the Japanese finance ministry because it was determined that technical processes and ideas from its Super machinery line had been used here, infringing Giori's patents. Giori simultaneously let all potential customers around the world know that every securities printing machine from Komori would immediately be confiscated by customs. Lausanne had no luck with its suit before the Japanese court against by far the country's most powerful government agency. The Komori machines showed small deviations from the Koebau-Giori models. The Japanese judge therefore ruled that these were independent Komori developments, not copies of Giori machinery. Lausanne also lost on appeal in the summer of 2002. After a decade and a half of litigation Koebau-Giori waived the right to approach the high court in Tokyo as the final legal redress. He who controls 95 percent of the world market can be magnanimous.

The threat of seizure had its impact. Who would want to battle the feisty Italian in court for years, perhaps while his valuable presses rusted in custody of customs authorities? Thus the export business remained difficult for the Japanese. National banks are careful with their outlays. The Komori technology for printing banknotes was untested abroad. Why take a risk? The first drum beat came in 1989 when Giesecke & Devrient ordered a small sample press from Komori. It was also suitable for printing very small series. Model notes that must be presented to the customer for final approval are printed on such a sampling machine. DLR Giori at the time had no such machine in its product line, although Komori could deliver from England immediately and at half the price. The alarm bells went off in Lausanne and Würzburg. Parallel to this, rumors circulated on the market that Komori had sold two intaglio printing machines to Gosnak, Lausanne's best customer, and that they were destined for the banknote printing center in Perm, Siberia. The Russians kept quiet, but Perm suddenly became a »restricted area,« even for experts from Lausanne or Würzburg. In the hot years of the Cold War it had been basically closed to foreign visitors. Gosnak obviously wanted to avoid not only possible reprisals from Giori. Perm had also had technical problems with the two intaglio presses from Komori and did not want to advertise the fact. Specifically, the printing plates had broken after the printing of just a few thousand sheets. The technicians from Komori needed nearly two years to repair the damage. Not until 1992 did Gosnak show Ludwig Selhuber, who was in charge of the Russian market, and other representatives of DLR Giori the two machines and recounted the debacle – during a work break for the Japanese. Gosnak contritely returned to the Koebau-Giori fold, ordering from Lausanne printing and production machinery worth more than 400 million Swiss francs, a big consolation prize. The palliative effect was diminished, however, when one payment installment of 35 million Deutschmarks was lost in Germany in transit from Russia to Switzerland. Executives of an import-export firm that was affiliated with Gosnak and had had close contacts to the defunct Soviet system had speculated with it in the foreign-exchange market. DLR Giori's bookkeeping department had been asleep at the switch, noticing the missing payment too late. A German employee went to jail, but Lausanne never saw the money again.

The South Koreans, who had repeatedly complained about Lausanne's lofty prices and had worked hard to establish themselves as the region's secure printer, also dared to buy a Komori machine, this time for background printing. That also remained an anomaly. While the Chinese urgently needed more paper money as part of their economic reform, not even they would do sustained business with the Japanese, although the People's Bank of China promptly bought several machines for background printing in Japan. These were offset machines from the commercial machinery line. And they weren't even supplied by Komori, but rather by Mitsubishi. The Chinese deployed them for printing their smallest denomination of yuan, which is printed on both sides in simple offset technique. Old mistrust and new anxieties on both the Japanese and the Chinese side saw to it that it was not nearby Tokyo that ran off with China's big business with intaglio printing, banknote numbering, and final packaging, but rather distant Lausanne. Even so, the spell was broken.

From Salboni to Abuja

In the early 1990s Reserve Bank of India (RBI) called for tenders on the rebuilding of two banknote printing plants. At that time India was running two high-security printers with thousands of employees. The finance ministry was in charge. One plant was in Nashik, near Bombay, in the vicinity of a large military complex. It is the oldest note printer in the whole country. The second printing center was located at Dewas, southwest of Bhopal. For a time it was known as the largest banknote printing facility in the world. Both plants were equipped with machines from Koebau-Giori. The one in Nashik had two complete printing lines, the other in Dewas had five. The machinery had been procured in the 1970s and 1980s. Yet, the Indian appetite for banknotes is gigantic. More than a billion Indians pay for almost everything in cash. The capacity of Nashik and Dewas was therefore no longer appropriate for the growth in the population. Printing performance was also diminished by the fearsome Indian bureaucracy. There were sporadic production outages, the causes of which remained mysterious. The lamentable physical condition of Indian rupee notes spoke volumes. The extremely filthy and tattered Indian notes have even created a form of employment among the poorest of the poor as exists in no other country of the world: the »torn note mender,« who somehow pastes and darns disheveled notes so that the tradesmen will again accept them. The Indian central bank has repeatedly had to place overspill printing orders abroad on short notice, each time for several billion banknotes. These orders usually went to the British banknote printer De La Rue, which still had the best contacts to the former British colony. These orders blew a big hole in the Indian foreign currency reserves.

The finance ministry and the central bank wanted to correct these discrepancies with capacity expansion in both of the existing banknote printing facilities, Nashik and Dewas, and by building two more high-security printing plants. The Reserve Bank of India, which was made responsible for this, chose as locations the southern Indian city of Mysore, near Bangalore, and Salboni, near Calcutta, in the northeastern part of the subcontinent. The costs of the two new money centers alone were officially given as 375 million dollars, of which 80 percent was supposed to go for machinery and equipment. In Lausanne they were salivating in anticipation of the »certain« order. Then they found out that Komori had energetically entered the bidding for the first time. Until then a call to Tokyo would have sufficed and Komori would have withdrawn. But this no longer worked. Hans Bolza Schüneman, then the chairman of Koenig & Bauer, intervened personally. He pulled out all stops, even going to the highest diplomatic level, in order to stop the Japanese. Lausanne was supposedly even more economical over all. It didn't help. India had received so much development aid from Japan that it would now simply have to take Komori into consideration, the former finance minister was quoted as saying. In the end Lausanne and Würzburg still received the lion's share of the project – and the logistically more attractive base of Mysore.

The contracts were signed in 1995. The Japanese offered an unusually long credit term for a machinery transaction and an extremely low interest rate. There were construction delays in Mysore and in Salboni. But Koenig & Bauer finally installed by the end of 1999 seven lines of printing machines in Mysore. In about the same period Komori installed its eight in the less accessible Salboni. Koebau-Giori was also commissioned to modernize the old plants in Nashik and Dewas from the ground up. India, not exactly among the richest of countries, had by that time taken delivery of altogether 90 major machines from Koebau-Giori since the opening of the business relationship. The technical printing capacity amassed there was gigantic. Just the two new banknote printing facilities of Mysore and Salboni could print nearly 20 billion notes a year when running with three shifts, a representative of Reserve Bank of India calculated for the 1999 Currency Conference in Sydney. In the same year only 6.7 billion unit notes were actually printed, although India's yearly need for banknotes was pegged at about 15 billion units. It was above all the shortage of qualified printing personnel that hindered India.

Komori landed a second order, this time from Nigeria. Africa's biggest country by population, Nigeria looked like nearly a copy of India with respect to its supply of banknotes. That applied to the rapid population growth and the banknote printing facility of the Nigerian Security Printing and Minting Company (NSPMC). This facility had never really worked, despite capital participation from De La Rue then amounting to 25 percent. As a debtor Nigeria didn't enjoy the best reputation then. So DLR Giori didn't exert itself much when the Nigerian central bank called for bids on the building of a second banknote printing plant in Abuja. Two complete lines of printing machines were involved. General Sani Abacha, the Nigerian ruler then, as well as his son had a strong personal interest in letting the contract that Komori was able to sign in 1997. This was an expensive project. The money center is supposed to have swallowed 135 million dollars, not counting the property costs, reported British broadcaster BBC, which cited Nigerian sources. The two installed lines of printing presses alone were said to have cost around 100 million dollars.

The plant was set to go on line in 1999. That schedule was rather tight in a country with such huge internal problems, from corruption through missing infrastructure to the heat. As the newspaper *This Day* in Lagos complained, Nigeria had to cover around 70 percent of its replacement requirement for banknotes with expensive imports – mostly delivered by De La Rue or Giesecke & Devrient. Nevertheless, it seemed that some local politicians were out to delay the project in Abuja. The problems with the building of the money center and the installation of the machines seemed to have no end. Either the parliament would refuse to allocate the money, or there were structural design problems with the new printing center, or finally the temperature control was missing from the printing hall. The project manager dispatched by Komori stacked arms in annoyance. The Japanese were threatened with loss of face. After the experience in Perm, Komori had had to assume an extra long contractual obligation for breaking in personnel and field-testing the printing presses. When both the new printing lines were finally up and running in the new Abuja money center in early 2002, production soon had to be stopped again for lack of materials, like paper and ink. With two large printing plants, Nigeria ran the danger of remaining dependent upon imports of banknotes in this way.

Warning from Munich

Then the outgoing millennium handed Komori a triumph. A digression into the not always simple relationship between Lausanne and Munich is needed here. Siegfried Otto had, as described, negotiated a very substantial discount in his agreement with Gualtiero Giori on technological cooperation. When Giori brought De La Rue on board in 1965, he also had to grant this banknote printer a price discount for at least its own requirements for printing machinery. But this one was considerably smaller, which was a perennial topic. Roberto Giori succeeded his deceased father at the Lausanne company in 1992, becoming president of the supervisory board. He had not, however, been initiated into the operating management, which his father preferred to delegate to his secretary. The son, a technically adept and passionate jet and helicopter pilot, had stood in the shadow of the almighty father whom he had admired. Roberto, called by *Time* magazine one of the richest and at the same time publicity-shy men in Switzerland, was regarded as impulsive and given to swings in mood.[9] As the new president of the supervisory board of DLR Giori, he now got the idea of finally cleaning up these discounts. He drove to Munich and demanded a price supplement for an intaglio printing machine that had been properly ordered by Giesecke & Devrient. He had been urged in Lausanne not to make this trip. Giesecke & Devrient put up a fight and also had the last word. Koenig & Bauer mediated. But the incident was not without consequences. Roberto had already annoyed Giesecke & Devrient previously by rejecting at the last moment a signature-ready contract for mutual development of a machine for quality control in note printing. The Munich firm had a head start of years in this matter and Lausanne could only have benefited from the cooperation. Roberto's decision from the gut didn't merely saddle his company with high development costs for a machine that no one later wanted. There was also a cooling of the relationship between Lausanne and Munich.

Giesecke & Devrient was not the biggest of Lausanne's customers among private printers; that was De La Rue. Over the years De La Rue had taken 45 major machines, Giesecke & Devrient only 38. This, moreover, illustrates the subordinate importance of the private printers in comparison with the state printing plants. Because of its high quality requirements in the printing of banknotes, however, the Munich company had a disproportionately greater technological significance for Lausanne. This customer had been permanently soured – and frightened with monopolistic innuendo. Giesecke & Devrient turned the tables, began complaining aloud of lagging innovation at Koebau-Giori, and demonstratively asked Komori about buying a simultaneous background printing machine. This was a low blow for Lausanne. Naturally it did not escape the trade circles that the Bavarians, for all the outrage they put on display, remained cautious in their choice of machinery. For of course one can also obtain replacement parts for a background printing machine from commercial printing machinery lines, if one day there should no longer be any securities printing machinery coming from Tokyo. Yet the breakup had occurred.

Yoshiharu Komori, the president and chief executive officer of the Tokyo company, regarded securities printing machinery as his personal hobby. For him this inquiry was a gift from heaven. It was not just a further discount from its preferential Lausanne price that he dangled before the highly prestigious customer from Munich. He also offered a machine tailored to Munich's requirements. State printers usually produce long-running series of national banknotes. The private printer, on the other hand, lives from exports, meaning he has to print a multiplicity of continually changing currencies. For these small series printing machinery must always be newly set up. That costs time and money. Komori offered a fully electronic control solution for plate changes and register calibration with his background printing machine. This saved plenty of time. Although the innovation stemmed from Komori's commercial line of offset machines, Koebau-Giori at that time did not yet offer electronic controls for its securities printing presses.

In his advertising Komori-san took full advantage of the decision of the Munich firm. After all, he had been successful with his machine in the country of origin of securities printing machines. It remained only an isolated victory in spite of that. When the Bureau of Engraving and Printing at the turn of the millennium called for tenders on the multicolor intaglio printing and simultaneous background machines already mentioned, Komori bid, citing his latest success in Munich. A Japanese printing machinery manufacturer was entering »open battle« for the first time in an industrialized country against DLR Giori, as one branch representative put it. Yet the battle was lost. After a hotly contested auction featuring powerful blows below the belt, the Bureau decided for its tried and true supplier. DLR Giori had energetically sought to preserve its »stranglehold on the market.« There was a demonstrative reticence among the central bankers to buy anything other than »Giori systems,« complained the English Nale Industries Ltd., a supplier to Korori.

The marketing access hurdles for securities printing machinery are insurmountably high, Munich's Hypovereinsbank once observed in an analysis of Koenig & Bauer. The fate of Komori confirmed this. Since its market entry in the mid-1980s, Komori had been able to book only a handful of foreign orders in this machinery segment. The branch in Britain cost a great deal of money. The relentless economic crisis in Japan, coupled with the slump on the world market for printing machinery, left deep scars in the balance sheet of the parent company. In autumn 2002 the Marubeni trading company unexpectedly withdrew from the joint venture in England. The lack of follow-up orders and excessive capacity after the euro investment rapture were cited as reasons. The retreat of this trading firm was registered in Würzburg and Lausanne with great satisfaction. Maybe they were not entirely uninvolved in this outcome. The departure of the Japanese from the ever tougher business with securities printing machinery was only a matter of time, some branch insiders speculated. Perhaps they did not sufficiently appreciate the pride of the Japanese.

Fat years, lean years

But the rafters were creaking not just for Komori. The last of the big purchasing countries –the former Soviet republics, China, India and the euro countries – had been supplied with new machinery. The market was showing symptoms of saturation. Eighteen unsold printing presses stood in the warehouses of DLR Giori at the turn of the millennium. Staff had to be shed under a social plan: an unheard-of situation for a company that had been accustomed to partake of plenty. There were tensions between Roberto and his British partner. That exchange-traded printer of banknotes had to issue a warning of falling profit at the end of 1999 – the result of a damage claim filed by Roberto for 125 million pounds because of unauthorized technology transfer. It was referred to an arbitration court. The charge of »unauthorized technology transfer« remained peculiarly vague. In hushed tones insiders related that the British partner had even generously served itself with the newly developed security features and production techniques from the research center of DLR Giori. The dividend disbursement of De La Rue – once the most important item in the profit-and-loss account – no longer spurted so briskly. In the end Roberto had blocked it with his litigation.

The announcement came in May 2001. De La Rue sold its 50 percent stake holding in De La Rue Giori S.A. of Lausanne for 50 million Swiss francs (20 million pounds sterling) to Koenig & Bauer. The business run by Lausanne no longer had strategic importance for De La Rue. At the same time the German company took over the remaining 50 percent from the other, unnamed owner. That meant Roberto Giori and his private investment firm, Dynavest Holding & Co. The price was a surprise. Accountants of Ernst & Young had pegged the total worth of the Lausanne company at 275 million Swiss francs only two years before. Roberto, who was staking out a career as an international financial investor with his share of the income – he was after all in touch with the best of contacts in high finance and the »new economy« venture bourse still beckoned – had at times entertained even higher price notions. Perhaps this explained the rumors that Roberto's friend, Olivier Dassault, a scion of the French aircraft manufacturing dynasty, or Prince Waleed bin Talal, the richest man in Saudi Arabia, had signaled interest in buying in. The fact was that the Würzburg company had the technological expertise, a rock-solid position in the worldwide market and a binding contract that would only last until 2007.

Agreement on an official selling price of 100 million Swiss francs was finally reached for the whole block of stock. The British had to make an additional lump-sum payment of 5.9 million pounds to Roberto Giori, a sign that his complaint was probably not entirely fabricated out of thin air. All the mutual claims before the arbitration court were then considered paid in full. This was probably the best outcome for Lausanne. Any investor other than Koenig & Bauer would have bought »only half its freedom,« Director General Olivier Beaumont had warned, because he would still have been dependent upon Koenig & Bauer. It was a remarkable change of command from a cosmopolitan proprietary firm to an internationally active joint stock company rooted in Germany. Three weeks later the business in Lausanne was renamed KBA-Giori S.A.

There was bitter infighting in Roberto's family over the disengagement. It meant the end of a unique industrial success story that was inseparable from the family name of Giori/Coen. The row temporarily caused a disruption of family ties. Two half-sisters also sued Roberto for a notable settlement, which was also awarded to them. Those directly involved maintained a stubborn silence even after the sale. Only Beaumont expressed his satisfaction with the outcome in a press release and emphatically assured Koenig & Bauer of »the full support of the entire management« for the change of ownership. He had in select groups repeatedly vented his dissatisfaction over the impetuousness and moods of his supervisory board chairman, Roberto Giori. The true extent of the problems in Lausanne was first made public in the group business report of Koenig & Bauer for the year 2001. Sales for the truncated, nine-month business year had shrunk to 117 million Swiss francs. Extrapolated to a full calendar year, that was only a third of the past peak figure. Moreover, a loss, the first in the company's history, went unquantified.

It had taken forty-seven years from the beginnings with the »Pilato« until the first 1,000 Giori machines had been sold. Lausanne required only another eight years, until the end of 2002, to sell the next 500 units. This pace could not be sustained. Now the belt also had to be tightened in Lausanne. For the future one counted on innovation under the slogans of cost savings and security against counterfeiting. At the 2002 Currency Conference in Honolulu, KBA-Giorio introduced a new software program, Computer-to-Intaglio-Plate (CTIP), with which one could execute all the preliminaries of intaglio printing on the computer, right up to the completed printing plate for an entire paper sheet. This process is known in commercial printing as Computer-to-Plate (CTP) and is now also supposed to find application in intaglio printing of banknotes with the use of the most modern laser technology. It saves time and delivers high quality – qualified engravers are also ever rarer – and with its extremely high image resolution it clears the way for quicker, yet highly accurate integration of security features in banknote printing without sacrificing originality. The new technology was put to the test by Banca d´Italia and by Orell Füssli; the private printer from Zurich had succeeded with the first fully digital draft of a banknote series in the early 1990s for the current Swiss franc notes. CTIP is regarded as expensive within the industry. Yet it has since been installed by Francois Charles Oberthur Fiduciaire and, surprisingly, by the American Bureau of Engraving and Printing.

Since mid-2003 Claus Bolza-Schünemann, the second son of Hans Bolza-Schünemann, has been responsible for the marketing of securities printing machinery as deputy chairman of the managing board of Koenig & Bauer. A difficult business and delicate decisions are in store for this certified engineer. Since the purchase of DLR Giori in May 2001 not a single order to set up a new banknote printing facility has been booked. Hopes for a printing plant in Baghdad, vague as they were, have faded with the deteriorating internal security in Iraq. Traditional lines of securites printing, such as stock certificates or postal stamps with intaglio-printing, have lost their importance or have disappeared altogether. Koenig & Bauer, therefore, is banking on replacement orders. The business with high security printing machinery is now subject to extreme swings and can make a profit only over a longer period of time, according to the company´s headquarters. Turning every penny over twice, Bolza-Schünemann has even shifted the production of the prestigious intaglio printing machinery to Mödling in Austria in order to achieve higher operating rates. Only the engineering, electronics and software still remain in Würzburg. The »fat years« are over.

4
Why Monsieur Amon had the same success with printing ink

Albert Amon and his SICPA printing ink factory must be mentioned at this point. Amon was practically Giori's twin brother in the lucrative business with banknotes. Monsieur Amon, a model of amiability and discretion in an industry that thrives on ugly rumors, was always ready to render great assistance to customers and friends. This won him a special position of trust in Giori's surroundings. Amon mediated when tensions mounted between business partners, helped out with funds when someone was in urgent need, and readily performed other friendly services. He did not always do himself a favor with this – as demonstrated by the story of Otto and his mystery-shrouded trading company, Security Printing S.A., as we shall see later. When Giori invited a hand-picked group of suppliers from the high-security printing field to Lausanne in autumn 1952 in order to lay down the rules of play and parcel out roles in banknote and securities printing, Amon was in this chosen circle. Siegfried Otto was the only printer there. This market cabal was to last forty years. In those days the securities printers made their own ink. Giori concentrated on intaglio printing. The special inks were expensive and promised to bring enormous business. Much to Otto's dismay, Giori assigned this business to his friend, Albert, who had already delivered the ink for the Piloto. Thereafter, wherever in the world Signor Giori sold one of his printing machines, he also saw to it that Amon would be considered as supplier of the special inks. A second quasi-monopoly was born. In one of its rare publications, the otherwise ever-so-discreet Association Internationale des Imprimeurs Fiduciaires (AIIF), about which later chapters will report extensively, listed the line of available inks: water-soluble reagent ink, which changed its appearance when treated with chemicals; visible or invisible luminescent ink, which glows in ultraviolet light and takes on new colors

Moneymakers, Klaus W. Bender

ISBN: 3-527-50236-X

in infrared beams; and finally magnetic and electrically conductive inks. These were exclusive products of SICPA. Even today the ink pails standing beside the demonstration machines in the Koebau-Giori technological center in Le Mont have paper labels with the abbreviation »SICPA« in extra large letters as their only marking. They can hardly be overlooked.

›Stradivarius‹ of printing inks

Société Industrielle et Commerciale de Produits pour l'Agriculture (SICPA), founded in 1927 by Maurice Amon, an immigrant from Lebanon, started out as a producer of milk fat and coloring agents for farm products. The one protected the udders of cows during milking; the other made butter more yellow and peas greener. With Giori's help, this outfit became the market-dominating supplier of special inks for banknote and securities printing. The family stock company is registered today as Société Industrielle et Commerciale de Produits Amon (SICPA). The purpose of the business changed; the acronym remained. The taciturn family company, to which *Neue Züricher Zeitung* with uncharacteristic disrespect attributed a disclosure policy like that of the Stone Age, made group sales of nearly 1 billion Swiss francs with 3,500 employees in 2004. This made the corporation one of the largest ink manufacturers in the world. Some 65 percent of the turnover came from Sicpa Packaging, which produces commercial inks for the packaging industry. That is a tough business, which is locked in a continual prize squeeze and ekes out slim profit – if any. The Swiss group reaped its earnings, high earnings, from special inks for banknote printing, inks that do not trade freely. These made up the rest of the group's sales, namely 350 million Swiss francs. There has been much speculation about SICPA's business with secure inks because there is no official information about it. One could make a ballpark estimate of production volume because a rule of thumb holds that it takes between three and four kilograms of secure ink to print 1,000 paper sheets of 40 banknotes each, depending upon the size of the notes and their design. For the estimated 90 billion banknotes that are printed in the world each year, at least 9,000 metric tons of secure ink are required for intaglio, background, and number printing if only single-side engraved printing is done. Half of the 90 billion notes are made by the four banknote great powers, the United States, China, India, and Russia. This portion of the requirement can be disregarded because the government printing plants make their ink themselves. The »available market« for secure inks therefore requires 4,500 metric tons a year. It is supposed to be open to bidders. Of this available market, the Swiss company claims a modest 85 percent. But even this figure is misleading. Of the four giants of banknote printing, only the Russian Gosnak is regarded as comparatively independent in its ink manufacturing. It imports only binding agent – not from SICPA but from Gleitsmann Security Inks GmbH of Berlin. The Americans, Chinese, and Indians operate joint ventures with the Swiss company. Local laws often forbid importation of special inks for note printing. There are, therefore, still a few countries, including Australia, Britain, Japan, and South Korea, that make their own ink. But comparatively small volumes are required by these countries, and they often depend upon SICPA for technology. Only Japan goes it all alone. Actually, SICPA largely controls the world market for secure inks, regardless of how »protected« or »available« it officially may be.

The prices are a secret that is no less stringently guarded. The consumer of intaglio printing ink for note printing has to dip deep into his pockets, for this ink has to be laid on thickly. Otherwise one would not be able to detect it at a touch, and the desired tactile security effect would be missing. One-third of the intaglio printing ink is lost as a result of the special printing process. The losses were once even greater. For this reason about six times as much engraving ink is required than is background ink, assuming that only one-sided intaglio printing is done. If engraved printing were possible on both sides, it would naturally be still more expensive, but the background is done with offset printing, which requires minimal ink, little of it lost in printing. It is striking that the technically much more challenging intaglio printing ink still costs much less than the background ink. This is intentional. If one seeks to popularize intaglio printing with its high ink consumption then one must not price the ink out of the market, for others could deliver the engraving ink in a pinch. All quoted prices are subject to sharp swings, depending upon the volume and the customer. At the end of the 1990s SICPA billed one customer 35 Swiss francs for the kilogram of engraving ink and 75 francs for the kilogram of background ink. If special markers, such as fluorine compounds, had been blended into these inks, the price could have risen to multiples of that. But the really expensive part comes first with the specialty of the house, the »optically variable ink« (OVI) that works through light refraction. This is color-shifting ink, about which much more will be said. In the early days it cost around 2,500 Swiss francs a kilogram. One can envisage that such a price is calculated with margins so high that they deserve only the epithet »unreal.« The business magazine *Bilan* (balance sheet) of Lausanne once likened the secure inks from SICPA to Stradivari – probably not simply because they are as good but also because they are as expensive as the instruments of the Italian violin maker from Cremona.

This market success did not take shape all by itself. Even Giori's obvious patronage could not have done that, if SICPA had not been so demonstratively innovative in this special field. What distinguishes the SICPA secure inks is their binding agent. The technology was poured into this, not into the pigments, which could basically be delivered by any other supplier. For the chemical authenticity and the physical durability of this binding agent added up to a tall order. The ink may dry neither too slowly nor too quickly. In addition, it may flake, rub off, or vanish from the note only within strictly prescribed limits in the washing test with hot lye in a washing machine or in the soiling and folding tests. The binding agent is decisive for quality in all these matters. The Swiss ink specialist had also achieved a number of significant advances in the field of secure inks. For instance, it had developed a procedure to determine their physical value and the fixing of universally recognized parameters for the application of these inks, such as those that already existed for commercial inks. The secure ink was for the first time standardized, made exactly reproducible, and with the aid of spectrographic analysis could be tested for authenticity in this way. And there was also the development of secure inks that water would remove: inks that could be washed away with water in a pressurized cylinder, although they could also withstand the caustic lye and high water temperatures of the washing test. Thanks to this invention, one could dispense with the health-endangering trichloroethylene by using leaching water for the cleansing of residual ink from printing plates. The introduction of the high-pressure machine with its unusually high compression was a further challenge. Special ink that dried very rapidly was required here for engraving ink that had to be laid on thickly. The sheets of banknotes would stick to one another without it. Until that time a blank sheet had been used as a sort of blotter that was »shot« in between two printed sheets. That was dirty work, time consuming, and entailed high costs. Only the Japanese with their flat steelplate engraving and the Americans with their thick dollar paper had no problems with it.

But with the latter, banknotes with ink smears were also being put into circulation. It was Haim Bretler, a veteran director of secure inks for SICPA, who solved this problem with his research team.

It was, however, the aforementioned »optically variable ink,« OVI, which found application exclusively in banknote printing, that combined technological triumph with commercial success for SICPA. The inspiration for this came from Interpol's sixth International Conference on Currency Counterfeiting in Madrid in 1977. The international police authority reported there for the first time about the copying of banknotes with the new color copying machines. The Japanese manufacturers were tardy with defensive measures. An import ban was being considered for their dangerous copying devices. Bretler took part in the conference as an observer. He spontaneously offered that SICPA would develop a totally new security feature for a visible portion of the banknote, one that could not be reproduced with color duplicating machines. After several years of research he found what he was looking for in a California laboratory. It was a coating used on the windows of the Space Shuttle and on the sunglasses of astronauts to screen out cosmic rays. Optical Coating Laboratories Inc. of Santa Rosa had such a substance, which changed color with the angle from which it was viewed. Bretler and his team developed the OVI. With it alone, a very limited number of fully changeable binary color combinations are possible.

Because of the extremely high price of this OVI color-shifting ink, the quest to reel in the first customer was commensurately difficult in the early days. No one wanted to be the first to use this expensive – and also untested – feature. Yet, at the seventh International Conference on Currency counterfeiting, held in 1987 at Interpol's headquarters in Lyon, there was no longer any doubt that the threat from color copiers from Japan had intensified considerably in the ten years since the previous conference had been held. SICPA lent coincidence a helping hand. The Bank of Thailand was planning to issue a banknote denominated as 60 baht to mark the sixtieth birthday of King Bhumipol in 1987. And this issue was to incorporate a premium that would be set aside for civic purposes. The unusual note in a square format, which was only to be issued in a protective jacket, is still to be found today in Buddhist temples, where the faithful like to fasten the notes to the altars as an offering. For this commemorative note SICPA offered its new color-shifting ink for free on condition that the Thai state printing plant would publish a report on the volume requirement and the printing characteristics of OVI. This caution was appropriate. Years later Oesterreichische Nationalbank had the painful experience of how ticklish the application of this special ink can be when the OVI color-shifting ink of the numbers of the value denomination flaked off its new 1,000-schilling notes. The note was lampooned in the media as »*Rubbellos*,« the German name for a popular type of lottery card from which the purchaser scrapes a coating off the concealed numbers to see whether he has won.[1] Following Thailand's example, the Nigerians put the color-shifting ink to use. This was associated with the fact that banknote printer De La Rue, which usually printed for this African country, held a one-third stake in Fidink, a SICPA trading firm for secure inks. Amon had made this stake available to the British after their link-up with Giori in order to make sure that the world's largest private printer would not go astray when procuring its ink. Fidink no longer exists. But a long-term delivery contract with special conditions still makes sure that De La Rue remains loyal to SICPA. The Bundesbank became a customer for OVI in 1992 after long hesitation. The parsimonious Bundesbankers, however, used the expensive OVI color-shifting ink only for their 500- and 1,000-mark notes of the last Deutschmark series (BBk III), and they did without the raised print of the precise intaglio process.

The market breakthrough did not arrive, however, until the Americans decided to use OVI color-shifting ink for their new 100-dollar note in 1996. The Bureau of Engraving and Printing had been using secure inks to print its dollar notes since the mid-1970s. These inks were supplied exclusively by Sicpa Securink Inc., the U.S. subsidiary of the Swiss company. The decision in favor of OVI was a triumph because the Americans take great pains in their banknote printing to avoid becoming dependent on foreign technology, treating this as an important aspect of national security. Siegfried Otto was stymied by this policy among other things when he initially tried at the start of the 1980s to sell the Bureau his innovative M feature that could be read by machine but was otherwise an invisible marking on the notes. To top off the story, media reports cropped up around the start of the negotiations between the Bureau and SICPA about the OVI color-shifting ink. Alleged irregularities with SICPA were reported to have occurred in the call for tenders for secure inks and also in its price calculations. There was also talk of influence peddling. The Senate had to become involved in this delicate matter. Once again a director of the Bureau was forced out of office.

The Bureau, which prints between 8 billion and 9 billion notes a year, was already the most important single customer for secure inks SICPA had at that time. The volumes of OVI required for the U.S. market were vast and the supplier relationship meant additional prestige. The Americans therefore succeeded in wresting unique concessions. Not only did a special OVI color pairing have to be reserved for the dollar, but the color-shifting ink also had to be manufactured in the United States and delivered at a price far below that which SICPA otherwise commanded for its security characteristics on the world market. The Swiss had to grin and bear it. A joint venture called Flex Products Inc. was founded together with the Californian OCLI laboratory for the manufacture of OVI pigments. The Swiss were granted only a minority stake of 40 percent. The OVI color-shifting ink was then mixed in the U.S. plant of SICPA. Still reserved today is the alternative OVI binary color of bronze-green and black for all dollar notes of the series issued since 1996, with the exception of the 1-dollar and 5-dollar notes. And the Bureau lays on this ink with demonstrative thickness.

This coup in the United States marked the breakthrough to the worldwide market. Around eighty countries, including those of the euro bloc, now use the OVI from SICPA for their banknotes. With the exception of the U.S. customer, all these countries are supplied with the coveted color-shifting ink exclusively from the company's main plant in Chavornay, Switzerland. And this ink is delivered only to customers who also purchase the other secure inks from SICPA. There are but two exceptions to this strict rule: Japan and Russia, two countries with large OVI needs and ones that SICPA would not want to do without. One other unusual customer of SICPA has to be mentioned here: North Korea. Pyongyang receives not only its secure inks from SICPA, it also obtains the expensive OVI color-shifting ink for its highest denominations, 500-won and 1,000-won notes, although the North Koreans basically do without the – relatively economical – security threads. Although this OVI color-shifting ink on the won notes is of miserable quality, it is greenish, like the OVI on the dollar notes of the archenemy, the United States. The North Korean regime suffers a chronic shortage of hard currency. The danger of counterfeiting in this repressive state with its ubiquitous informants ought to be minimal. Even the act of taking the home currency out of the country or bringing it in is severely punished. So, the application of OVI remains a luxury of the North Koreans that is hard to grasp. That matter will be revisited later.

The market climate is changing

The business with secure printing inks is highly profitable. Nevertheless, there is hardly any competition. That's odd because the technical barriers in the development of the product do not seem insurmountable. Even the strict security requirements for production and storage really ought not to be a deterrent. As far as the euro is concerned, the ECB keeps an eye out to see that precautions are taken at SICPA's Chavornay plant, for example. Apparently the reticence of the ink industry is linked to the fact that the commercial hurdles for entering the market with secure inks are extremely high.

The purchase of secure ink actually entails a public contract, for which public tenders must be solicited when a government printer is involved. Perhaps this is also done. But it is no guarantee that the most economical bid will be accepted. With its annual need for more than 400 metric tons of secure ink, heavily populated Pakistan is regarded as an interesting market. Ever since DLR-Giori delivered the first sheet-fed printing machine to the Pakistan Security Printing Company (PSPC) of Karachi in the 1960s, SICPA has also gone along for the ride as ink supplier. How that came to pass is illustrated by the following case: In 1998 PSPC solicited tenders for 119 metric tons of secure ink. Sweden's Akzo Nobel and Germany's Gleitsmann Security Inks responded to the solicitation. SICPA won the contract – but it had not even filed a public bid. A review revealed that the bid from Akzo Nobel had been around one-fifth below SICPA's price and that SICPA had already started to deliver when the public solicitation was still in progress. The Swedes took that to court in Pakistan and won the case – but not the contract award.[2] For the Swiss had participated with PSPC since 1995 in a joint venture, Sicpa Inks Pakistan Pvt. (SIPL) of Karachi and had a long-term, exclusive contract with the Pakistani state printer. Moreover, it was for this reason that PSPC had stopped making its own ink. The case created a stir. The auditor general of Pakistan in the Government Accounting Office in Islamabad examined the background of the joint venture in a special report. According to this report, the venture could be traced back to the 1993 participation of the Pakistani prime minister of that time in a »seminar on direct investment in Pakistan« in Zurich.[3] The auditor determined that there were conflicts of interest in public office on the part of PSPC employees. The auditor's report expressedly mentioned the delivery of used machinery at an inflated price, above-average increases in price since the start of ink deliveries by SICPA Ink Pakistan, and in general delivery prices from the joint venture that were above the world market level. The report also found that SICPA had taken advantage of the business relationship with PSPC to open the Pakistani market for its commercial inks. The devastating verdict of this special report ended with a recommendation to terminate the joint venture as soon as possible. The contract came up for renewal in 2000, yet the auditor's report has had no consequences so far. Except one: Akzo Nobel pulled out of the Pakistani market. Competing bidders also came up short in Egypt. Although the government printer solicited tenders for the ink requirement for a single denomination, it awarded the contract for delivery of the security ink directly to SICPA for all other denominations.

There are concrete reasons for so much customer loyalty. Central banks are conservative and it is hard to cause them to switch suppliers as long as their banknote production with the inks of a given manufacturer proceeds without problems. In order even to consider a change, the emitting institutions and their state printing plants demand proof that banknotes have already been successfully printed with the new ink. Should complications arise, the consequences could be grave, ranging from the costly interruption of production to, in an extreme case, a shortfall in the national supply of paper money. For example, when VEB Wertpapierdruck of Leipzig mixed a local product with the expensive intaglio ink of SICPA in the making of the East German 50-mark notes with two-sided steelplate engraving in the mid-1980s, the presses had to be stopped. Yet, it is precisely the private note printers that shy away from the printing test required by the central banks, although they are the logical ones to conduct it. The business risk is usually too great for them. Moreover, Printer A doesn't give a hoot about the printing test successfully completed by Printer B. On top of that, many central banks insist that separate printing tests be conducted with every single ink – and there can be a dozen of them on one note – and for every single note denomination. That can take years. So, the snake here has bitten his own tail.

Our quasi-monopoly is the best guarantee of security in this delicate business, goes the simple argument advanced by the Swiss. The consistent quality of ink and a globe-spanning market presence undoubtedly give SICPA big advantages. Whenever a problem arises somewhere, this enables the customers to be informed quickly. Also helpful are the personal contacts that have developed over the decades and are carefully cultivated by SICPA. They reinforce its market position with respect to challengers. Should some product crop up somewhere that could nevertheless disrupt SICPA's arrangements, the Swiss would then buy up the innovation or the innovator whenever possible. Ovart Nitithantprapas, a chemist with the central bank of Thailand, achieved in this way a very high, lifetime stipend. With local raw materials he had developed an intaglio printing ink that – as one hears in Bangkok – measured up to the quality of the competing SICPA product at only a fraction of its cost. According to the inventor, who has since passed away, the product would have been particularly suitable for the printing of U.S. dollars. This was apparently not an unusual case. The report of the government accounting office in Islamabad also determined that the development work of PSPC on a fast-drying intaglio ink, called P-5, was rolled back by SICPA with the help of the local joint venture.[4] It is easily conceivable in such an environment that an employee could be tempted to defect with his knowledge to the competition. SICPA takes action against such eventualities with all the means – and meanness – at its disposal. Written into the hiring contract, this approach includes an injunction – of questionable legality – against other employment in the field for several years after severance from the company. A former SICPA chemist who struck a deal with Sun Chemical in the 1990s and had wanted to help the Americans set up their own production of secure ink wound up in prison. Such draconian action was taken against the man that even the responsible judge in Geneva took pity.[5] Quite a bit of money was at stake. The market power of SICPA is really intimidating. Germany's Bundesdruckerei made a virtue of adversity by signing over the exclusive distribution of its electroluminescent secure ink, Elu, to the Swiss company. Nothing more was heard of this color-shifting ink, which had been developed with EU assistance.

Such suppliers as Akzo Nobel and BASF's Kast & Ehinger have in the meantime withdrawn from the difficult business with secure inks. The market has become more fluid, nevertheless. In the production of banknotes, on one hand, there are signs of a shift along the value chain toward alternative security features. In their search for easily recognizable and easily verifiable security characteristics for the citizenry, the central banks have started to encourage alternative security features such as the hologram or iridescent stripes with pearly sheen. For reasons of austerity there are many, among them the United States, Britain, and Germany

(DM-notes), which have changed to one-sided engraved printing, or, like France (Franc-notes), have done away with intaglio altogether. On the other hand, they are starting to keep their eyes peeled for other suppliers of secure inks. This has been a rather half-hearted quest and the outcome has been commensurately meager. The complete line of secure inks is offered today by Hunolt Tintas S.A. in the Basque city of Beasain and by Gleitsmann Security Inks, a unit of Michael Huber München GmbH. Hunolt has so far not succeeded in supplying ink for the printing of the euro. Gleitsmann, however, has struck a deal with Giesecke & Devrient for replacement printing of the euro in the 10-, 20-, and 50-euro denominations. Before the Second World War, at a time when Gleitsmann was still primarily a purveyor of commercial inks, this company had already supplied Giesecke & Devrient in Leipzig with special inks for banknote printing. Since then Gleitsmann has concentrated entirely on secure inks. As mentioned, it supplies Gosnak with binding agents for its own production of secure inks. The Berlin company is also the exclusive ink supplier to the state printing office of the Philippines, where its bid was far more reasonable than that of SICPA in a procurement solicitation. And Bangladesh, one of the few countries that always solicit public tenders for procurement requirements, is also regularly supplied by Gleitsmann. This company regards itself today as the second biggest supplier in the world, commanding by its own estimate a share of 12 percent of the »available market« for secure ink.

SICPA has reacted cautiously to these developments. For example, a few production facilities for secure inks have been set up abroad as joint ventures or simply as franchises that still have to obtain their basic products from Switzerland. Efforts to lock up long-term supply contracts have also been redoubled because public bidding is then rendered superfluous. The prices have been lowered somewhat. In the case of euro printing especially, SICPA has had to make price concessions on a broad front with its security inks. But this does not mean that everyone now automatically pays the same price. Only for the OVI color-shifting ink was a uniform delivery price of 1,250 Swiss francs for all member countries agreed upon at the insistence of the ECB. That is still considerably more than the price the U.S. Bureau of Engraving and Printing has to pay – but it is below the world market price for this special ink. The OVI color-shifting ink remains the resplendent golden goose of the SICPA.

Family crisis

Yet even monopolistic revenues are no protection from corporate crises. Like many another family companies, SICPA learned that a transition from one generation to the next can be painful. Charles Bossert, the veteran director general who had played a substantial role in SICPA's success with secure inks, left the company at the end of the 1980s. Albert Amon, the senior executive who had become accustomed to success, missed the opportunity to place the operating direction of the greatly expanded group in the hands of professional managers. His two sons, Maurice and Philippe, now the third generation of this entrepreneurial family, took over the operating leadership instead. What then transpired was reminiscent of the drama played out by the Seagram whiskey dynasty of the Canadian Bronfman family. Maurice and Philippe plunged SICPA helter-skelter into an expansion program financed with bank loans. Snapped up for inflated prices across the world were companies that were either losing money or did not fit into the core business. On top of that came the suspected involvement in several scandals about which the media reported with delight. The tight-lipped family business was suddenly dragged through the gossip columns of the tabloid press. The group plunged deeply into the red. Bank debt mounted. The situation grew so precarious by the mid-1990s that the survival of the company seemed in jeopardy. Albert Amon had to put his stock in escrow. Reports circulated in the media that the U.S. investment bank Goldman Sachs had received a mandate to find a buyer. That was quickly denied. But the two house banks, Swiss Bank Corp. (SBV), today part of UBS, and Banque Cantonale Vaudoise (BCV), forced the Amon family to withdraw from the running of the business. Albert Amon had to exchange his post as chairman of the supervisory board for a presidency emeritus. Sons Maurice and Philippe moved from the managing board to the supervisory board, which for the first time was chaired by a president who was not a family member. At the insistence of the banks, Hans-Jörg Loeliger was called in as a troubleshooter. Loeliger, a manager with extensive professional experience in U.S. big business, became simultaneously chief executive officer and president of the general directorate.[6] Thus empowered, he unloaded all of the participations that did not belong to the core business in order to restore liquidity. One such participation was the stake held in Flex Products Inc. in the United States. This divested share capital was acquired by OCLI, the U.S.

laboratory that held the majority in that joint venture. In this way Loeliger was able to reduce indebtedness in a comparatively brief period, bringing the ink manufacturer back into the black. The strong earnings still generated by the secure inks made the decisive contribution to the successful turnaround.

This success bred intemperance in the family. The conflicting interests of the Amon family and the creditor banks had repeatedly engendered tensions with the troubleshooter as well. At the end of the year 2000 the two sons managed abruptly to oust the unloved turnaround specialist, who had preferred to take action autonomously. The father had previously signed over his stockholding to the three children. Maurice and Philippe were installed as relative majority shareholders, and daughter Monique received a smaller stake. In the event of a seizure of the stock, Swiss equity law ensured that the Amon family as nominal owner was able to continue to exercise voting rights. Shortly thereafter the financial director, Daniel Meyer, also left. Leading a consortium of a dozen banks, Goldman Sachs took over the refinancing, replacing the company's two house banks. Maurice and Philippe are fully engaged in the company again today. Yet the banks have imposed a strict regimen. The consortium continues to have an important say. In late summer of 2005 the two sons had to do that which was repeatedly advised and which they had steadfastly refused throughout the years: SICPA beat a complete retreat from the business with packaging inks. With sales of 600 million Swiss francs, a worldwide workforce of 2,800, and a market situation that was stretched thin, Sicpa Packaging was sold for an unnamed price to Siegwerk Group International of Siegburg, Germany. This enabled the German company to bolster its position as world market leader for upscale packaging inks. SICPA henceforth will concentrate fully on the business of secure inks and security systems for printing banknotes, said a terse press release. The secure ink to supply the world market will be manufactured only in the main plant in Chavornay, and the secure ink for the Bureau of Engraving and Printing at Springfield, Virginia. This dramatic turn of events makes sense from an earnings standpoint. The business with secure inks remains highly lucrative. But for Albert Amon, the senior member of the clan, this has to have been a bitter pill.

Moneymakers II

5
What caused De La Rue's imperial aura to fade

De La Rue plc. of Basingstoke, near London, is not the oldest private printer of banknotes in the world. The Dutch Joh. Enschedé en Zonen beat the British to this title by decades. And even Giesecke & Devrient can claim to have been engaged in note and securities printing a few years longer than De La Rue. Nor is the British company any longer the leader in sales among the world's private high-security corporations. The Munich rival is now in front by a nose.[1] But no other private firm prints so many banknotes for so many countries as the tradition-steeped British firm, nor does any other deliver so much secure paper. The list of countries that obtain their banknotes or their banknote paper from it includes 150 names, De La Rue has said. In the almanac of high-security printers, the name of De La Rue has the most prominent place.

Urbi et orbi

The origins of this private high-security printer go back to the year 1813. It was then that Thomas de la Rue, a descendant of Huguenots who fled France for the channel island of Guernsey and there published the newspaper *Le Miroir Politique,* opened a stationery store and an adjacent printing shop in London. He initially printed playing cards. Tax stamps and postage stamps followed in 1853. In 1860 the first banknotes were printed for the government of the island of Mauritius. De La Rue was excluded from the printing of British banknotes, except during the First World War, but was allowed to print pound notes for Scotland and Northern Ireland. As a substitute for printing the domestic currency, the British dominions, especially India, provided a much more lively demand for its products, be they tax and postage stamps or banknotes. Even then the Lon-

Moneymakers, Klaus W. Bender

ISBN: 3-527-50236-X

don private printer lived from exports. Foreign business ties that had grown up during a century were later to bear rich fruit again when the British colonies were given their independence. Nearly all the new countries of Africa and Asia that wanted to have their own banknotes and postage stamps after decolonization let De La Rue do the printing as an obvious choice.

Equally advantageous proved the arrangements under which De La Rue printed banknotes in London for the numerous governments in exile there from the countries of southern and eastern Europe during the Second World War when those countries were occupied by German troops. Greeks, Yugoslavs, Poles, Czechoslovakians, and Norwegians paid their resistance fighters at home with banknotes produced by De La Rue. And these were often »delivered« by the Royal Air Force. Only the French didn't have this problem. After the First World War Banque de France as a prudent precaution moved its banknote printing facility from Paris to Chamalières, near Clermont-Ferrand in central France, where the printing establishment remained in fact long untouched by the German occupation during the Second World War. The countries once occupied by the Germans naturally turned to De La Rue after their liberation at the end of the Second World War. And this happened on an even larger scale after the fall of the Iron Curtain when more countries wanted to swap their worthless socialist paper money for capitalist banknotes with buying power.

The British banknote printer landed such orders frequently and comparatively without effort. And there was a great flurry of business in the immediate postwar years. Both of these conditions might have contributed to some negligence with regard to the security and conscientiousness otherwise commonplace in the industry. In any event, a mishap[2] unique in the history of banknote printing then came to pass. In 1951–52 the Greek government set forth a stabilization plan that also included a currency reform. The economy had been ravaged by hyperinflation. The net outflow of capital exceeded the assistance payments from the West. It appeared that the inflationary spiral could only be arrested with entirely new money. The printing of new drachma banknotes was initiated in this spirit, financed by funds from the Marshall Plan and supervised by Ed Tenenbaum with his team of experts. The young American had made history as the father of the West German currency reform of 1948. Although American Banknote had printed the Greek notes exclusively from 1861 until the 1930s and had also produced a portion of the notes for the German currency reform, De La Rue received the contract. It was worth 100,000 pounds sterling, then a considerable sum, and it included the production of a complete series of notes, from drafting through the engraving of the printing plates to the printing of the notes. But the program conceived by Tenenbaum for stabilizing the economy had been so successful that the newly elected government in Athens did without the currency reform. And in April 1953 it was able to risk the – politically more dangerous – devaluation of the existing drachma currency. Fifty billion old drachmas corresponded to two new ones! The new note series that had been printed by De La Rue was obsolete. It was stowed away in a warehouse in Britain – and promptly forgotten. Not until years later, after many a persistent inquiry from members of the long since disbanded Tenenbaum team and after tedious investigation were the dusty crates of freshly printed notes rediscovered. These notes had to be laboriously burned in Britain in a special furnace. Then there was no more risk-taking. Two representatives of the U.S. government were present until the last note had turned to ashes.

De La Rue Company Ltd. was already a globally active corporation at the end of the 1950s when Giesecke & Devrient was laboriously staking out a new lease on life with the printing of the first Deutschmark notes for Bundesbank. De La Rue then had sales of 22 million pounds sterling. According to the Bank of England, that would be worth fifteen times as much in today's pounds. It had twenty-four plants in fourteen countries and ten thousand employees. More than a billion individual banknotes each year left the printing plant of De La Rue in London's Bunhill Row in those days. This market dominance of the British printer was to increase still more, following the operating debut in the early 1960s of a huge new high-security printing plant in Gateshead by Newcastle, far in the north of England. In the best of times seven lines of printing machinery operated there, including three of the especially high-performance Super line, and all of them from Koebau-Giori. Who but the »House of De La Rue« could have afforded to publish a type of world atlas for its 150th anniversary, instead of the usual company chronicle? De La Rue, »urbi et orbi«! No other company could claim to pull such weight on the world market for banknote and securities printing. Employees still rave today about the annual »diplomatic dinners« held at London's Dorchester Hotel for central banks' governors and ambassadors of the customer-countries. Always in attendance was a member of the royal family or the British prime minister. Those events were done away with decades ago. The company was considered a jewel of British industry. In its own self-awareness it was also a demonstratively British company, directed by »gentlemen« who knew one another well from college or military service and who naturally appeared for work wearing the distinctive ties of their »public school.« This high-security printer or one of its subsidiaries won the coveted Queen's Award for Enterprise for outstanding achievement nine times.

Beyond Malta

As time past, though, the corporation became somewhat unwieldy. Stake holdings that had not a thing to do with secure printing belonged to the group. For example, there was a rubber products manufacturer in the United States, a British manufacturer of heating boilers, and a specialist in refrigeration engineering. This was corrected in the 1970s by Peter Francis Orchard, the legendary chief executive of De La Rue who had earned his spurs in securities printing. He tossed the exotic ballast overboard and refocused the group on the core business of printing banknotes and securities. He simultaneously pressed forward in setting up banknote printing facilities abroad. De La Rue at that time already had overseas printing plants for securities in Brazil, the United States, and at times in Mexico. Its printing of banknotes had been done exclusively in Britain, however.

Although that was also needed for reasons of security, Orchard's predecessor had already broken with this principle in 1974. The first banknote printing plant of De La Rue outside England was then erected in the independent island republic of Malta. In the course of his tenure, Orchard added a whole list of other foreign banknote printing facilities. Their locations – Ireland, Sri Lanka, Singapore, and Hong Kong – stretched out like a string of pearls to remote Southeast Asia. Added in the 1990s after Orchard's departure were Kenya, Nigeria, and Portugal, although excess capacity on the market was already shaping up at that time. One had hoped to derive basing advantages from these late-coming branches, especially in the emerging African market. De La Rue showed that it was ready to take risks and was not averse to forging politically sensitive alliances with local state printers. Sri Lanka, Nigeria, and Portugal were joint ventures, partly even with minority participations. In the beginning the geographic diversification followed no strategic plan. The foreign units had been only a reaction to the mounting conflict with the English printers union, whose implacable stance was finally to cause mass closing of printing establishments in the British Isles and the notorious »death of Fleet Street.« But relocation in low-wage countries that also offered tax incentives bestowed cost advantages. On Malta De La Rue balanced payroll costs that are still considerably lower today than those of Giesecke & Devrient, as is averred in Munich. This secured for the British a margin before interest and tax of 15 percent to 20 percent in the core business of banknote printing. No wonder the competition viewed this earning power with envious admiration. Gateshead remained the center with the highest quality for the printing of banknotes. Paper production was uninteresting. A printer doesn't make paper; he buys it, as De La Rue used to say.

By farming out printing, De La Rue freed itself from the dictates of the unions but heaped numerous logistical problems upon itself. The response to changes in demand and the ad hoc use of fallow capacity for printing banknotes became more complicated. Once the secure paper for a special currency was on its way overseas by ship, it was hard to make changes. The relocation of production also caused problems with quality. Although British technicians directed the production at the site, there were complaints about printing quality. That often resulted in the loss of a customer.

This relocation and the simultaneous run-up in printing capacity were accompanied by a deliberate strategy of market shakeout. Disturbing competitors were bought out whenever the opportunity arose. Massive restructuring costs were often accepted when this happened. Waterlow & Sons in 1961, Bradbury, Wilkinson in 1986, and Harrison & Sons in 1997 vanished from the market in this way. Their printing capacity was mothballed. One exception was Harrison's stamp-printing plant in High Wycombe, which had been purchased because of the strong business with stamps. De La Rue was even interested in taking over Giesecke & Devrient at one point. This was in the 1960s when the »newcomer« had forced the British out of the important Mexican market for secure printing. The Munich company politely declined.

The Portals debacle

De La Rue was outstandingly positioned in the market at the start of the 1990s. Jeremy Marshall, the chief executive of the British Airport Authority (BAA) who switched to De La Rue the end of 1989, had led the company quickly out of a slump, restoring to it stable growth and rising earnings. With the collapse of communism, the note printer had desired to secure for itself a disproportionately large share of banknote printing, especially in the CIS countries emerging from the wreckage of the Soviet Union. Printing volume of more than six billion notes had touched its historic peak there. Insiders even talked of eight billion. The business with printing machinery for the countries of the imploded Soviet empire was also running encouragingly. De La Rue profited from this not just through the rising dividend disbursement of its participation in Lausanne. The financially potent banknote printer also became directly involved in the building of printing plants for selected eastern countries, for example the Ukraine, Kazakhstan, Uzbekistan, and Bulgaria. And lastly, the newly launched British state lottery »Camelot,« in which De La Rue had been granted a notable stake holding, promised fat profits.[3]

Net reserves carried in De La Rue's balance sheet at the end of the financial year 1993–94 amounted to 270 million pounds sterling. That corresponded to nearly half of consolidated group sales. This caused an outcry in the City of London. These funds must be invested »productively,« demanded a swelling chorus of analysts. De La Rue lacked vertical integration in production and a stable paper supply. The Portals corporation offered both. It made banknote paper based on cotton in Overton and secure paper for passports and check blanks in Bathford. The founding of this company could also be traced back to a Huguenot émigré. It had exclusively supplied the paper for the pound notes of the Bank of England since 1724, the reason why Bank of England also held a 30 percent stake in the paper factory. For a long period Portals had claimed to be the leading private producer of secure paper in the world. Naturally, Portals was also the most important – if not the only – paper supplier of De La Rue. Conversely, De La Rue was its most important single customer among all the world's private printers.

The market for secure paper is tight and is controlled by a few large manufacturers. There are no official figures on it. Experts estimate the global volume of production at 140,000 metric tons a year, of which somewhat less than half is supplied to the »available market« and the rest is covered by state-run paper factories, which predominantly concentrate on their own governments' needs. Around 70 percent of this available market today is divided by a trio, composed of Portals, the Louisenthal paper factory, and the Anglo-French paper group Arjo-Wiggins, the only one that also produces commercial goods.[4] The unusual concentration is explained, for one thing, by the lofty technical requirements for this special paper, which shares only the name with commercial available goods. Responsible for this difference is, secondly, the large investment for a secure paper-making plant that far exceeds the comparable cost for a conventional paper factory. The investment even for a small plant, such as the one in Uzbekistan, with its capacity of 3,000 metric tons, is more than 100 million dollars. To cover these costs, however, a secure paper plant has to produce at least 4,000 metric tons a year of banknote paper. One could cover the need for banknotes of nearly half a billion people with that. This tight market therefore wheezes under chronically excess capacity.

Portals erected its first foreign production facility for banknote paper at the start of the 1980s in Hawkinsville, Georgia, in the United States. This was a bold gamble because the paper market for the dollar is tightly sealed off from all foreign competitors by technical barriers. For starters, the Americans produce their dollar paper on a machine called Fourdrinier, after its French inventor. This machine works with much longer pulp fibers, while the rest of the world makes short-fiber banknote paper with the cylinder mold technique. What's more, to manufacture their dollar paper the Americans add 25 percent linen from undyed dungaree refuse to the usual cotton pulp, something no one else does. The result is a much thicker and firmer dollar paper. The typical sound associated with handling American banknotes is explained by this. As if that alone did not offer enough protection against undesired import competition, the Bureau of Engraving and Printing is allowed to use only dollar paper produced domestically. This still did not seem to suffice for some politicians. At the behest of the late Rep. Silvio O. Conte, a Massachusetts Republican, the so-called Conte Amendment was enacted in 1987. Since then, any manufacturer of dollar paper has had to be at least 90 percent controlled by U.S. capital.

Crane & Co. of Dalton, Massachusetts, a family-owned company, alone fulfills this condition. Its origins date back to the late 18th century. Crane is an institution. When the White House sends out invitations, they go on handmade paper from Crane & Co. And when the U.S. government complains again to its European partners about unfair trade practices, it will be done with great probability on stationery from Crane & Co. But the Crane family makes its money with the dollar paper, although the strictly secret share of this in its overall sales might be rather small. The »greenback« has been around since 1862. Crane & Co. has exclusively supplied the paper for the dollar to the Bureau of Engraving and Printing since 1879. Again and again there have been disputes over the price of paper between Crane and the Bureau of Engraving and Printing, such as occur in monopolistic pricing. Congress became upset and called for competition. Portals began to hope that the capital clause would be relaxed so that it could do business with the Bureau of Engraving and Printing through a local subsidiary as an additional paper supplier. Rep. James Kolbe, Republican of Arizona, even wanted to earmark 100 million dollars as startup financing for this. That was a capital mistake because it delivered ammunition to the opponents of a market opening. The Crane family showed not even the slightest inclination to share such a comfortable and lucrative monopoly with somebody else.[5] Crane & Co. threatened layoffs and mobilized diehard political allies locally and in Washington. As a venture launched only half-heartedly by overhauling a U.S. custom papers factory with used machinery, Portals' attempt to open the U.S. market was a complete flop. After a year-long tug-o-war the proponents' two bills – one to render assistance, the other to lower the U.S. capital requirement to 50 percent – were routed on Capitol Hill. Democratic Sen. Edward M. Kennedy of Massachusetts, another true ally of Crane & Co., celebrated the defeat of an »outrageous proposal,« and Democratic Rep. John W. Oliver of Amherst, Massachusetts, proclaimed the »victory of fair competition in America.«[6] The British had long since struck their colors. Cumulative losses from the American campaign, according to industry insiders, came to more than 50 million dollars. That was not a financial problem. But the self-confidence of the exchange-listed British paper manufacturer had been shaken.

Amid this depressed mood De La Rue boss Jeremy Marshall made the owners of Portals a takeover bid at the start of 1994. According to media reports, he offered 650 million pounds sterling, which corresponded to a premium of around 50 percent on top of the price at which the Portals share had been trading. Portals' management rejected it, nevertheless, with the support of the staff. The tradition-rich company did not want to lose its independence. The price of the Portals share then buckled, while the share of De La Rue soared. This reaction on the exchange should have served De La Rue as a warning of impending trouble, but the signal was overlooked. Marshall's pride was injured. And perhaps he was also worried that another investor could buy into this strategically important supplier. Reports that the chief executive officer of Portals had resided for years in a luxurious country manor suddenly cropped up in the media. The notional yearly rent for the estate was estimated in the newspapers as more than 100,000 pounds sterling. »Laverstoke House« belonged to Portals, but not a word about all this had appeared in the financial statement. The line of defense began to waver. De La Rue went on the offensive, saying that the technical expertise of two leading companies in the banknote and securities business would be combined, allowing them to achieve great synergism in the development of new security characteristics for banknote paper.[7] Portals would then benefit from the banknote printer's closeness to the customers. They struck a deal in December 1994. De La Rue took over 100 percent of Portals' capital, paying 720 million pounds for it, according to internal calculations made in the City. Around two-thirds of this was to be paid in cash. A stock swap would be made for the rest of the shareholders – including many employees of Portals who had received stock distributions.

The stock exchange became unnerved. In the previous business year, 1993, Portals had made a pre-tax profit of 31 million pounds on consolidated sales of 198 million pounds. That was respectable – but sales and profit had been stagnating for years. A premium amounting to 31 times earnings per Portals share was regarded in the City as too high, especially since De La Rue had to go deeply into debt to finance the takeover. The purchase was completed in just a few weeks, during which De La Rue quickly took advantage of the historic high price of its own share, namely more than 1,000 pence, to orchestrate a large capital hike. Exactly one month after the triumphantly announced takeover, De La Rue issued a warning of an impending profit decline for the business year in progress. And it let the perplexed financial world know that one could look forward to a negative profit contribution for at least the next two years after the acquisition. The price of the De La Rue share went into a free fall, shedding nearly half of its market value within a few months. It was small consolation that Portals would be the only company in the De La Rue group that would be able to keep its own name. The subsidiary was, after all, one hundred years older than the parent company, and tradition was duty.

The worries were more than justified. It had been apparent for years that the market was in flux – and mainly to the detriment of Portals. When Giesecke & Devrient undertook in the 1960s to build its own plant for secure paper, the competition was still able to refuse to deliver the technology for special papermaking machinery. Giesecke & Devrient was forced to develop this engineering know-how by itself with the help of machinery manufacturer Dörries. The Munich company became autonomous in this technology in the end. The others had not wanted that. It was logical now to admonish the Louisenthal paper factory to be circumspect about passing on its valuable technology. Louisenthal was then working with large losses and naturally had no desire to kill off its own export market. The established competition still controlled the prices on the world market. A price war would have been injurious for the Munich company.

But Louisenthal slowly worked its way up, becoming an important international supplier of secure paper. Then it became no longer just a matter of passing on technology. It now had to worry about prices and markets. What was more logical in an oligopolistic market plagued by persistent excess capacity than to band together in secrecy? Siegfried Otto was not shy in such matters. Such delicate negotiations come more easily when one meets in pleasant surroundings, such as under the warm sun of Tuscany. The outcome was the »Italian agreement,« in which the big three committed themselves to offer no less than their production price when exporting and in certain cases – such as a country which one producer regarded as »his« customer – to stay clear voluntarily. It became repeatedly apparent in later public solicitations for paper bids – also for note printing, for example – that a supplier would make an attractive bid for certain denominations, although he would practically catapult himself out of the auction with unfathomably high prices on others.

This was initially only speculation. Yet rumors were continually nourished, for example in connection with the window thread developed by Portals some years later. With window thread, the security thread of transparent polyester that is otherwise completely embedded in the paper intermittently surfaces, just as in a window. Only when back-lighted does the continuous path of the thread become recognizable. This polyester thread is »demetallized,« meaning its surface coating of aluminum or a precious metal is partly interrupted at regular intervals, but without breaking the electrical conductivity of the thread. This makes it possible to place minute black writing on a white background. Originally it could only be seen in the negative as white writing on a black background. That is an additional and effective security feature. Portals transferred the license for this invention to Louisenthal without charge. It certainly also played a role in this decision that the customers were reacting with increasing reluctance to stitch close ties to just one supplier and also didn't want to become dependent through an exclusively offered feature. But the view in the marketplace was that Portals was no longer strong enough to make a success of its new security feature all by itself. Crane & Co., the maker of the dollar paper, detected a threat to its own export business in the agreement between Portals and Louisenthal. In the second half of the 1990s the Americans, who were now running a second paper mill, Baystate, with conventional cylinder-mold technology for export, took Louisenthal to court for alleged patent jumping. They failed across the board, losing even the modest patent protection they had had to that point. It had been unwise to fight before a court over a process that they had not even mastered technologically.

Gentlemen's agreements are, of course, easy to make. Whether or how long they will be honored then becomes another question. Chronic excess capacity visibly limits their value. For when in doubt, each supplier thinks first about the use of his own capacity. For example, India was by tradition a special market and also an especially important one for Portals. It had built a paper factory for rupee notes in Hoshangabad, near the huge Dewas banknote printing complex. Since India had at its disposal all the materials required for manufacturing banknote paper, from cotton to chemicals, it had hoped to reduce its dependency upon expensive imports of paper. But Hoshangabad, which today produces nearly 4,000 metric tons a year, was too skimpily dimensioned initially and was not in any way equal to the sharply rising Indian demand. It was also plagued by strikes and technical disruptions so frequently that even the experts were surprised. In order to meet its requirements of currently around 12,000 metric tons a year, India still had to rely on imports. This made – and still does today – a welcome contribution to the operating rate of the Portals plant in Overton.

With its huge requirements, India obviously was a highly attractive sales market for the Munich company. Louisenthal first managed to sell paper to India at the start of the 1980s. Then there was a delivery hiatus of a decade and a half before the otherwise tight-lipped Munich company reported in near triumph the signing in autumn 1998 of its biggest export contract for banknote paper, a deal with India worth nearly 100 million Deutschmarks. Louisenthal is today among the standard suppliers to the subcontinent. And after the Indians proclaimed their policy of the »clean banknote« at the turn of the millennium, their business relationship with Giesecke & Devrient has become ever closer. Munich has now delivered its banknote processing system to India in large numbers. It was even able to install its sensors for the control of printing quality on the Komori machinery in the new Salboni printing plant. And according to industry reports, Munich is in talks with private Indian financiers to build a large paper factory. This could mark the end of Portals' deliveries to India. But the Munich printer is in no hurry with this paper factory in India. Who is eager to lose such an important customer?

With the takeover of Portals, Marshall had in mind the example of Giesecke & Devrient and its profitable paper factory. Yet the entry into the paper business came too late and at an exorbitant price. People in the City console themselves today with the thought that De La Rue would no longer be viable as a banknote printer without Portals. The shift from printing to paper in the chain of added value and the inclusion of highly technological security characteristics in the paper substrate confirm the validity of this strategic decision. Price pressure and the strong British currency remain a burden on Portals, to be sure. The purchase decision was correct but the purchase price was 300 million pounds too high, Chief Executive Officer Ian Much once remarked to colleagues about the De La Rue takeover in retrospect. The price of the De La Rue share has never recovered from the Portals debacle.

Efforts toward an additional business line

The British high-security printer had naturally diversified early on into an additional line of business with machinery. De La Rue was one of the first in the industry to recognize the significance of banknote processing. But the British did not specialize in the business with central banks but in the automation of cash disbursement by the commercial banks instead. This promised greater sales volumes. In the late 1960s De La Rue had already installed the world's first automated teller machines in London, ATMs from which bank customers could withdraw cash around the clock. Machines to count and sort cash at the teller windows as well as fully automated note feeds to the automatic teller machines followed. De La Rue occasionally laid claim to market leadership here.

In building up its machinery business, however, De La Rue relied less upon the power of its own research and development, pursuing expansion instead through targeted purchases of technology and markets. This saved time and money, permitting a quick market entry – if one were lucky with the purchases. The takeover of Sweden's Inter Innovation at the start of the 1990s was one of these strokes of luck. The company developed and produced dispensing mechanisms for individual disbursements of banknotes. Small manufacturers, which make a business with cash dispensing machines only as systems integrators, need to buy these devices. The leading suppliers of ATMs, IBM, NCR, and Diebold of the United States; Germany's Wincor Nixdorf; and Japan's Fujitsu develop and produce such devices themselves but do not sell their technology to third parties. The takeover of Inter Innovation enabled De La Rue to enter this niche business as a so-called original equipment manufacturer and secured for it sustained sales success in Europe, Africa, and Latin America. The worldwide market presence of De La Rue proved to be the trump card here. Sales increased disproportionately right after the takeover of the Swedish company, soon surpassing those of traditional banknote and securities printing.

But the big drawback of a market strategy based on purchases is that it obstructs the development of one's own capability. This weakness had surfaced earlier when De La Rue began to take an interest in high-performance systems for banknote processing. The importance of that demanding market was perhaps not appreciated in a timely fashion. Not until it became impressed with the development work in Munich on the »automation-capable banknote« and the complementing banknote processing systems (BPS) did De La Rue follow suit. Crosfield Electronics had been purchased in the 1970s. It was a supplier of control systems and was then conducting development jointly on an optical inspection system for banknotes with Recognition Equipment Inc. of Dallas, actually a U.S. specialist for postal sorting systems. The system then offered by De La Rue was greeted with only scant interest in the market. It was too slow and had difficulty inspecting dirty notes. Crosfield was sold again.

The outlays of this high-security corporation for research and development remained comparatively low. At the beginning of the 1990s they amounted to just 2 percent of sales. Even today's ratio of 2.7 percent of group sales corresponds to less than half the ratio Giesecke & Devrient has been investing in its research for years. In Munich, however, the cost-intensive field of cards is included in the figure. In the first half of the 1990s De La Rue even lowered its research spending in the machinery sector. When the outlays were raised again with the approach of the euro, the effort came too late. De La Rue profited from refitting of cash dispensing machines in the euro sphere and made record sales in the business of »payment systems.« But the British company played scarcely a role with testing systems for central banks and large commercial banks. It has been practically shut out of this special business in the euro countries.

De La Rue again sought salvation in acquisition, deciding upon the takeover of Currency Systems International (CSI) of the United States. CSI had already had a checkered past at this point. The company had been carved out of the previously mentioned Recognition Equipment at the start of the 1990s, when that business had just failed with a contract from the Federal Reserve to develop a capable system of processing banknotes. Some employees then assumed the risk of a management buyout in order to continue the development on their own with the available technological knowledge. CSI machines were also sold to some central banks – Australia, Canada, Israel, Malaysia, South Africa, and Taiwan. Yet the sensor technique and working speed in inspecting banknotes remained a problem. The desired market breakthrough continued to elude the chronically underfinanced company. In this way the majority of capital in CSI was finally sold to the company G+D (no relationship to Giesecke & Devrient) in Bologna, an extremely secretive company that was regarded as one of the world's leading suppliers of packaging machinery for cigarettes. The prosperous Bolognese wanted to diversify into a second business because of the crisis in the tobacco industry. But they soon found the financial as well as technological turnaround of CSI to be too expensive. CSI therefore wound up with De La Rue in the end.

The Texas company was acquired for 55 million dollars, including debt, only months before the euro was introduced. But De La Rue soon discovered that putting two invalids together didn't add up to one healthy unit. The integration of CSI, the realignment of production bases, and the development of new technological solutions proved unexpectedly difficult. The costs exploded. Just after De La Rue's takeover of CSI, Giesecke & Devrient succeeded in getting its foot in the door of the central banks of Australia, New Zealand, India, and other countries with its large banknote inspection systems. It even garnered large customers among banks and casinos in the United States. De La Rue had to concede openly that it had miscalculated the market. It wrote down the goodwill of CSI. But the British did not give up. Shortly after the euro's introduction, De La Rue bought Papelaco, a specialist for banknote processing automation on the Iberian Peninsula, in order to climb into the new business with direct cash recycling. This is a promising business branch, although the move was now unfavorably timed. It was the banking crisis that caused sales of the new subsidiary to collapse in its two most important markets, Spain and Germany. Again the British had to write down the good will of a recently acquired company. Despite its respectable sales volume, the machinery business remains the Achilles heel of the British high-security group.

The underestimated competition

Back to banknote printing. This is a highly sensitive business in which it does not suffice to have a good and maybe even a better product. Political considerations play a central role in the decision on who may print notes for a certain country. De La Rue for a long while had the best cards there. Contacts at diplomatic and secret-service level came into play and the »old boys« network worked well. When push came to shove, one requested discreet assistance to tie a knot in the tail of a disagreeable competitor. The political sensitivity of the banknote business and the power of the British private printer can be illustrated particularly well in the case of Poland. Shortly after the fall of the Berlin Wall, Warsaw decided to issue a fully new series of banknotes as part of a currency reform. Narodowy Bank Polski, the Polish national bank, had its own state-owned high-security company in the form of banknote printer Polska Wytwórnia Papierów Wartosciówych, (PWPW). PWPW would have been able to print the new zloty; its capacity was taken up by the routine printing of still valid banknotes, though. Moreover, the printing of the new notes was supposed to be a strict secret so as to avoid upsetting the people even more as they grappled with the difficulties of transformation. Therefore, the decision was made to print abroad. Giesecke & Devrient had built a modern paper factory for PWPW in the 1970s. It also often obtained paper there, which provided Poland with foreign exchange. Polish delegations often visited Munich and personal contacts were very close. So the Polish national bank made a contract with Giesecke & Devrient to print 550 million zloty banknotes, an arrangement worth more than 30 million Deutschmarks. Playing a big role in the letting of the contract were assurances that the new Polish banknotes would come with the same security features as the new Deutschemark series BBk III, which was just being made ready for issue by the Bundesbank. Giesecke & Devrient had been engaged to handle half that printing and had exclusively delivered all of the paper for the new D-mark notes, on which the security features were regarded as especially effective in the battle against counterfeiting. For this reason the paper for the new zloty notes was also supposed to come from Louisenthal. In return, the Munich company placed a major order for banknote paper with the Polish paper factory for the printing of notes for Zaire. The designs for all nine zloty denominations – from 1 to 500 zlotys – were obtained from two Polish graphic artists. The technology center of De La Rue Giori in Sévelin was tasked with providing equipment, namely the making of the originals and printing plates. Stefan Tyminski, the director general of PWPW and an internationally recognized expert for banknote security, traveled repeatedly to Lausanne at the start of the 1990s to monitor the progress of work on the originals. The printing took place at Giesecke & Devrient. The proofs were given unblemished approval on the Polish side. The printing contract was executed to full satisfaction. It was, as several independent experts unanimously confirmed, a note printing with impeccable execution.

Poland's economy was still suffering from the reconstruction difficulties of the post-communist era. There was a highly inflationary adjustment. The Polish national bank therefore didn't want to issue its new currency until the announced reforms of economic and fiscal policy had taken hold. It was therefore decided to warehouse the new zloty notes initially. That was supposed to be done in Germany for reasons of secrecy and security. The Bundesbank made the storage space available free of charge for the 600 metric tons of banknotes. But the reforms stalled and Poland's economy slipped into an ever deepening crisis. Governors came and went in rapid succession at the Polish national bank until Hanna Gronkiewicz-Waltz was appointed governor in 1992. That's when the problems began. For reasons that were not entirely transparent, the new zloty notes were a thorn in the side of the new governor. Representatives of the Polish national bank suddenly found fault with the security features of the zloty banknotes stored in Germany, asserting that they did not meet the latest level of security against counterfeiting. Even a special report from the Deutsche Bundesbank was unable to convince Warsaw that these zloty banknotes, with security that was the technical equivalent of the new German D-mark notes, would not pose a heightened risk of counterfeiting. It was maliciously rumored in the industry that the name of the predecessor of her predecessor on the zloty notes irritated her worth of office.

The competition had never been pleased that Giesecke & Devrient was allowed to print the first banknotes for Poland after it was liberated from communism. De La Rue ostensibly backed the security objections but asserted simultaneously that the Polish state printing facility was technically unprepared to print modern notes – and it offered to print the new ones. The Polish national bank agreed, much to the amazement of the industry. The 550 million zloty banknotes, ready for issue and stored in Hesse, had to be hauled back to Munich and destroyed by Giesecke & Devrient in an expensive operation. Only a small number were overprinted as cancelled by Warsaw and offered to international collectors. The Polish national bank also paid the Germans for their services without objection. Yet the equivalent of more than 35 million Deutschmarks – that's how much the whole flap with the unloved notes had cost from printing to destruction – had gone up in smoke in the truest sense of the word. It was a strange decision for Poland, which had been conducting difficult negotiations on debt restructuring with its foreign creditors at that point and lacked even sufficient hard currency for vital imports. The complete new zloty series designed by De La Rue, but now for only five denominations, was printed in Malta. It was put into circulation at the end of 1993. But the British banknote printer did not have much joy with its coup. Some notes found their way into circulation that actually should have been destroyed as deficient. After only the first issue the Polish national bank pulled De La Rue's printing contract, recovered all the backup materials, and has since printed its banknotes itself.[8] Moreover, nothing became of the desired takeover of PWPW, which De La Rue had wanted to use as a base in an opening eastern Europe. This project foundered on objections from the government in Warsaw. That was doubly annoying because it is now looking as though PWPW may, under the circumstances, be allowed to print the euro notes for Poland and the Baltic states, if they enter the euro currency sphere.

The international banknote market was in a state of flux. While the volume of notes to print was stagnating on the available market, the Internet increasingly made this secretive market more transparent than had previously been conceivable. The price consciousness of the central banks mounted. New suppliers muscled their way onto the international scene. They were private printers from small countries, such as Switzerland's Orell Füssli AG in Zurich and the Dutch Joh. Enschedé en Zonen of

Haarlem, which exploited their impeccable printing quality to target export markets with limited note requirements. Both had solid financial and technological credentials as printers of their national currencies and sought additional business in order to put to work printing capacity that was insufficiently occupied by the national currencies. Their impact on the internationally available banknote market was comparatively small in terms of volume.[9] To this competition had to be added France's Francois Charles Oberthur Fiduciaire (FCOF), which was only founded in the 1980s and which printed only for export. With their aggressive pricing policies, these private printers succeeded in short order in penetrating traditional markets of De La Rue in Africa, Central America, and Southeast Asia.

Giesecke & Devrient had also blossomed into a potential competitor in note printing, although it had long played a subordinated role, in contrast to its significance with paper. Under pressure from the continual appreciation of the Deutschmark, this company had traditionally concentrated on the top segment of note printing where it could also command high prices for its high quality. The demanding technical specifications for D-mark printing as well as the accommodating price policy of the Deutsche Bundesbank were the essential conditions for this strategy. De La Rue had lived long and well from high-volume business, occasionally taking on a contract that returned little or no profit in order to make better use of its huge printing capacity. That changed radically in the last decade of the 20th century. It was at the beginning of the 1990s that the Munich competitor, as noted, increasingly entered the internationally available market – and it did so »aggressively,« as it also conceded in its company history.

Perhaps it was the complacency of its own strength that caused De La Rue to pay too little attention to these changes, to make too little of its strengths in the core business of banknotes, and instead to fragment its power with the hectic pursuit of news fields of business. In any event, De La Rue gradually lost customers in Africa, the Near East, and Asia. The loss of Malaysia as a customer in banknote printing to Giesecke & Devrient was a heavy blow to De La Rue in the 1990s. For two decades it had battled against this with all the means at its disposal. Yet the shifting balance of power really became apparent again in the case of India. At the end of 1997 India solicited bids on 3.6 million rupee notes, the biggest »overspill« contract it had ever let. De La Rue had regarded India practically as a »home market« and anticipated receiving the award. Yet following a marginally transparent bidding war, which made waves in media and politics (which will be covered in detail in the chapter on the Bundesdruckerei) the British received the award for only 2 billion notes. The rest were printed by Giesecke & Devrient. This was the first printing contract from India for the Munich company. And it was not the last defeat of this sort for De La Rue. Shortly thereafter, Nigeria, Africa's largest country with a huge requirement for banknotes, sought tenders for the printing of 4 billion naira notes. This was then the largest »overspill« contract ever let in the history of international banknote printing. De La Rue was excellently positioned in the West African country and held a blocking minority in the Nigerian state banknote printing facility. Although the Munich company had previously delivered its banknote inspection system to Nigeria – for a handsome price, incidentally – it had only been allowed to print banknotes once before for Nigeria. Yet Giesecke & Devrient was awarded the contact. The Munich company, however, subcontracted somewhat more than half of the whole volume to De La Rue, explaining this officially with »capacity problems.«

The Nigerians had long been looking for a foreign banknote printer as a partner in their ailing state banknote printing plant. They now redoubled their efforts. At one time they even seemed to have found one in Spain's FNMT. Yet the preliminary contract was derailed by the extraordinary declaration that there was no one among the Spaniards with knowledge of the English language. De La Rue and Giesecke & Devrient showed polite reticence, which was possibly prompted by something more than the notoriously difficult environment in Nigeria. They have since been permitted to carry out further giant banknote printing orders for Nigeria, while Nigeria's own banknote printing plant has been sitting idle. In the meantime, the Nigerians have shelved all plans to privatize or bring a foreign partner on board, preferring to have the printing done abroad in emergencies.

Faded glory

By the second half of the 1990s it could no longer be overlooked that De La Rue had come under increasing margin and volume pressure in all of its businesses. Only the stakes in Camelot and DLR Giori were still making strong profits, but they no longer belonged to the core business. The company has been listed on the stock exchange since 1947 – an exception in the secretive world of high-security printers.[10] The legal form of a joint stock company entails obligations, regarding for example the disposition of profit and the duty of disclosure, that are hard to reconcile with the discreet work of the banknote printer. The compelling expectations of investors may have encouraged De La Rue to pursue its traditional strategy of buying up companies and then selling them again after a brief period, if they did not quickly measure up to fixed expectations. For example, a stake holding in American Banknote Holographics (ABNH) was sold back to the original seller in this way after just five years – for exactly the same price. There were other cases like this. Such a strategy generates costs, ties up management capacity, and agitates a company. In the second half of the 1990s and through 2004, De La Rue's costs for restructuring, modernization, and plant closings – sometimes the same factories that had just been expensively modernized – added up to an amount in the three-digit millions of pounds sterling.

Therefore, the »painful decision« to reduce the superfluous capacity in banknote printing by 25 percent took shape at the start of 1998. Chief Executive Officer Marshall simultaneously announced that he was pulling out of his contract. The *Financial Times* wrote of »three final years of ill health.« Marshall's successor, Ian Much, came from mechanical engineering and enjoyed the reputation in the City of a »tough-as-nails turnaround specialist.« His approach was directed strictly toward »shareholder value,« a rather unusual strategy in the conservative banknote business that emphasized the long term. The new chief executive replaced sixty ranking managers. This clean sweep of personnel was even mentioned with praise in the annual business report. But it meant that De La Rue had lost in one fell swoop at the leadership level nearly all managers experienced in the complex business with banknotes. Even Michael Pugh, who had grown up with securities printing, departed prematurely. As the managing board director responsible for secure paper and printing, he had been over the years the open adversary and discreet negotiating partner of the unloved competitor from Munich. The new chief executive also reorganized the business divisions and created a special division of »global services.« Not everyone immediately understood the mission of the new global services. Its sales progression remained disappointing. The division was soon disbanded again.

The incumbent chief executive went about the reduction of the crushing debt with the same brute force. Besides a raft of small subsidiaries,

Much sold De La Rue Card Systems, which had long been celebrated in the group as the bearer of hopes. The whole cards business, with sales of 140 million pounds, went to French competitor Francois Charles Oberthur for 200 million pounds. The divestment coincided with the peak of price euphoria on the stock market and the selling price was commensurately attractive. But not much remained in the treasury. At least half of the proceeds had to be passed on to the grumbling De La Rue shareholders as part of a special dividend disbursement. Also, sold again was Philips Cartes et Systèmes, which had only been bought the previous year for more than 56 million dollars. Giving up the cards business was hotly contested within the company. Speaking for the sale was the small market share, especially for the chip cards that were so promising, and the small profit contribution of the division. An expansion would have tied up management and engineering capacities. And it would have required a large investment in research and development, resources unavailable to De La Rue at that time. The global crisis in the cards business after the disposal may have justified the sale in retrospect. But in the opinion within the industry, De La Rue had cut itself off from a significant source of technology with the cards sale, seriously weakening its own market position with modern ID systems, a business with a future. The new chief executive was at least able to redeem the whole debt burden with these sales of companies.

Much went to work with no less energy on the capacity shakedown that had been announced before he took office. It was initially supposed to affect only banknote printing with the help of a new approach to the high-value market segment of note printing. Predecessor Marshall had already sold the banknote printing plant in Hong Kong. That came, incidentally, only ten years after it had been built. Now capacity was reduced to a single Super line in Gateshead, once the pride of the group with its seven lines of printing machines. Since there were also considerable cutbacks in securities printing of checks and stamps – Enschedé and Francois Charles Oberthur were gunning for De La Rue's old customers there – capacity reductions were also imposed here. This spelled the bitter end of the securities printing plant of High Wycombe. Specialized in stamps, this printing facility had just been modernized at great expense. But, around the same time House of Quest, a small specialist in stamp printing, was purchased.

All that seemed rather impromptu and hectic. And yet it was still not the final word. De La Rue surprisingly announced in 2002 that it was closing the banknote printing plant in Singapore, which had been running for twenty years. And it very quietly withdrew from the joint venture in Nigeria as well. The Singapore closing was officially explained by logistical problems that actually existed. But it was also learned that EU membership candidate Malta had demanded the creation of additional jobs on the island in return for renewing a taxation agreement with De La Rue. In fact, most of the machines from Singapore were brought to Malta, doubling the printing capacity there to two Super lines. The rest of the machinery went to the securities printing plant in Kenya, where De La Rue then wanted to concentrate on the intaglio printing of passports along with check printing. The domestic political balance of Kenya is not very stable. There is also suspicion that cells of the terrorism network Al Qaeda are at work there. The danger that authentic passports could one day turn up in the hands of terrorists is not likely to please some customers of De La Rue. At the end of the day De La Rue was left with only three bases for the printing of banknotes: Gateshead, Malta, and Sri Lanka.

De La Rue has gone to the mat several times but the company can in no way be counted out. At the start of 2003 De La Rue unexpectedly pulled off a coup with the takeover of the Debden Printingworks of the Bank of England. From then on the private printer was allowed to produce all the pound notes for the Bank of England in Debden under a seven-year management contract. For this arrangement, the printer took over the printing machinery in Debden, while the premises are only being rented. Considerable advantages for De La Rue accrue from the fact that the central bank remains the owner of the high-security plant and continues to conduct its own services there, such as cash processing. The expense of the security apparatus, installations, and personnel in such a high-security printing facility easily makes up 5 percent of the total manufacturing cost of a note. In the case of the Debden printing works this cost continues to be borne by the Bank of England. There is even a supplier guaranty for the first five years for around 1 billion pound notes a year, an amount that would fall slightly thereafter.

Experts regard Debden as modern and efficient. Depending on the number of shifts and based on the long-running British issues, as many as 2 billion notes can be produced there with two Super lines and 230 employees. Fewer than a billion notes are currently being printed in Debden in a two-shift cycle. Britain has only four denominations for its pound notes, reducing the time lost for refitting the printing machines. The existing reserve capacity, therefore, may be used by the private printer for jobber printing for foreign countries, according to the contract. Thanks are probably due Alex Jarvis for bringing about the advantageous Debden contract. He served as an adviser to De La Rue – and to the Dutch shredder machine manufacturer Kusters – shortly after his retirement as director general of Debden.

The capability of Debden was tested a few months after the takeover by the printing of new banknotes for the American-controlled Iraq. As consortia leader, De La Rue received the contract for the superbly remunerated printing of around 2 billion notes. Only a few months were allotted, however, for the printing of the six Iraqi denominations, done with one-sided intaglio engraving and equipped with relatively modern security features. De La Rue, which printed in Debden, had to farm out a considerable portion of the order because of the deadline pressure and the gigantic quantity of paper. Shipment required twenty-seven jumbo jets, each with 90 metric tons of banknotes. Since Spain had belonged to the war coalition against Saddam Hussein, its state-owned FNMT received first consideration. But Giesecke & Devrient – in all secrecy – also received a respectable contingent, which it produced in Leipzig. One year before that, the Munich company had been awarded the printing of the new banknotes for the transitional Afghan government, namely around 1 billion notes counting the initial replacement printing run. In that instance it had in turn farmed out a contingent to De La Rue. This had been the share of 5 percent, which the U.S. paper factory Crane had secured for its new Swedish subsidiary Tumba, formerly Tumba Bruk, but then had decided not to print.

Yet such successes do not alter the fact that the former market dominance of De La Rue has been eroding in the decade of the 1990s. According to an internal study by the Bundesdruckerei, De La Rue in 2000 held a share of only 54 percent of the available market by the number of printed banknotes, compared with 78 percent in 1990. Giesecke & Devrient on the other hand had been able to raise its share in 2000 to 25 percent from 10 percent in 1990, the study showed. Munich is circumspect in its comments on market share, assuming a ratio of 35 percent against 45 percent for De La Rue. A British expert even estimated that De La Rue printed only 3.2 billion units in 2002 after the closing of Singapore. That would be little more than Giesecke & Devrient produced the same year. The printing output of De La Rue would then have halved since the middle of the last century. This cannot be verified because De La Rue has provided no more data on its banknote printing since the operating shutdown in Singapore. In any event, no later than the expiration of the seven-year arrangement for Debden, De La Rue will have to make the painful decision on which of the two printing facilities it wants to close: Debden, with its model technical security and location near London, or the extremely large Gateshead plant in the far north of England. The two printing bases can hardly coexist in the long haul.

The erosion of the former dominance of De La Rue is also recognizable in other numerical comparisons. At the end of the 2004–05 business year, group sales were barely above those of 1994, the last year before the Portals takeover. But Portals had then boosted sales by 200 million pounds. Taking the divisions of paper, banknote printing, and securities printing together, their sales today are way below the value De La Rue showed in just banknote and securities printing before the inauspicious Portals acquisition. A sober assessment has fallen over the City. The »dotcom« euphoria, which had lifted the price of the De La Rue share, has evaporated in thin air. According to the City's assessment, the earnings on paper and note printing were supposed to have financed diversification into new businesses. The voluntary departure of a young, highly qualified chief financial officer in the summer of 2002 after only three years, and the long search for a replacement have alarmed the City, sowing more worries in the wake of further staff changes in important divisions. A large-scale buyback program of its own shares was taken as a sign that the management of De La Rue no longer had a concept. In February 2003 the share price plunged by 32 percent in one trading session on publication of an alert of lower profit to come, the third such warning in six months. Around 200 million pounds sterling of De La Rue's market capitalization was wiped out on this one day.

The market capitalization of the whole De La Rue group on the exchange today amounts to less than the sum the group had paid to acquire Portals. Once the figurehead of the *Financial Times* stock index, it has long since lost much of its glitter. Under pressure from the City, Ian Much was replaced by Leo Quinn in early 2004. No easy task awaited this branch novice as the new chief executive of De La Rue. Excluding the cards business, the British company is still one-third larger than its German competitor in »paper, banknote printing, and payment systems.« But this matchup includes the sales-heavy machinery business of the British, which continues to suffer from fragmentation of production and run-away costs. A rational use of the shrunken printing capacity for banknotes together with a simultaneous concentration on the upscale market segment could give a boost to De La Rue's note printing, which is profitable anyway. The Debden effect cannot be underestimated, especially since the Bank of England wants to strip the three Scottish and four Northern Irish state banks of their historic privilege of issuing »their own« pound notes. That intention was explained by a sensational robbery of banknotes worth 26.5 million pounds at the Northern Ireland Bank in December 2004. Such a change would raise the operating rate of Debden somewhat. With its note printing in Malta, moreover, De La Rue now has its foot in the door of euro printing. Malta now belongs to the EU and is regarded as a promising candidate for an early entry into the common currency group. The first financial statement presented by Quinn and covering the business year 2004–05 showed signs of improvement. Quinn had probably benefited here from the streamlining measures initiated by his luckless predecessor. The strong results and Quinn's announcement that De La Rue would henceforth concentrate on those activities in which it was knowledgeable was cheered by the British business press. The *Financial Times,* otherwise given to understatement, called for »a round of applause« for the new chief executive. The media really hasn't been spoiled with good corporate news from De La Rue during the past ten years. Poorly led companies are the traditional prey of private equity funds. Such rumors have also dogged De La Rue at various times in the past. Two attempts at hostile takeovers have in fact been made in the history of De La Rue. The first was made at the end of the 1960s by the U.S. Rank Organization, the second about twenty years later by the British Norton Opax. As De La Rue's principal stockholder, publisher Robert Maxwell at that time is supposed to have been so concerned for his stake of 21.7 percent that he sounded out De La Rue's arch competitor in Munich for assistance. Peter Orchard was incensed. De La Rue has recently raised the collective share of its five largest investors – De La Rue calls them »stable investors« – to nearly 51 percent from the previous 35 percent. The empire strikes back.

6
How Giesecke & Devrient struggles for technological leadership

It was an exuberant group which sat together under the ceremonial tent erected in the Kaiserhof courtyard of Munich's Residenz palace on a rainy June evening in 2002. The Bavarian state government had issued a special permit to allow them to gather for a gala dinner in a place under protection as an historic monument. The 1,700 guests – representing governments, central banks, commercial banks, industry, international organizations, and business associations – were there to celebrate the 150th anniversary of the founding of Giesecke & Devrient. Strictly speaking, the part about »150 years of existence« was not quite accurate. Although the company had survived the Second World War with 80 percent bomb damage, it was then seized by the communists and later nationalized. Giesecke & Devrient had ceased to exist. Thanks solely to the daring and determination of Siegfried Otto, the traditional name was revived. During the war he had married the youthful Jutta Devrient, very much against the wishes of her family. After the senior boss, his father-in-law Ludwig Devrient, perished in the deprivation of a Soviet penal colony, Otto moved the company's headquarters to Munich from Leipzig shortly after he was released from Soviet captivity. That was 1948 and Munich was located in the economically liberal Bizone, as the occupation zone jointly administered by the Americans and British was then called.

In fact, this was a new founding – and a new beginning under the most difficult of circumstances: without capital, without skilled workers, without printing machines, and without customers. Franz Helmberger, the veteran technical director of the home plant in Leipzig, had warned Otto strongly against beginning anew. The company of Giesecke & Devrient had »died honorably in Leipzig,« he had informed the »young man,« and everything that was started there in Munich would be »doomed to fail.«

Moneymakers, Klaus W. Bender

ISBN: 3-527-50236-X

Otto disregarded this advice. He went to work with a borrowed typewriter in an apartment under the eaves. And his success then proved him right. Giesecke & Devrient is today the world's leading high-security printing corporation. The group in 2004 made sales of 1.16 billion euros with 7,300 employees and as a holding company controlled 38 fully consolidated subsidiaries in 27 countries. Yet the name of Siegfried Otto, who had died five years earlier, was mentioned only in passing at the festivities held under the motto »value in changing times.« Much was said of the innovative high-technology corporation and the challenges of the future but little of the man who, with his great entrepreneurial achievement, had refounded it. In the expensive and richly illustrated company chronicle published especially for this occasion, one looked in vain for a photograph of Siegfried Otto.

In labore virtus - The puritan work ethic

The company Buch-, Kupfer- und Stein-Druckerei Giesecke & Devrient was founded in 1852 in the book publishing city of Leipzig by Hermann Giesecke and Alphonse Devrient. Art books and cartography were its printing specialty. Only four years after the founding, however, it received its first printing order for banknotes. It was 10-thaler notes of the ducal government of Altenburg, soon followed by treasury bills of the kingdom of Saxony. The privilege of issuing then belonged to the banks. The next order came from Bayerische Hypotheken- und Wechsel-Bank for the printing of 10-guilder notes. These notes were printed on both sides to increase protection against counterfeiting. Shortly thereafter, however, the Bavarian customer nervously demanded its printing plates and related materials back from Leipzig. Bavaria's king wanted to go to war against Prussia on the side of Austria. The Munich bank feared that Saxon Leipzig would be occupied and that the printing of its guilder notes would be used by the Prussian enemy for economic sabotage. Tales of the »old Europe.«

The Leipzig Officin für Geld- und Werth-Papiere, as the firm now called itself, received its first printing order for export in the 1870s from some Swiss cantons. The first foreign order from beyond Europe came from Peru. At home the high security printing company was only allowed in exceptional cases to print notes for the German empire and its Reichsbank, for example the notes for some of the colonies as well as the so-called Rentenmark during the hyperinflation after the First World War. A particularly critical moment came at the outbreak of the Second World War, when the Hitler regime decided to embark upon economic sabotage against Britain by printing phony pound notes. The technical director, Helmberger, was especially dispatched by the board of Giesecke & Devrient to Berlin. He could only with difficulty turn down the scheme to get the internationally respected banknote and securities printer involved. The forged British pound notes of Operation Bernhard – history's biggest counterfeiting action by a state to destabilize the economy of an opponent – then had to be done by inmates of the Sachsenhausen concentration camp under the supervision of a special SS unit.[1]

Siegfried Otto, who took up the baton again in Munich, was an autodidactic person in matters of secure printing and an autocrat in corporate management. Near the end of the Second World War he had served as an officer in an armor unit and had seen action on the eastern front.[2] His outlook on the world was emphatically conservative. Despite assertions to the contrary, the former Reichswehr officer had been neither a member of the NSDAP nor had he belonged to the SS.[3] Otto had not only courage, dynamism, and determination, which one might have expected from someone with his experience, but also a keen entrepreneurial instinct. Even contemporaries who were not enthralled by his personality described him as a »dynamic entrepreneur« in the best mold of Schumpeter.[4] The way he dealt with his employees left little doubt that he was a former military officer. Otto did not like to be contradicted and had no patience with lengthy discourse that didn't get to the point. But he also knew how to motivate. Because of the dearth of trained personnel, the schooling of newcomers then played a central role at Giesecke & Devrient. Even today, many who began as young draftsmen, engravers, or printers in Munich still describe Otto's strong personal charisma and enthusiasm, which he radiated to them for their demanding activities. Doing business means, in a nutshell, driving the competitor out of the market if possible and maximizing profit. As the company's boss as well as in private life, Otto pursued both of these objectives with marked aggressiveness. The daily handling of money confers immunity against its blandishment, people in the industry like to say. Not a trace of this immunity could be detected in Siegfried Otto. To some, this made him seem coolly calculating, a person who planned every move right down to sacrificing a pawn to check a king – should that become necessary. Others recalled more readily Otto's frequent decisions based on gut feelings. Indeed, he made a number of decisions that actually did not have to be made and in retrospect were hard to fathom because they damaged Otto himself.

The pet slogan of the two founders had been *in labore virtus,* »in labor virtue,« the puritan work ethic. Otto readily made it his own conviction. »If you want something done, do it yourself,« was the way he looked at things. With his sensitivity to color combinations and graphic design, he personally poured over every last detail of a planned banknote or any other printed paper of value. There was no draft that would not be scrutinized on his gigantic desk before it was finally approved. He was a regular and expertly critical visitor to the originals department and the printing bays, frequently even by night and also at the paper factory. It wasn't long before the banknotes and securities of Giesecke & Devrient, which were for decades drafted by Spaniard José Lopez, drew attention for their proficient graphics and outstanding printing quality. Experts normally recognized at first glance a printed product of Giesecke & Devrient.

The timing of the refounding was auspicious. Printing orders poured in because of the German currency reform, a subsequent overhaul of Germany's securities law, the decartelizing of the German economy – from the coal and steel sector through I.G. Farben chemicals to the large banks – and the outcome of the London agreement to regulate Germany's foreign debt. Equity shares, bonds, covered mortgage bonds, and other debt securities had to be printed anew in D-mark denominations. So did all the external bonds of the defunct German Reich. On top of all that came the demand for bank checks and travelers checks because the wanderlust of the Germans had been reawakened. To keep up with the deluge of work, Giesecke & Devrient, which had found temporary quarters on the premises of Munich's Riem airport, quickly had to conduct its first capital increase. Since the stockholders of the family corporation had no money, Deutsche Bank and Bayerische Hypotheken- und Wechsel-Bank, both old customers of the securities printer, initially took a large part of the new shares on their own accounts.[5] Otto cunningly used the opportunity to secure for himself the absolute majority in the high-security printing company he was directing. The slow withdrawal of the founding families had begun. Otto had to borrow the money for this. A photograph of Hermann Josef Abs, later the chairman of Deutsche Bank for a long stretch, promptly appeared on his desk. This bank, with its enormous stake holdings in German businesses and its dominance in German securities trading, was the ideal partner for Otto. Because of this the bank for decades provided the chairman of the supervisory board of Giesecke & Devrient from the time of its re-establishment until an abrupt parting of the ways in 1997.

As early as 1955 the *Frankfurter Allgemeine Zeitung (FAZ)* reported that Giesecke & Devrient in Munich had »again matched the capacity of the former technical operation in Leipzig.«[6] The printer at that time had just won its first postwar order for banknote printing, again an order for Peru. And these notes in sophisticated multicolor intaglio were supposed to prove that Giesecke & Devrient was technically fully capable of printing German banknotes – if these were again to be printed in Germany. Otto had earlier proposed just that in the quoted memorandum for the Bank deutscher Länder.

Yet, banknote printing remained a distant objective, while the printing of securities was a reality. Numerous providers jockeyed for orders in this field. Otto devoted his characteristic determination to this problem. The new formulation of Germany's »Guidelines for the exchange listing of securities« was adopted on his initiative. Giesecke & Devrient had been instrumental in shaping the original version of this regulation in the 1920s. It prescribed the graphic design and printed characteristics of securities as a condition for admission to trading. The revision was made necessary by technical advances in the threat of counterfeiting. Otto promoted the revision of the guidelines in the hope that a common, uniform technical language in securities printing could be found for all Europe. He wanted to involve foreign securities printers in this through cooperative agreements, doing business as a license issuer and materials supplier. The existing import barriers would be elegantly overcome in this way, he hoped.

His next step was the founding in 1958 of Security Printing S.A., a holding company based in Glarus, Switzerland, together with a local securities printer. The operating company Security Printing Aktiengesellschaft of Zurich followed three years later. The purpose of this company was to develop new printing systems for secure printing and to purchase licenses and stake holdings. The prevailing guidelines for securities printing prohibited the use of offset printing presses because of the supposedly greater counterfeiting threat. Sheet-fed printing machines for simultaneous background printing from Koebau-Giori were too expensive for securities printing. Otto envisaged a more economical sheet-fed press especially for securities. Machinery manufacturer Roland, today MAN Roland, at his order developed the »Roland Zweifarben Security Printing Press« (RZSP) for indirect, two-color, raised printing. Zurich's Securities Printing was supposed to distribute such machines. Giesecke & Devrient officially held 49 percent of the registered shares of the holding company in Glarus. This 49 percent stake was sold to unknown buyers in 1976. The holder of the majority of the capital had never become known publicly. It was suspected that this could have been Albert Amon and his SICPA. All trails, however, led to Otto.

In a third move, Otto founded Giesecke y Devrient de Mexico (Gidemex), the Munich company's first and for many years its only foreign printing base. Gidemex printed securities but no banknotes. The founding of this company was notable not so much for its strategic importance, although it was supposed to work the emerging South American market, as it was for its private considerations. Siegfried Otto, deeply marked by his years in Soviet captivity, did not exclude the possibility that the communists would one day come to power in Western Europe. The Mexican subsidiary, he thought, would protect him from losing everything once again.

Otto's securities plans didn't quite click into place. The German securities guidelines were unable to prevail in Europe despite extensive technical help from Munich. Nor did the Roland printing machines really find a foothold in the market. This cheered Gualtiero Giori, who had followed Otto's activities with dismay. Only the securities printing plant in Mexico was an unexpected success. It soon forced long-entrenched De La Rue out of the market, causing the British to close their local subsidiary. Otto's hope of also doing business with the Mexicans as their banknote printer went unfulfilled, however. Much to the chagrin of American Banknote, its traditional note printer, the Mexican central bank decided to erect its own printing facility and engaged for this the director of Gidemex, Ludwig Selhuber. Otto promptly banned him from the Munich premises for »disloyalty.« The peso banknotes produced under Selhuber's technical direction were of high printing quality. One could even make out the time on a clock tower on the reverse side of the 1,000-peso notes. The idea for that came from the U.S. 100-dollar note with its bell tower. As their time, the Mexicans chose 2:10 p.m. instead of the 2:20 on the dollar note. That would show the Yankees. Once powerful in Central and South America, American Banknote lost its last big foreign customer for banknote printing and was never to recover from this shock. It had slept through the advent of multicolored intaglio printing. The once renowned printer of banknotes and securities went down after long agony in a maelstrom of litigation for fraud and creative accounting. Only recently has American Banknote re-emerged as a securities printer of checks and passports. Chapter 11 allowed the company to shed all its accumulated debt of more than 100 million dollars.

Back to Munich. The new Deutsche Bundesbank signaled that it wanted Giesecke & Devrient to take part in the D-mark printing. Initially involved was only 290 million mark notes for the first supply. The other half was reserved for the Bundesdruckerei, the government's printing facility. But the Bundesbank set conditions. It insisted upon reserving a line of printing machines in a separate printing hall exclusively for the printing of the D-mark notes, although Otto already had such a printing facility, now located within Munich's city limits. Otto promptly began the expansion, even though he still had no contract from the Bundesbank.[7] For the plant's grounds in Munich's Steinhausen district, incidentally, the municipal property register imposes a »ban on prostitution-like operations, gaming, betting, and religious sects« as restrictions on use. That was Otto's soldier's sense of humor. Moreover, the Bundesbank required Giesecke & Devrient to revert to the legal form of a limited liability company, GmbH, from the joint stock company form, AG, it had had for nearly thirty years. This was officially explained by problems with the financial statements – an unhealthy ratio of own-to-borrowed capital. The Bundesbank was disturbed that its banknotes would be printed by a company subject to a certain disclosure requirement, although it was not listed on the exchange. The central bank, however, agreed to the retention of the supervisory board as an additional control organ. This would help the vigilant Bundesbank to keep an eye on developments in Munich.

In retrospect, the two conditions imposed by the Bundesbank proved to be a stroke of good fortune. The dividing of the D-mark printing order between Berlin and Munich involved the public pricing scrutiny to which D-mark printing was subject. This meant in practice that Giesecke & Devrient, which could print more economically, could hide for decades behind the price demands of the Bundesdruckerei, which was more expensive, although technically the Bundesdruckerei printed with the greatest precision. And the legal form of a family company shortened the decision-making processes, eased long-term planning, and allowed, when necessary, even a »risky« project to be financed. Such a project, be it a capacity increase or a research endeavor, could now be financed without immediately exposing the boss to critical questions from the stockholders.

He wins who dares

Otto knew how to take entrepreneurial advantage of his latitude as the main stockholder of Giesecke & Devrient. At that time no German paper factory was able to make banknote paper. The paper for the D-mark notes had to be ordered abroad, from France's Arjomari for Giesecke & Devrient and from Britain's Portals for the Bundesdruckerei. Without even having a supply contract with the Bundesbank, Otto in 1964 bought a rundown paper factory in Gmund on the Tegernsee lake and rebuilt it for the production of security paper. It was regarded in the industry as highly unusual that a banknote printer would supply itself with paper. With its Papierfabrik Louisenthal (PL) the high-security printer was entering technical terra incognita. The Bundesdruckerei was to fail with its parallel attempt – leaving it tied to Louisenthal as the exclusive supplier. Since the leading foreign manufacturers of security paper had denied Otto access to their technology, as mentioned, Louisenthal had to develop this technology painstakingly by itself. Assistance was rendered by a technician hired away from Sweden's Tumba Bruk. Gmund hadn't even mastered the technique of the watermark. It depended for this upon help from experts of Italy's Cartiere Miliani di Fabriano (CMF). Worse was to come. The first banknote paper, earmarked for the 5-Deutschmark note, proved not to be firm enough. Also, the starting capacity of Louisenthal of 1,800 metric tons a year was below a profitable production level, but was still much too high for Germany's need. The Bundesdruckerei and Giesecke & Devrient together needed not even half of this amount for their D-mark printing. For this reason the paper factory for years created such high losses that they exceeded investment. The parent company, which was still not financially secure, seemed at times endangered. In this difficult situation, Otto turned over the direction of the paper plant to the young Manfred Beck, who had returned from Egypt in the meantime. Beck succeeded in improving Louisenthal's operating rate with export orders. The first of these paper orders came from Indonesia, followed quickly by Thailand, Vietnam, and South Africa – all traditional Portals customers. The paper for South Vietnam was even delivered to De La Rue because this company printed the South Vietnamese banknotes. It's not hard to envisage the mixed feelings with which the British, who had until then controlled the market, followed the initiatives of this newcomer. This market entry by Louisenthal was no small feat, not only because of the entrenched competition, but also because of the cost pressure from the continually appreciating D-mark. The distribution organization built by Beck for banknote paper laid the groundwork for later expansion of the high-security printing corporation into foreign business, but at that time printing banknotes for export played only a marginal role in its business.

It was the concept of Eurocheque that finally put Louisenthal into black figures.[8] Differences of opinion arose here with the British private printers over the technical aspects of the check blanks. The British wanted engraved printing. Otto regarded this as too expensive for a form that would be used only once. He suggested as an alternative security feature a multi-tone, localized watermark. He wanted high security and strong use of the forms because he was thinking of the fallow capacity of his paper factory. He had his way. Used in combination with a special check card as a guarantee, the Eurocheque developed into one of the world's most popular check systems, accepted nearly everywhere in Europe. Otto's stake in this business was therefore secure, even if the demand for banknotes should ever fall. And the banks loved the concept because it forced their customers to carry a comparatively high running balance to suppress interest charges on their checking accounts, if they wanted their Eurocheques to be covered by a guaranteed amount. This was initially 300 Deutschmarks, later 400. In the heyday of the Eurocheque, Louisenthal produced expensive secure paper for as many as half a billion check blanks a year. These 500 metric tons offered a welcome additional use for the capacity of the paper machinery. But the project of introducing a standardized European traveler's check, which Otto pursued energetically, failed. The dispute over the technical aspects of the Eurocheque had one other side effect. Upon Otto's initiative the Association Internationale des Imprimeurs Fiduciaires (AIIF) was founded. It was originally conceived as a confidential discussion forum exclusively for European private printers and, only later, for overseas printers in its ranks. Its mailing address, the offices of Security Printing in Zurich, underscored the nearness of AIIF to Giesecke & Devrient.

Since the printing machinery project had faded to insignificance, the company Security Printing had become a hub of international trading in the banknote and secure paper of Papierfabrik Louisenthal. It even distributed paper of Cartiere Miliani, a gesture of thanks for its help. Forcing Louisenthal to go it alone in technology proved to be a boomerang for the competition. Over the years the paper plant called attention to itself for a number of innovations in cylinder mold technology for the making of security paper. The speed of the machinery was raised many times over and the width of the paper belt was enlarged. The paper machine was also changed for throughput, operating twenty-four hours a day, seven days a week. Louisenthal itself became a supplier of turnkey plants for secure paper. A significant part in this early success was played by the technical director of the paper factory, Paul Kling, and the chemist, Claus Jung, who is engaged worldwide today as an independent expert in setting up secure paper factories. Although the plant engineering business is being run on a low flame in deference to the company's own paper exports – and to the nervous competition – at least a dozen paper plants have been modernized or built abroad. Giesecke & Devrient only managed to accomplish that in exceptional cases with banknote printing plants.[9] What applies to a modern banknote printing facility actually applies to a greater degree to many of these expensive paper factories: output capacity of their high-performance machinery far exceeds national requirement. In the final analysis, they too are prestige projects done at taxpayer cost.

It proved to be an advantage that Security Printing, like Organization Giori, operated out of a neutral and discreet country. This was helpful in negotiating with politically sensitive customers in Eastern Europe, even if the Soviet Gosnak itself had never registered objections to dealing with the German supplier. The construction of a paper factory in Poland, which the competition had torpedoed with political arguments, became possible in this way after a decade and a half of tough talks. These plant engineering deals were settled for a long time through the tiny trading firm in Zurich, while the commercial and technical consulting on all these activities was handled by experts from Munich. Finally, Security Printing still functioned as an agent for special machinery for banknote production. Even the Bundesdruckerei, operating under direct orders from the Bundesbank, had to follow this cost-driving route through Zurich. The arrangement with Security Printing offered ideal conditions to expatriate earnings. In comparatively advantageous Switzerland, Glarus offered even more favorable tax rates. Since there was also a profit-surrender agreement between Glarner Holding and the trading firm in Zurich, it presented a further advantage. The acronym SP of Security Printing soon came to stand for »Siegfried's Provision,« which is German for Siegfried's commission. How profitably Security Printing must have worked was revealed much later when Siegfried Otto allowed himself to be talked out of 220 million D-marks by a property speculator, who had married the daughter of Otto's second wife. That much money had accumulated as profit from various sources in the account of the Swiss trading firm.

Papierfabrik Louisenthal was still not on solid footing when Otto embarked on his next project. He got together with Helmut Gröttrup, a scientist from the former staff of rocket researcher Wernher von Braun in Peenemünde. He took over this man's insolvent engineering office along with its staff of technicians and founded Gesellschaft für Automation und Organisation (GAO). This 100 percent subsidiary of Giesecke & Devrient became the research and development center concerned with cashless payments traffic.

The cashless transfer of wages and salaries was introduced in Germany in the mid-1960s. The growth of circulating notes flattened steadily. There was much talk of a coming »cashless society.« A market study of the Bundesbank showed, however, that the absolute number of circulating notes would keep increasing with strong economic growth. In those days all banknotes had to be checked individually by hand for authenticity and physical condition. Around five thousand persons at Bundesbank and its branches were entrusted with this Sisyphus task. It was foreseeable that the processing of a rising tide of paper money would have to create increasing problems of quality, payroll costs, and secure storage space. As a solution, Otto envisaged making the banknote fit for automated inspection. This would be done without changing the appearance of the banknote. Inspection would take place with absolute reliability by means of a special reading machine to determine authenticity and condition in one work process, thus deciding whether the banknote could be returned to circulation. The Japanese electronics corporation Toshiba is supposed to have sparked the idea. It had been working for years on a reading device for banknotes. Otto succeeded in convincing Bundesbank and in recruiting financiers for its project.

Automatic inspection for authenticity proved to be the technical hurdle. The researchers of GAO solved that problem with lanthanoids. These compounds belong to the family of rare earth metals and their isotopes. Their Greek name, meaning »to be hidden,« betrayed their peculiarity. As inorganic substances, lanthanoids are distinguished by high instability and extremely rapid chemical reactions, in contrast to their organic sister isotopes. When exposed to a flash from a strong source of light, they emit a band of light in a split second. This display disappears just as rapidly. With this repeatable, characteristic light band the banknote can be identified by a reading device beyond doubt as authentic or phony. Should a lanthanoid then be covered by another isotope, such as a metallic crystal, for protection, decoding then becomes nearly impossible for unauthorized persons. Should a counterfeiter with a highly modern laboratory try to define the substance, he might even succeed – but he wouldn't find that substance which alone permits the authenticity to be checked. He would be deliberately led astray. Known as the M feature – *M* for machine readable – the inorganic oxide is colorless and can be integrated in the paper, in the security ink, or in the security thread without causing any change in the appearance of the banknote. The more, the better.[10] By comparison with other security features this substance was a technological and commercial masterwork for Giesecke & Devrient.[11] It did not suffice to put the M feature just anywhere on the banknote. The central banks also required special sensors to recognize the M feature. These sensors were also supplied exclusively by Giesecke & Devrient. The Munich company earns doubly with this expensive powder.

Otto was able to present his automation-capable banknote to the Bundesbank in 1975. Two years later he also demonstrated the banknote processing system that went with it in a semiautomatic version, ISS 300.[12] The Bundesbank started employing the new substance on its superficially unchanged banknotes by using the security thread as a carrier. Today the powdered M feature is blown onto the still moist paper belt in a trail that is changed according to note denomination. It is also mixed into the printing ink.

The reaction on the market was rather tepid, especially in the Anglo-American sphere. Although the U.S. Fed sought a machine for the processing of banknotes, it rejected the semiautomatic device from Giesecke & Devrient because of unsatisfactory performance. The Bundesbank, which had ordered the first semiautomatic devices at the end of the same decade, also had difficulties in the beginning, but of another sort. The labor unions resisted the new technology for fear of losing jobs. The Bundesbank, therefore, pulled out of the subsequent development to full automation, which Otto had pressed for. The high outlays for GAO's research and development were always a bone of contention within Giesecke

& Devrient. After the setback in the United States, more voices were heard that called for a cessation of the development work on the fully automatic inspection system for banknotes. Otto prevailed with the comment that he was, after all, »dispensing my own money,« witnesses reported.

Developments made him right again. In the final twenty-five years of the past century the number of notes in circulation increased an average of 4.6 percent a year in Germany and 6 percent in the United States. Processing of banknotes was indeed becoming a problem. When the Fed later went looking again for a banknote processing machine, Giesecke & Devrient showed up with its ISS 3000, a high-performance system it had developed in the meantime. This fully automatic device identified and sorted by different currencies *and* denomination in a single working process. It checked simultaneously as many as 40 (freshly printed) banknotes a second for authenticity and condition. This processing speed is the equivalent of an Olympic 100-meter record. Notes that are no longer suitable for circulation can be destroyed in the process – namely, without human intervention that could invite abuses. The Munich company in America won the competition but lost the bidding. To blame was the Buy American Act. Otto, however, was not easily deterred. He had his prototypes installed with the Fed in Baltimore and began searching for local manufacturing possibilities. American Banknote offered its assistance but was apparently more interested in the technology than in the distribution of the new banknote processing machines. The cooperation contract was hurriedly dissolved again.

Then Fortune smiled. Recognition Equipment, an American company, had received the initial award but had to return the contract to the Fed because of technical problems with the throughput performance. There was a second solicitation and the Munich company received a huge contract for 102 of its fully automated banknote processing systems at the start of the 1990s. The order was then raised to 133 units, including replacement parts and a long-term maintenance contract. The total contract amounted to more than 250 million euros. This price tag made it the largest contract ever let by the Fed. It corresponded to nearly the entire annual turnover of Giesecke & Devrient at that time. The payment conditions of the Fed were excellent. In the phase of high interest rates at that time, one could profit by investing the prepayments. Nevertheless, the Americans decided against the M feature and also insisted upon local manufacturing. Therefore Giesecke & Devrient took over ECA Electrocom Automation, a U.S.

subsidiary of AEG AG. This company had made the machines in Germany for Giesecke & Devrient. Only the system control and the sensors came directly from GAO. The huge Fed contract marked the final breakthrough to the world market and secured the Munich company's place as an internationally active high-security corporation. Some 3,300 banknote processing systems from Giesecke & Devrient are installed today in nearly 100 countries. This number includes around 240 high-performance BPS 2000/3000 models that are exclusively made for central banks and, in a modified version, for printing plants. Despite the initial skepticism, the M feature also caught on. Today, it is integrated in the banknotes of 40 countries. Hans Wolfgang Kunz, who was responsible for this business division for years, said he knew of no case of counterfeiting eluding this system.

The formative expansion phase of Giesecke & Devrient was capped by its entry into the cards business. GAO had been involved in the technical design of the first check cards for the Eurocheque. Otto's pet project in which the Eurocheque was supposed to be used for cash disbursement at money dispensing machines had failed, despite costly field trials. Therefore, the check guarantee card was equipped with an MM code that afforded forgery protection similar to the M feature at the end of the 1970s. And it was personalized by means of a new laser technique. It became a payments medium. Just by inserting this card, one could now obtain cash at the automatic teller machine of any bank. The person's account would simultaneously be debited. This was the beginning of the wide-ranging application of the new card. A banknote printer with body and soul, Otto always kept a certain distance from the card business. It was initially assigned to Lutz Devrient, the last direct descendant of the founding family and later built up nearly single-handedly by Jürgen Nehls.

The crisis

Siegfried Otto was at the pinnacle of his success at the end of the 1980s. Under his leadership, Giesecke & Devrient had grown into the world's only vertically integrated high-security corporation. With the exception of printing ink, it produced nearly everything itself, from banknote paper to note shredders that were immune to abuses. The son of a Prussian policeman had become one of Germany's richest men. His invitations to golf tournaments were gladly accepted even by federal German President Roman Herzog – not to mention by the golf enthusiasts of the Bundesbank. *Forbes* business magazine estimated Otto's fortune at 2.4 billion D-marks in 1990. Other estimates were even higher. Yet, the patriarch had missed the proper time for his departure from the direction of the company. A struggle for money and power, fought with great bitterness within the family, plunged Otto and his company into a deep crisis. The dispute became ever more bitter, for it was later accompanied by a smear campaign in the German media.

The drama began in private. But since Otto was the principal stockholder of the company, this also pulled Giesecke & Devrient into the maelstrom of events. A second marriage to a considerably younger woman, Ursula »Bambi« Burda, had caused the latent tension between the father and his own four children, who had to fear for their inheritance, to erupt openly. The family crisis – comparable to the melodrama of the American TV soap operas *Denver* and *Dallas* – reached its crescendo with the revelation of massive irregularities in the settlement of deals handled by the two sons. As sources associated with the supervisory board later said, this involved deliveries of banknote processing systems for Nigeria, for which Tilmann was responsible, and the machinery order of the Fed, which Yorck had handled. Yorck, the younger but more energetic of the two sons, had actually been favored to succeed his father. Yet the dispute ended with the involuntary departure of both sons from the company. They were bought out generously. Michael Endres, a member of the managing board of Deutsche Bank AG who had just taken over the chair of the supervisory board of Giesecke & Devrient, then worked toward a separation of management from capital, finally persuading Otto to withdraw from the management. Otto went to the supervisory board. Endres brought tax expert Thomas Rademacher into the company. The new chief executive took all too literally Endres' assignment to end the era of Otto. He went to work with little finesse among the executives and his actions paid little respect to the aging patriarch. Now gravely ill, Otto broke with him in a last exercise of will and finally also severed ties with his second wife.

Just at the time of the breakup with Rademacher, rumors began to fly in the company about illegal arms exports by Giesecke & Devrient. Moreover, an employee of the important internal security department died under circumstances that initially seemed mysterious. This also was promptly linked to the supposed arms export. Beck had the confidence of the patriarch and saw to it that all suspicions were reviewed with great care by the Munich office of the federal prosecutor. All of them proved »unfounded« and as the »product of posturing and fear of professional loss of status,« as stated in one of the two rulings that dropped the probe.

The reports of »arms exports,« »contract murder,« and Rademacher's dismissal kicked up dust devils in public just the same. In this charged atmosphere, the Frankfurt business information newsletter *Czerwensky Intern* suddenly came up with spicy details about the tax scandal that had not been aired in public at Security Printing. The source – or sources – for the damaging material was never determined. But there must have been access to the files of the management in Munich. The drum beat of this information service's pointed reports on the matter soon resonated in media across the country. The media criticism called forth a full-blown publicity crisis in this otherwise highly self-confident company. Its response took on an accusatory tone. The company said that for the first time in its history the developments had put the family company into the headlines, particularly in the tabloid press. It preferred to blame the bearer of bad news for the missteps.[13]

As if that were not enough, a former employee of Giesecke & Devrient now came forward, accusing his former employer of fraud against the Bundesbank. Business ties with the Bundesbank had always been the exclusive domain of Siegfried Otto, and this matter was already a decade old. It concerned the placement of a marker on the security thread of the Deutschmark notes, an issue resolved in 1988. The savings from rationalization here had not been passed on to the customer, the Bundesbank, although Giesecke & Devrient had been contractually obliged to do that. In lieu of this, a fictitious production step had been rolled in with the help of SICPA in Switzerland. And it had been billed.[14] It was an incomprehensible story that didn't become any more palatable with comment that the Bundesbank was represented – which is uncommon – in the public price audits and had remained silent. The same Bundesbank, which had over decades helped and favored the rebuilding of this banknote and securities printer, was »charged for costs unrelated to any appropriate service,« as this was delicately phrased in Munich. This kicked up big waves in Frankfurt. Giesecke & Devrient had to pay back nearly 40 million marks. Since it had no long-term contracts running with Munich, the angry Bundesbank explored the possibility of changing paper supplier and note printer. That proved to be difficult for paper, with its tailored specifications. Louisenthal had a de facto technical monopoly. The conversion to another supplier would have taken at least eighteen months. And, indeed, tight printing capacity in Berlin stood in the way of a change in printers – for which the Bundesdruckerei actually had been hoping for years. The Bundesbank also had to concede that a program of massive cost reduction had been introduced in Munich under Beck's reorganization of the divisions of paper and note printing. With this the D-mark notes made in Munich cost less at the end of the 1990s than they did at the start of that decade, despite the rise in payroll costs and inflation in the interim. The Bundesbank finally was ready to issue a public statement in which it confirmed its desire to maintain its business ties with Giesecke & Devrient.[15] This declaration helped considerably to settle matters both at home and abroad and it nipped a potentially dangerous development in the bud. The danger of losing the D-mark business had been banished. Under pressure from the Bundesbank, however, Otto had to turn over his entire stake holding in Giesecke & Devrient to a trustee. And he had to withdraw from operations completely. The separation between management and capital was completed in the seventh generation of the founding family, although at a high price. Siegfried Otto died shortly thereafter. His two daughters, Verena von Mitschke-Collande and sister Claudia Miller, who lived in New York, inherited the family company in equal parts. In the same year Endres vacated the chair of the supervisory board. The era of Deutsche Bank had ended.

In dealing with the crisis concerning Security Printing and in step with the dramatic change in power within Giesecke & Devrient, blame was ascribed to outsiders. Apparently this was supposed to divert attention from the actual cause of the debacle and to protect the family's name. It is normal for an industrial corporation to deal through a trading firm, if one ignores the particular tax issue in this case. The crisis of Security Printing in truth concerned the fact that the principal owner of the family corporation, Siegfried Otto, had for decades deliberately made incomplete statements in his personal income tax declaration. And he had even confirmed these falsehoods in writing.[16] It was stated in a company memorandum that Otto made a declaration of his own culpability to the fiscal authority in June 1993 in order to settle his personal tax liability and to avoid involving the company in the matter. *Der Spiegel* told the rest: Otto did not voluntarily cite himself for culpability, thereby avoiding punishment, until his first wife and some of the children had threatened to have him charged during the aforementioned family dispute. And this charge would have cited his ownership of Security Printing.[17] Security Printing had been »fully owned by him for years,« it was reported.[18] Otto had to pay 135 million marks in accrued back taxes, it was privately estimated. Endres, who had been the supervisory board chairman at the time, had pondered whether Papierfabrik Louisenthal would have to be sold. The money was then raised in lieu of that from the company and its subsidiaries through extraordinary dividend disbursements. Security Printing went into liquidation.

Long forgotten, this whole affair surfaced again on the eve of the company's celebration in 2002, when the two sons all of a sudden publicly demanded a huge hike in their settlement from the two sisters, ostensibly because the company had been wrongly valued.[19] Hidden between the lines in two planted newspaper reports but plainly apparent to those versed in the subject was the accusation that the tax authority had let Otto off too easily. It was also insinuated that the Bundesbank still might have open claims of reimbursement from Giesecke & Devrient in the three-digit millions for inflates invoices. Tax issues linked to Security Printing, as explained, had played a pivotal role in the father's break with his two sons. Hans-Christoph von Mitschke-Collande, the husband of Verena, a member of the board of Giesecke & Devrient before these events took place, had told the author that the tax case was not yet settled. According to him, the company continued to pay penalties in connection with the SP tax-fraud affair. If this were true, why then was the family trembling again? In any event, Bavaria's fiscal authority and the Bundesbank shrugged off the matter. Thanks to the company's clever publicity approach, the media quickly lost interest in the renewed family squabble. But it has not been buried. It is, alas, Yorck who keeps after this matter with marked tenacity and doggedness. One could assume that he is pursuing a far more ambitious goal than just topping off his settlement.

The bid for technological leadership

Many another company would have been damaged by these financial – and psychological – burdens. It says something about the dynamism of Giesecke & Devrient and its employees that the corporation experienced a remarkable upswing in just these turbulent years. Otto had always managed his strongly expanded corporation as though it were still a big industrial crafts workshop. The reorganization into business divisions finally gave the corporation an appropriate internal structure. Although this coincided with the peak of the company's crisis, it set free growth forces, which were deliberately directed toward foreign business. Largely through organic growth, Giesecke & Devrient was able to double its sales to more than a billion euros between 1994 and 2002. Only part of that could be attributed to the euro boost. In 1990s, for example, the Munich company counted barely a dozen countries as customers for its export printing. In the interim it has printed notes for more than 80 countries. And Louisenthal has delivered banknote paper to nearly 100 countries. With paper capacity of 16,500 metric tons a year and printing capacity of around four billion notes, it is hot on the heels of De La Rue. Only in their machinery business for cash systems are the British still clearly ahead in sales.

Solving the problem of bottlenecks in printing, however, was a precondition for any expansion abroad. As a starter, all banknote printing was concentrated in Munich as part of the building of the new corporate headquarters at the beginning of the 1990s. That unnecessarily expensive project, which had still been supervised by son Yorck, outran all cost projections. The new building on an expensive urban plot swallowed several hundred million marks, making it a lasting cost burden for the corporation. The concentration of all high-security printing on the property of the company's paper factory on Tegernsee would have been more sensible, both in costs and for physical security considerations. But the new printing plant in downtown Munich augmented printing capacity considerably. Then the Paperfabrik Königstein in Saxony was purchased, followed by VEB Wertpapierdruck of Leipzig, which was obtained from the federal reconstruction trust. Westphal, the former technical director of Giesecke & Devrient who inspected the eastern printing facility, reached a favorable conclusion in his report. The high-security printer even had a line of printing machines from Koebau-Giori, along with some IBM computers, acquired by circumventing the Cocom embargo list, Westphal reported. Otto embarked upon the re-acquisition of the historical premises of Giesecke & Devrient with no show of emotion, however. The operation merited only one visit from him and he complained he was supposed to buy something that had always belonged to him. It was more difficult still for Beck to persuade Otto to buy the old paper factory. This was mainly supposed to forestall an acquisition by De La Rue-Portals or the Dutch VHP. Both had shown interest in the printing plant and the paper factory. Both eastern companies were reasonably priced and their eastern German workforce was capable as well as eager to work. They had already demonstrated their capability for the citizens of collapsed East Germany in connection with the unification »welcome money« provided by the federal government. This cash was mainly distributed in 5-mark notes, which were in little demand in western Germany and were therefore scarce. The Bundesbank had 50 million notes in this denomination printed by the Leipzig securities printer. Of course, both companies had to be modernized at considerable cost. And an environmental cleanup had to be done at the paper factory, where not just an additional increase in capacity but also more flexibility in production was sought. But in the end they both became rare instances in which the purchase of companies in the new eastern states led to the creation of stable jobs. Surprisingly even the cooperation with Irmgard Ulrich, director of the Leipzig printing works, developed favorably. The director, who had worked her way up through the ranks, was initially the object of great skepticism in Munich.

One further step in the expansion of production capacity, in 1999, was the takeover of the stricken British American Banknote (BABN) in Ottawa, Canada. It was the first foreign base for banknote printing that the Munich company ever had. Now modernized, BABN prints half of Canada's banknotes, produces cards for Canadian banks, and provides a printing venue that is less vulnerable to foreign-exchange swings within NAFTA, the North American Free Trade Agreement. This was, incidentally, the last project handled by Beck. He retired at the end of 1999 after nearly fifty years with the company, leaving the management of Giesecke & Devrient and Papierfabrik Louisenthal. He had left an indelible mark on the expanding corporation in good times and bad. An official statement saluted him for »great accomplishments for the company.« The expansion of production capacity continued, however, after his departure with the building of a plant for making strips of film on the property of Papierfabrik Louisenthal and the erection of a banknote printing facility in Kuala Lumpur. The Malaysian project was one that De La Rue had tried to prevent with all means over many years. The plant went on line at the end of 2003 as a joint venture between Giesecke & Devrient and FIMA Corporation Berhad Kuala Lumpur, Malaysia's leading security printer. Giesecke & Devrient holds a 70 percent majority of the capital and is responsible for technical direction. The Malaysian central bank has given no guarantee to purchase from this venture, however. While the aforementioned manufacture of strips of film extends the chain of added value – and independence – in the production of banknotes, the printing venture in Malaysia offers the advantage of wages that are far below the German level.

With used and overhauled machinery from Koenig & Bauer, this engagement of Giesecke & Devrient in Malaysia has succeeded beyond expectations so far, although it still lacks an exclusive contract with Bank Negara Malaysia and currently prints less than half of Malaysia's 1 billion banknotes required annually. In the summer of 2005, the banknote printing plant announced it was operating at full printing capacity, thanks to brisk export demand. A doubling of capacity to 2 billion notes a year was envisaged in the medium term, the company statement added. The announcement was obviously a subtle hint to the Malaysian central bank that capacity for its note requirements would always be reserved in spite of the rising production for export, probably associated with the relocation of printing contracts from bases with less favorable cost structures. But other note printers are also interested in Malaysia. Malaysia isn't just an impressive 12th on the IMF list of the most competitive countries. This strongly nationalist Southeast Asian country with its 23 million inhabitants offers an attractive domestic market because of its favorable economic policy. A Dutch-Malaysian consortium advised by Britain's Secura Monde International wants to build a second high-security printing plant in Malaysia. Joh. Enschedé will handle the technical consulting. The Dutch will take initially a 5 percent and »might« increase their stake to 15 percent later. The rest of the capital is held by the Malaysian Focus Equity group. The banknote printing plant is supposed to be equipped with brand-new machinery from KBA. The targeted capacity is 1.8 billion notes a year and the total cost will be around 100 million British pounds. The printing-works is scheduled to start operating in January 2007. It is the intention of the investors to produce not only all banknotes for Bank Negara but also, to serve export markets, especially in Muslim countries. The consortium is clearly counting on the influence of local politicians to cause the hesitant central bank to issue the required permit. A memorandum of understanding between the partners was ceremoniously signed in the presence of Malaysia's prime minister. But contrary to the relevant statement of the Focus group, there is no machinery order yet with KBA for or from Malaysia. The Würzburg company has also been talking for many years with the Malaysians about this project, but with no success so far.

It would indeed be a spectacular development in the embattled world of high-security printing if an anonymous group of investors would be authorized by a central bank to buy these tightly controlled banknote printing machines.

And there is more trouble in the offing for Giesecke & Devrient. Also, there are reports circulating in Kuala Lumpur of another Malaysian consortium planning to build a factory for security paper. The project seems to involve the building of a paper factory with a final capacity of 6,000 metric tons of banknote paper a year. Just the machinery and technical plant would swallow 100 million euros on top of the costs of buildings and grounds. Since this huge capacity far exceeds Malaysia's own requirements, the consortium hopes to sell part of its paper on the world market. The Reserve Bank of India would be a potential customer. India has so far covered its gigantic import requirement for banknote paper primarily with supplies from Louisenthal and Portals. The required authorization from Malaysia's finance ministry and central bank seems to pose no problem.

Both plants, if built, would not only put Giesecke & Devrient in a vise, but they would further aggravate the chronically excessive capacity on the world market for secure paper and note printing. With the huge cost advantages these projects offer, they might knell the beginning of the end of private banknote printing in Europe.

Back to the turbulent 1990s. At the peak of the crisis, Hilmar Dosch, the former chairman of Heidelberger Druckmaschinen AG, was recruited for a new, temporary posting as chairman of business management. With the title came tremendous power and the challenging mission to calm the agitated workforce. During his three years in office, Dosch, a kind father-figure, succeeded in this mission although not without difficulties. It had not been his task to review the strategic direction of the high-security printer after the departure of Siegfried Otto. This was the job given to Willi Berchthold, who replaced Dosch at the end of 1998 as chairman of business management for Giesecke & Devrient. Berchtold, however, had not been the candidate of choice. There had been another eligible person, whom the two owners would have preferred. Yet this person had demanded a great deal for taking this difficult assignment; too much, in fact, for the two heiresses. Berchtold had most recently been business manager of IBM Deutschland Information Systems and general manager of its services business in the German-speaking countries, in Russia, and in all of central and eastern Europe. He had been molded by his long career in the

U.S. multinational corporation and understood that his arrival in Munich was a signal of cultural change for the corporation: performance was supposed to count henceforth, not tradition. Berchtold gathered the comparatively autonomous divisions into two »systems« under a leadership that was again strongly centralized. Apart from paper, security features, and printing, the »banknote system« also included banknote processing and destruction. In the »card system« were concentrated all activities of the card division, including devices to read and personalize them. Berchtold began strengthening research and development by hiking the R&D outlays, sometimes to nearly 8 percent of group sales. And in Munich he built a new technology center, which now employs more than 450 technicians. The two systems - banknote and card - currently have nearly the same turnover and each receives half the funds for research and development. It was Berchtold's stated aim to make Giesecke & Devrient the technological leader for highly secure products and to rebuild the company, which had always been product-oriented, as a supplier of complete systems for banknotes and cards and of the information and expertise necessary for their operation. Giesecke & Devrient was supposed to become a service provider, something that has long been commonplace in the branch of information technology.

In contrast to the Deutschmark days, Giesecke & Devrient no longer needs euro printing contracted out by Bundesbank in order to take up the slack in its printing capacity. Attention has now turned to the growing demands of printing and physical security, connected with the outlook that the euro could become the world leader for security among banknotes. In the banknote division the emphasis in research has been placed on enhancing security against counterfeiting. This is being pursued with new, three-dimensional or optically variably security features, as well as with the development of paper types with longer useful life. Also, possible substitution of plastic for the traditional banknote paper made of cotton is deterred. Instead, Louisenthal has developed two types of paper that, thanks to a special surface coating, repel dirt and moisture. Soiling and physical damage are the main causes of banknotes having to be prematurely removed from circulation and destroyed. In addition, a transparent polyester strip embedded on both long edges of the note protects it from tearing. This surface coating of the banknote is not new, although there are frequent difficulties with it, it was the cause of the Bank of England's problem with the ink rubbing off from its new 5-pound notes. In the battle against counterfeiters, Giesecke & Devrient wants to introduce a new security feature for banknotes at each of the coming annual meetings of the World Bank and International Monetary Fund. That is an ambitious goal for their researchers because the competition isn't snoozing. It could easily induce people to decant some old wine from new skins.

The market saturation in the business with banknote processing systems for central banks has forced Giesecke & Devrient to rethink its strategy in this field, too. To supplemental central banks business, it increasingly offers its processing systems to commercial banks, gaming casinos, department stores, food market chains, and money transport companies. The whole line of systems was extended downward to match their requirements. In the process the first fully functional banknote processing device in desktop format was brought to market. Thanks to their decades of accrued knowledge of processes, the Munich people see themselves out in front with direct cash recycling. They also want to include the administrative »back office« in their automated cash processing. The system was tested in a field trial in a big German department store. The cashiers put their day's receipts in the machine, which counted the notes and checked, sorted and bundled them into a secure cassette. Because the system is connected with the bookkeeping cycle of the department store, it also registers the balance on account even and sends a message to the armored-car service when the full cassette is ready to be picked up. The money transport, therefore, occurs at irregular intervals, which is an effective protection against holdups and armed robbery. Although the market for this sort of business is regarded as large, the business is still in its infancy. The entire cash processing of all the Munich branch offices of Hypovereinsbank, including its two hundred ATMs in the city, has been taken over by Giesecke & Devrient. While the business with cash management is developing gingerly at home, Giesecke & Devrient succeeded in establishing itself with these new services in Dubai, Morocco, and South Africa. For a real breakthrough, providers of the new service will have to demonstrate that it works not only as reliably as their customer would, but also that the system is considerably cheaper, maybe causing Giesecke & Devrient to kiss off the high profit margins that were once the norm in the business with banknote processing systems. And it will have to sell quite a number of small processing devices in order to match the turnover of a single high-performance system. The smallest processing device costs 12,000 euros, while the most elaborate version of the processing system 2000/3000, designed for the printing works of the central banks, would bring 4 million euros.

The stable and profitable business with banknote paper and banknote printing presently is the backbone of Giesecke & Devrient. The corporation earns its money here. Two appointments were supposed to help the Munich private printer play a leading role in this business later on. Wim Duisenberg, the former ECB president, who recently died, had been recruited for the company's advisory board on strategic issues. And Peter Walter, who formerly directed the Bundesbank's central treasury and took part in the planning of the next euro series even after his retirement, was also named to this panel. But Berchtold was absorbed with his second pillar, the »card system,« the memory card, and the advanced version of the processor card. The processor card with its computing capability in a central processing unit (CPU), also known as a smart card, is among the few products with which Europe still has a clear technological edge over the United States. Berchtold saw this as the true challenge and future of the high-security company he was leading. This particular engagement was illustrated by a boost in related research spending to more than 50 percent of the company's outlays for the sector of cards from just 2 percent during Berchtold´s period in office. The financial efforts have been remarkable and the technological expertise is high. Yet the situation of the card business is fundamentally different from that of the business with banknotes. With the latter, Giesecke & Devrient has been able to carve out a unique position on the world market as a systems provider of everything from paper and note printing to processing systems and even the shredder. It has something decisive to say there about market prices. Whether the same position can be achieved with cards is questionable, to say the least.

According to industry estimates, 2.264 billion chip cards were produced around the world for a value of roughly 3 billion euros in 2004. That volume included 1.41 billion microprocessor cards. The French lead the world market here. Market shares of 25 percent to 30 percent each are held by France's Gemplus, which made headlines in a U.S. takeover attempt, and Axalto (ex Schlumberger). Giesecke & Devrient followed, with around 17 percent of the market. France's Oberthur Card Systems was in fourth place.[20] A 20 percent market share is regarded in this branch of industry as the critical mass. The French competition leans more toward volume business, while Giesecke & Devrient concentrates on the more demanding segment of processor cards with their own computing capability. This business is divided into the following segments: payments traffic, commercial and government, including health care delivery, and telecommunications.

It is a hotly contested market. Exactly that business vigorously pursued by Munich with identification systems, such as ID and access cards, is proving difficult. Showcase projects are needed. No country wants to use some standards in building a national identification system that could later prove to be incompatible internationally. The standards include encrypting procedures, algorithms, and biometrics. In the absence of international standards on the technology, development is retarded by technical and legal differences of opinion on the matter of biometric recognition characteristics, namely fingerprints, the shape of the face, or the iris. It is also retarded by the differences over securing of electronic messages and application forms by means of the digital signature. The Americans are going their own way, confronting the world with done deeds in such things as, in any event, the selection of biometric data on a proposed new passport. And it is still unforeseeable whether and to what extent China will go along with international cooperation on these key technologies.

The first foreign order for Giesecke & Devrient in the field of identification cards, namely Project Delta, was a disappointment for all concerned. The public solicitation called for the building of a decentralized system of data banking for 42 million Egyptians and the issuing of identification cards with chips. The company won the bidding in the second round during the mid-1990s. Yet Munich was not sufficiently prepared with its technology. Missing infrastructure, including data conduits and data-bank software, an overtaxed public administration at the scene, and the difficulties the Egyptian security organs had in handling the new technology added to the burdens. Deadlines were missed and costs exploded. Project Delta was a loss-maker. Used for this project, the personalizing laser device Luchs later had to be withdrawn from production because of high manufacturing costs and too small a market share.

Concerning cards for payments traffic and telecommunications, Giesecke & Devrient has attractive customers under contract. They include the German savings bank association and the customer tracking center of Deutsche Telekom for all of Europe, now operated by the Munich company. But the Geld Karte, a stored value card developed by Munich as an e-purse, has not caught on so far in the market. Another project, the development of an electronic payments terminal, ZVT 900, had to be terminated after considerable investment. The availability of access devices in adequate numbers is one of the deciding factors in spreading card-based payment systems. But compared with the Italian and French competition, Giesecke & Devrient was too late and too expensive.

Size alone is not enough in the business with identification systems. The example of Finnish card manufacturer Setec OY has just proven that. Setec, which now belongs to Gemplus, was the first company to offer Europe an identification system with biometric characteristics. For primarily political reasons, such a success in Germany has eluded the Munich company. Giesecke & Devrient is even excluded from the lucrative business with biometric passports and personal identification documents in Germany. This production is reserved exclusively for Berlin by a long-term contract between the federal interior ministry and the federal printing works. But the Munich company has been able to land contracts for several more projects abroad. Half a million citizens of Chinese Macao have received a personal identification document with biometric identification characteristics, including a snapshot and prints of all ten fingers. Also, twenty-four million Taiwanese are equipped with multifunctional medical insurance cards, also containing biometric recognition features. The eight million Austrian health insurance cards come from Giesecke & Devrient as well. Finally, the building of a personalization center for passports and identification documents has been agreed upon with Lithuania. Apart from Taiwan and Austria, all these projects are of a modest size. But at least they could serve as important working examples in later public solicitations. Munich's gaze is now directed toward the pan-European introduction of UMTS standards for cellular telephony. It is still unclear here, however, to what extent this will generate additional demand for SIM cards. The hopes for the planned German health insurance card are more concrete. Giesecke & Devrient could benefit here from the crisis of the former subsidiary of the Bundesdruckerei, Orga Kartensysteme. The latter company has now been sold to Sagem, a French holding company engaged in the fields of electronics and armaments.

Another trend is also becoming clear in Munich. Giesecke & Devrient is entering the cards business increasingly as a systems provider, which buys its components and assumes responsibility from the customer for the system's proper functioning. That offers larger profit margins. But Giesecke & Devrient will probably remain dependent upon external sources for certain key technologies. That applies to data banks and computing systems. It also applies to biometrics, for which Munich has no technology of its own and must procure it. The leadership there is with France's Sagem, Japan's NEC, and Siemens-Infineon. All of these are corporations with considerable market power, against which Giesecke & Devrient could hardly prevail in a crunch.

The cards business may have a high potential for the future. At the moment, though, it requires considerable financial exertion, especially since acquisitions of companies are also likely to be unavoidable to strengthen the technological basis of Giesecke & Devrient. More concentration among European players is very probable. The planned merger between Gemplus and Axalto into Gemalto, announced at the end of 2005, will have a profound impact on the world cards market. Gemalto will have a turnover of 1.8 billion euros and a market share of 50 percent in the global chip cards business - that is three times the size of the cards business of Giesecke & Devrient. Yet Munich believes it is armed for this challenge. The corporation is de facto debt free and has respectable financial reserves. Whether they are sufficient in the long haul to undertake large projects with ID systems and to put up the required financial guarantees remains to be seen. Oberthur Card Systems and Axalto went on the exchange to obtain capital. The legal conditions for eventually going public with the cards business were created in Munich by the formation of Secartis AG as a 100 percent subsidiary. But Secartis was then sold to Secunet AG of Essen. In return Giesecke & Devrient took a 47 percent stake in this exchange-listed specialist for software for information technology. Will Giesecke & Devrient be able to stay on its own, or will it, one day have to turn to some powerful international financier?

The Bundesbank has expressed the hope several times in the past that Giesecke & Devrient would float part of its capital on the exchange. But Verena von Mitschke-Collande feels a duty to her family's tradition. The high-security printer is, therefore, expected to continue to be controlled exclusively by the family. An exchange listing isn't necessary because the debt capital market is now open to the company, she has said. Of the two heiresses, she alone is on the supervisory board and represents both owners with a seat and a vote on the advisory council for corporate strategy. The mother of several children, she is increasingly enjoying her role as an entrepreneur. Conflicts of interest or strategy, which have arisen under similar circumstances at Bertelsmann AG and Springer AG, cannot be ruled out there. In autumn of 2004, only a year after his contract had been renewed for four years in difficult negotiations, Berchtold left Giesecke & Devrient. His abrupt departure followed intensifying friction with Verena von Mitschke-Collande. Her chief executive was becoming too independent, it was rumored. The departure reminded observers of Rademacher's case. This matter must have cost the company another small fortune because Berchtold was paid his salary for the full length of his contract, not to mention his retirement claims.

Karsten Ottenberg became Berchtold's successor after a lengthy vacancy. The comparatively young physicist came from Philips Electronics. In the Netherlands he had initially been responsible for sales in the field of semiconductors, then later in the consumer products segment. It is obvious that the new chief executive will especially look after the cards business at Giesecke & Devrient. This remains promising and enjoys priority, even if its earnings contribution has been highly unsatisfactory so far. The company has improved its earnings power in the fields of paper and banknote printing by means of productivity boosts and the shifting of printing venues. But the cards business suffers from continued positioning in the cost-intensive German base amid simultaneously mounting price pressure. The announced resignation of Franz M. Haniel, who was in charge of the cards business, as well as the departure of his chief of production of cards, have given rise to new rumors about personal tensions and conflicting strategies in Munich. Haniel had worked for several years for the French cards group Gemplus and had been considered as a candidate to fill the top job at Giesecke & Devrient.

Giesecke & Devrient is now a global company but it still adds 70 percent of its value in Germany, while only 15 percent of its sales accrued are domestic. Particularly in view of militant trade unions, the management of the high-security printer will demand of Ottenberg plenty of entrepreneurial courage and vision. It will also demand – especially in internal relations – a high degree of diplomacy. An exchange-listed high-security printing company like De La Rue may have encountered certain problems because of its legal form. The pure family company of Munich has no fewer problems – only problems of another type. Whether these problems pose less of a challenge for the long-term development of Giesecke & Devrient time will show.

7
Where hard work and politics helped Francois Charles Oberthur Fiduciaire

It is fairly evident that the two heavies of the industry – De La Rue and Giesecke & Devrient – now divide the banknote market between them, denying access to others. But there were certainly attempts by outsiders to become involved in the 1980s, when the banknote business still yielded highly attractive profits. One such attempt was undertaken by the Frenchman Jean-Pierre Savare with his company, Francois Charles Oberthur Fiduciaire (FCOF). And he was unexpectedly successful. A second bid was made by the Ciccone brothers of Argentina with their Ciccone Calcográfica. But they were shipwrecked because of their greed. And there was the highly respected Bundesdruckerei, the German federal printing works in Berlin, which failed miserably with its expansion abroad. The last two bids for market entry are treated separately in later chapters; this one is about Francois Charles Oberthur.

›Phoenix from the ashes‹

Jean-Pierre Savare got into banknote printing rather by accident. The educated software specialist had dealt with industrial basket cases for years at Banque Nationale de Paris (BNP), specializing there in shipbuilders and printers. At the start of the 1980s he was assigned to work up a concept for the finance ministry for the rescue of the secure printer Oberthur in Rennes-Chantepie, Brittany. The 140-year-old family company produced a colorful assortment of printed materials: reference works, a popular calendar, lottery tickets, check blanks, and especially a small portion of the banknotes that Banque de France made for the former African colonies, the franc zone of today's Communauté Financière d'Afrique (CFA). The printing establishment, in which Swiss ink specia-

Moneymakers, Klaus W. Bender

ISBN: 3-527-50236-X

list SICPA held a capital stake of 50 percent, was insolvent and was supposed to go into liquidation. Savare found »a diamond in the rough,« as he later related. Instead of preparing the rescue concept for the finance ministry, he bought the secure printer for himself for the symbolic price of one franc, quitting his bank job in 1984. What then occurred resembled the emergence of the »phoenix from the ashes.«

Savare was not a complete novice. He had gained his first experience in this branch of industry as the owner of Éditions de Chiffre, a small printer of check forms and bookkeeping pads on the outskirts of Paris. From his job at the bank he also had contacts to officials in key positions. For example, the mayor of Rennes was at the time holding a ministerial office in Paris, which was helpful in matters of »preservation of jobs.« And finally, Savare had ties among the conservatives, among them Jacques Chirac, who later became president of the French republic. Political contacts play an important role in the business scene of many countries. In France they decide everything. The order books of Francois Charles Oberthur Fiduciaire, the traditional name under which the company was re-entered in the trade registry, were soon to fill up encouragingly. The first stroke of luck came shortly after this relaunching with the introduction of the »tac-o-tac« lottery. Oberthur was already involved with a small role in the printing of the national lottery. But now its successor company was receiving an award for the printing of two-thirds of the new lottery tickets from which a purchaser scratches off a surface coating to see if he has won with the numbers concealed underneath. Instead of a few hundred thousand lottery chances a week, several million tac-o-tac chances now had to be produced each week in Rennes. The second and even bigger slice of good fortune came shortly afterwards. It was the decision of Banque de France to give up printing banknotes for the African franc zone at a time when it was coping with strikes and technical refitting of its printing works in Chamalières. It decided to give the work to a subcontractor. Even before its takeover by Savare, Oberthur had been allowed to print a small portion of these banknotes. Now the new owner had received the contract to print all of them. Thirteen African countries and the Comoro Islands were in CFA. The zone's combined population was 93 million. Their yearly requirement for banknotes was in the neighborhood of 1 billion. This order secured for Rennes a stable, high operating ratio. Banque de France also paid handsomely for the notes. Naturally there was again gossip in the branch.

From its inception Rennes operated with rapidly rising sales and eye-catching profits, which long remained free of tax as well. The losses carried forward from the insolvency could be used to offset tax liabilities. It paid tribute to Savare's wisdom as an entrepreneur that these profits were reinvested in modernizing the printing establishment. Various banks, to whom he had to grant a one-third interest in his holding company, loaned him additional capital. At the beginning of the 1990s Rennes already had two highly modern Super printing machine lines with a capacity of around 2 billion units a year. For a newcomer to this branch, that was breathtaking printing capacity. And sometimes it was even running flat. When the need arises, the printing machinery in Rennes runs with three shifts around the clock, six days a week – just like its role model, the Bureau of Engraving and Printing in Washington. Savare was soon feared by the established competition equally for his aggressive market entry and his tightly calculated banknote prices.

And Savare, the workaholic, expanded. Because he recognized that the future of payments traffic would belong to the bank card, not the check blanks he was printing in great volumes, he got into the cards business just three years after his takeover. He entered into a temporary joint venture with the electronics concern BULL as a supplier of chip cards. Oberthur Card Systems (OCS) had begun. When the U.S. antitrust authority demanded the sale of a printing plant before approving the planned merger of American Banknote and U.S. Banknote, Savare acted immediately by buying Banknote Corporation of America (BCA) in New York. Though BCA no longer printed banknotes, this purchase made the Frenchman the principal supplier of the U.S. Postal Service. With 10 billion stamps a year it was the largest stamp producer in the world. More giant steps followed. When Ottawa's struggling British American Banknote (BABN) had to sell its lottery business to regain liquidity, Savare was there in a flash. He had to cough up the purchase price in installments over many years. But this step paved the way to the lottery business abroad. This was the origin of Oberthur Gaming Technologies. Yet Savare's quantum jump was made just before the millennium turn with the takeover of the entire card business of De La Rue. Savare had previously been given the brush-off by Germany's Orga Kartensysteme in Paderborn. The Bundesdruckerei had snapped up this prize in front of his nose. The Frenchman more than made up for that slap with his coup in Britain. It made Oberthur Card Systems the world's third-biggest cards supplier in one stroke. The takeover wasn't just another proof of Savare's entrepreneurial daring. It also proved his technical skill in financing. Although he paid a high takeover price, he promptly floated a small share of the capital on the stock exchange. At the high point of the IT share-price euphoria, he raked in such strong proceeds with this that he nearly got back his purchase price. Savare controls his entire group through a family foundation. But he gave the operating direction of this sole exchange-listed subsidiary to his son Thomas. The direction of the international lottery business and the financing of the fast-growing concern were turned over to the two daughters, Emmanuelle and Marie. The holding company does not publish consolidated results. It is known, however, that in 2003 the group made sales of 652 million and a net income of 18.2 million euros, with 4,700 employees. Of these group sales 66 percent were in cards and 15 percent in lottery. Banknote printing came in a distant third with barely 9 percent.

Challenges

Jean-Pierre Savare, who grew up in humble circumstances as the son of a Russian immigrant, had advanced to the top of his game. Within just a decade and a half he had succeeded in joining the list of the one hundred richest Frenchmen. At the company's Paris headquarters, a palatial mansion on Boulevard Malesherbes, the elegant furnishings and valuable 18th-century landscapes of Italian and French masters in his imposing office bespoke the pride of the patriarch in this achievement. Although accustomed to success, this entrepreneur also had to endure setbacks. One of the first was in the second half of the 1990s when Banque de France, with which he liked to feud, took away part of his lucrative banknote printing for the CFA countries. He was allowed to keep the largest group of West African countries served by Banque Centrale des États de l'Afrique de l'Ouest (BCEAO), but he had to surrender the smaller Central African group of countries served by Banque des États de l'Afrique Centrale (BEAC). That could not have come about based on price alone, because the third quota went to the Swiss private printer, Orell Füssli – which is known for high printing quality and commensurately high printing charges. Savare had tried to get around the Banque de France by contacting the countries directly, it was said in the industry.

This involved only the loss of 300 million banknotes a year. But the experience prompted Savare to look for allies on the increasingly difficult market for banknote printing. He had two high-performance printing lines to keep busy. And the European common currency was taking shape on the horizon. He would, as he must have feared, remain excluded from euro printing. After all, Banque de France, all its own problems notwithstanding, had always categorically refused to let both him and the old security printer, Oberthur, participate in the printing of French franc notes. Savare initially sounded out Giesecke & Devrient in Munich. Perhaps he believed he would easily have his way with the two heiresses, who had little experience in business matters. Nothing became of that. With a quick decision he turned next to the small Dutch printer Joh. Enschedé, whose participation in euro printing was certain. He offered a merger of the two secure printers, with a stake-holding ratio of 70:30. There had already been several takeovers between private secure printers, but never a merger of equals. The border-crossing industrial marriage was announced with appropriate fanfare. But it ended a few months later in mutual recriminations and insults. That was partly attributable to the relative competitiveness of the two printers. With nearly 300 employees, Oberthur produced an average of 1.2 billion to 1.4 billion units a year. With 100 employees, Enschedé managed to print just 160 million. But the break-up was also caused by a clash of key personalities and the corporate cultures they represented, French branch expert Guy Durand was able to say from close observation. The officious and somewhat rigid Dutchmen, who had been earning their money comfortably for nearly two centuries by printing guilder notes for the Nederlandsche Bank, hardly meshed with the aggressive and agile self-made man from Paris, who disliked back talk and quickly lost patience. Savare was left alone in the end with his banknote printer, which also painfully lacked any vertical integration, from paper manufacturing to banknote processing machinery.

The new millennium held more unpleasant surprises for the senior boss. First the share price of Oberthur Card Systems collapsed, and then its card business. Losses and debts rose alarmingly. This was not an isolated instance. The whole card branch went into crisis. That cost the son, Thomas, his post as boss. He withdrew angrily from the operating leadership and the direction of the cards division was turned over to Pierre Barberis, an acknowledged expert for difficult rescue operations. He led the card business back out of the red comparatively rapidly. Oberthur

Cards Systems is now especially well positioned on the French market in cards for banks and cellular telephony. It is also a supplier of applications related to security in the field of ID cards, with which the company is internationally active. This subsidiary of Francois Charles Oberthur Fiduciaire is regarded as promising, despite the tough battle over the card market.

Savare has had to take more heavy blows in the interim. First he lost the stamp printing contract of the U.S. Postal Service to competitor Ashton-Potter. It must remain only speculation that the disruption in the U.S.-French relationship over the Iraq war might have played a role. Next, and probably worse for Savare and his concern, was that Banque de France also terminated his remaining printing contract – the one for the BCEAO countries – at the end of 2003. The central bank apparently needs the printing of these banknotes to absorb its own fallow capacity, which recently expanded to handle the euro. Conspicuously, however, the Swiss private printer Orell Füssli has so far been allowed to keep its smaller printing quota. The consequences for Francois Charles Oberthur Fiduciaire could be serious. The comparatively heavily indebted French private printer has lost in one blow not only around half its volume of banknote printing in Rennes but, above all, a well paid long-term order. The impact on the margin of Savare's banknote business appeared to be taking shape, especially since Savare finally had been allowed to participate in the primary euro-note printing, but then was excluded from printing replacement euro notes, as shall be explained later. FCOF did indeed operate at full printing capacity in 2004, producing around 2 billion units. Yet this could only be done thanks to an aggressive marketing policy, which took its toll of earnings. The loss of its biggest stamp customer by far is also likely to leave its scars. Specialized in expensive engraved printing, the U.S. stamp printing plant of Banknote Corporation of America in New York had to be sold at the end of 2003. With that, the card business gained even more prominence in securing the future of the company. Perhaps the politicians will again rally to the side of the hard-pressed private printer. Savare had been interested in taking over the Bundesdruckerei in Berlin. While he has no use for its capacity to print banknotes, this would secure his access to euro printing. Berlin would also be valuable in the development of his own weak business with upscale ID systems. For the time being, however, Berlin has warded off Savare's overtures. But the final decision will not be made in Berlin. Domestically the »English solution« tried with

Debden could even inspire Banque de France, causing it to turn over its grossly inefficient state printing works in Clermont-Ferrand to the private Francois Charles Oberthur Fiduciaire under a management contract. There have often been rumors of some such arrangement with this private printer. The proud Banque de France would, however, have to swallow its pride, not to speak of those militant union officials in Clermont-Ferrand for whom the returns-oriented private entrepreneur is likely to have the effect of a red cloth waved at a bull. But putting such a deal together would also take an energetic and politically savvy actor on the side of Francois Charles Oberthur. Yet Jean-Pierre Savare, who had built up his business with such intense personal involvement, is slowly withdrawing from daily operations because of advancing age. He has long since signed over his company to the children. And after the withdrawal of son Thomas from the operating management amid the cards debacle, the leadership of the individual subsidiaries has been transferred to professional managers. Perhaps one day people will think only of cards when the name Oberthur is mentioned.

Money Losers

8
What brought Bundesdruckerei to the brink of ruin

The business with high-security products has become difficult. The value of the »license to print money« has fallen steeply. The case about to be described still deserves special attention. A respected government enterprise, equipped with large reserves of liquidity and perhaps the world's most modern production plant during the period in question, was privatized. Within one year it was maneuvered to the brink of ruin with noisy posturing, lack of vision, and rapaciousness. The case is unique in German postwar history, *Manager Magazine* also concluded.[1] Yet the most scandalous of the scandals that swirled around Berlin's Bundesdruckerei is perhaps the indifference concerning this drama. No one felt guilty in retrospect. No one from the business world or politics betrayed even the slightest self doubt, let alone a feeling of culpability. The Bundesdruckerei, a mirror of the Federal Republic?

For 125 years the Berlin high-security printer has produced German banknotes and can look back on a resplendent past. It came into being in 1879 as the Reichsdruckerei at the initiative of the Prussian postmaster general, Heinrich von Stephan. The Reichsdruckerei was the product of a merger between Geheime Oberhofbuchdruckerei von Decker and Königlich-Preußische Staatsdruckerei of Berlin-Kreuzberg. Most of its print works and offices were destroyed in the final days of the Second World War. After the war ended, it was turned over to Berlin's city administration as Staatsdruckerei Berlin because it happened to be in the western part of the divided city. It came into the possession of the West German federal administration in 1951 and was henceforth run as Bundesdruckerei, acquiring the insignia of the new Federal Republic of Germany. Four years later it was permitted to print the first federal German banknote, the 5-Deutschmark note picturing Europa on the Bull. British De La Rue,

Moneymakers, Klaus W. Bender

ISBN: 3-527-50236-X

which had been printing these notes for Bank deutscher Länder, made its original printing plates available for this. At the end of the same decade the Berlin establishment was entrusted by Deutsche Bundesbank with the printing of half the new D-mark notes. When the Cold War became hotter and the Berlin Wall, strong and tall, was built, worries mounted about the future of the free part of the city. The printing plant grounds bordered directly on the Wall, which was regarded as impregnable and was even used for that reason as part of the printing plant's external physical security. Bundesdruckerei, completely encircled by the communist territory, had to build a fallback base of printing at Neu Isenburg, near Frankfurt, for its D-mark banknotes. From then on only 10-mark notes came from Berlin. These notes had to be flown out of the city. Bundesbank's desire that Giesecke & Devrient, the company entrusted with printing the other half of the D-mark notes, set up a second D-mark printing plant as a backup, could be fended off by Munich, incidentally. After the fall of the Berlin Wall in 1989, the proportionally allocated printing of mark notes by Bundesdruckerei was concentrated in Berlin. At the same time the liberal-conservative Christian Democrat-Free Democrat coalition government of Helmut Kohl decided to put 49 percent of the capital of Bundesdruckerei into private hands at a time still to be determined. With the conversion of the state operation into a GmbH corporation with limited liability under commercial law, »the signals were set for a future in free competition,« the business report for the truncated year 1994 announced. The government plant from now on was supposed to receive more latitude in its actions and become more independent in its investment policy. The responsible budget committee of the Bundestag lower chamber of parliament had, after all, repeatedly criticized the occasional efforts of Bundesdruckerei to obtain export orders because the Berlin plant had offered to do this at marginal costs. With full costing it would stand no chance. These efforts angered the private Munich company, which was well-connected politically. The same budget committee had withheld funds for building up the state plant's own research department, saying that research was already being carried out in Munich. Bundesdruckerei was asked to stop any further research activities. The printing works was also supposed to be freed from the shackles of tenure and pay requirements of the civil service, and made more flexible in tailoring the salaries of top management. On the way into the free market economy it needed qualified staff, and that cost money. Since the retirement of the serving chairman of business management, Rüdiger Bock, was approaching, Ernst-Theodor Menke was appointed director of operations and later business manager. He hailed from private industry, including posts with Unilever and Dornier.

The »blastoff into a difficult market,« as the 1994 business report colorfully described this, began with an overhaul. Although Reichsdruckerei had once printed banknotes exclusively for Reichsbank, and later also made postage stamps, tax stamps, and identification documents for the empire, it had always been subordinated to the postal ministry. This arrangement continued when the printing works was turned over to the federal government. Bundesdruckerei was placed under the supervision of the minister for post and telecommunications. This ministry was regarded as a particularly unwieldy federal bureaucracy, and the state printing works absorbed this spirit. Although it was not a postal operation, it served the postal ministry as a sinecure. The position of president of Bundesdruckerei was a post coveted by veteran ministerial bureaucrats. And bureaucratic thinking set the agenda at Bundesdruckerei. The federal printing works presented a strange picture, to say the least. The padded workforce – 4,400 persons in 1990 – was paid above union scale and could not be fired. There was a works council functionary who drove a Porsche, while at the same time a revolutionary »red cell« was active in the printing works. The plant had the highest level of days lost to sickness of any industrial operation in Berlin. An attempt to improve the quality of management with professional advancement courses led straight into the arms of the Scientology sect, of all things.

The products of Bundesdruckerei enjoyed a worldwide reputation for technical proficiency in printing. In the making of printing plates, Berlin was even superior to Giesecke & Devrient in some ways. But it was too expensive. The high costs in Berlin were to blame that the production of Deutschmark notes for a long time was among the most expensive in the world. The state printing works was a competitor and a customer of the Munich company at the same time. It depended, for example, totally upon Louisenthal and its price edicts for the special D-mark paper. That also made life difficult for the Berlin operation. Giesecke & Devrient could print more cheaply, yet it liked to hide behind the higher costs of Berlin in billing its share of mark printing. This didn't even require the ineptitude of a Bundesdruckerei boss, who once left his documents on price calculations lying on the table at the end of a conference in Munich. Even after

Bundesbank in the early 1980s introduced public price reviews for D-mark printing, Berlin's cost structure still remained an advantage for the private printer. Many an episode leads one to suppose that there was a certain »leakage of information« from the auditing commissions, for the auditors met simultaneously in Berlin and Munich. This did not change until the end of the decade, when Bundesbank started to look more critically and to take heed of costs. The parochial bureaucrats in any case were no match for Siegfried Otto, the self-confident boss in Munich. Klaus Spreen, who was promoted from press spokesman for the postal ministry to president of Bundesdruckerei, recalls a visit to Otto on the Spanish island of Ibiza, where the private printer had a country residence that looked out over a private bay. Spreen conceded that he was somewhat intimidated by the material opulence on display there. He mentioned during the conversation that his ambition as president of Bundesdruckerei was to retrieve all German banknote printing to Berlin, as had been the rule during the Reichsbank days. Otto became very upset at this audacity and threatened to break off the conversation immediately. The subject was never raised again.

Global dreams ...

The postal bureaucrat squad at Bundesdruckerei regarded the breakthrough to competition as a simple question of equipment with the means of production – paired if necessary with a cautious adjustment of the workforce. Modernization and expansion were done with corresponding generosity – when necessary, even misleading the responsible parliamentary budget committee with concocted figures. A new banknote printing works was completed in the first stage at the end of 1996. It set new standards in banknote printing for the production process, security precautions, energy use, and environmental protection.[2] Its imposing production hall with open interior aroused the envy of the competition. Its high-security vault, unusual for being built at ground level because of the high level of the Berlin water table, was the biggest and most modern industrial vault installation in all Europe. This giant vault featured computer-controlled storage in high racks that could have accommodated sixty-five intercity train cars. Parallel to this building project, the production of identification cards was relocated to a separate, highly secure building. Applications and identification blanks now no longer needed to leave this section of the building until the identification documents were produced. And for good measure, a new administrative building with 15,000 square meters of floor space was constructed. Tallying up all these measures, from the new money center to the new energy supply, at least 135 million euros were invested in this modernized, enlarged, and beautified Bundesdruckerei. A technically more perfectly equipped high-security printing facility probably did not exist in the whole world – everything paid with tax money. Now Berlin could, depending upon the number of shifts, produce 1.8 billion banknotes a year, 7 billion stamps, and 7 million passports and identification cards.

When Menke arrived at Bundesdruckerei, it was producing all the German stamps, passports, personal identification documents, drivers' licenses, application forms, excise tax labels, patent descriptions, and parliamentary publications, along with half the D-mark notes. Those were all government orders, lucrative no doubt, but derived from a »protected field.« Menke envisaged the creation of a concern with broadly diversified holdings at home and abroad. It would be able to offer the global market products and systems all across the high-security spectrum with its credentials of closeness to the German government. Only in this way could the costs be lowered and the profit margin raised. That was a tall order in view of the structural weaknesses of Bundesdruckerei. It had only a narrow line of products and a short value chain. It was everywhere dependant upon suppliers and its workforce was too large.

Menke quickly succeeded in acquiring a controlling stake in Maurer Electronics of Munich, which specialized in image processing and production as well as in the development of security technology for identification systems. Similarly, he gained a majority interest in Munich's HSM-Holographic Systems, a specialist in holograms and optical electronics. Then the founding of Berlin's D-Trust as a trust center for digital signature followed, initially in concert with a subsidiary of Deutsche Telekom. Finally, Menke was able to obtain the capital majority in ORGA Kartensysteme GmbH of Paderborn, for which he had a right of first refusal for the purchase. France's Francois Charles Oberthur Fiduciaire had sought to buy this in vain. Menke acquired 75 percent of the shares for 70 million D-marks (36 million euros). But his strategy then lost its momentum. Together with Arnim von Schwedler, who was responsible for Bundesdruckerei's international relations, he knocked on many a door. There was a meeting with the Spanish state paper maker and note producer FNMT, a feeler toward the private Joh. Enschedé in Holland, talks with Banque de France about closer cooperation, and an assessment of whether to purchase Papierfabrik Sihl in Landquart, Switzerland. Also pondered was the takeover of CSI, the Texas supplier of banknote inspection systems – an American base is always good – or a participation in ABN Holographics, the subsidiary of American Banknote in the field of hologram production and that of kinegrams, which display a different image as the viewing angle changes. Incidentally, the latter failed because of an objection from Crane & Co., which had a stake in ABN Holographics. For a while, Bundesdruckerei even considered getting into building a paper factory and becoming involved in note printing with Indonesia's state-owned Perum Peruri. Indonesia is a country with low wages and a high note requirement, but also unfortunately a very unstable domestic political situation. Somehow all this came across as though Menke was trotting with a shopping cart through a supermarket of the high-security industry. In the end, all the talks and feelers proved futile. Even the small but fine Finnish banknote printer and chip card manufacturer, Setec OY, begged off politely after initial interest.

The time for border-crossing mergers in this extremely sensitive business with highly secure production was not yet ripe, later concluded Schwedler, who today runs Fiduciaire Mondiale Ltd, a trading firm in the high-security field with offices in Berlin and London. Bundesdruckerei's attempts to make a splash as a global supplier of banknotes and identification documents also met with little success. Traditionally strong contacts existed to Venezuela. When that country's central bank ordered 200 million Bolivar notes in the early 1990s, the order was routed in all secrecy to the securities printer in Leipzig, which had not yet been privatized. And that was the first order for banknotes in many years for the federal printer. This detour was justified by Berlin's own preparations for the planned issue of a 200-mark note, which incidentally had little popularity as a denomination and was issued with a limited volume. For Leipzig, which had lost all its customers in the socialist brother countries in one stroke, this was a welcome order in difficult times. Berlin could also be satisfied because it had squeezed Leipzig's price down and earned well on the trade. Eyebrows were raised only in Caracas because there were technical problems with the printing. A bit later Berlin received an order from Venezuela for a new national identification system. What was supposed to be a triumph ended as a disgrace. Bundesdruckerei demanded, according to newspaper reports, 480 million dollars for an identification system, which the British competitor was ready to deliver for 117 million. The news media in Caracas reported about massive corruption. According to these reports 150 million dollars was supposed to go to politicians as bribes. There was a fractious hearing in parliament. The government in Caracas expressed consternation over the behavior of the German state-owned company and withdrew the contract, which had been ready for signing.[3]

Worse things followed. At the beginning of 1997 Reserve Bank of India solicited bids for the »overspill« that had been mentioned previously, amounting to 2 billion units of 100-rupee notes and 1.6 billion units of 500-rupee notes. Bundesdruckerei took part in the international auction. It turned in the most favorable bid in the field. The »price wonder of Bombay« was not the result of rationalization successes in Berlin, however. Rather, Bundesdruckerei wanted to print only 700 million units by itself – according to the planning, at least – passing on the rest to the state printers in Ukraine and South Africa. The alarm bells went off at both Giesecke & Devrient and De La Rue. Berlin was not only one-quarter cheaper, but it was also proposing a security configuration that paper factories other than Portals and Louisenthal could have delivered. A real mud-slinging contest ensued. Giesecke & Devrient unleashed the supervisory board representative of its senior employees, who was an experienced professional. He complained to the federal government that the state-owned printer was causing the loss of German jobs. This thrust drew blood. Then De La Rue and Giesecke & Devrient reminded the Indians of the suffering of the Indian minority under the abolished apartheid regime in South Africa and expressed doubts about the reliability of the Ukrainian state printer using the catchword »mafia printer.« That also worked.

Bundesdruckerei began to worry about the loyalty of its lawyers on the scene. In this overheated atmosphere the details of the solicitation and the individual bidding prices of the printers were leaked to the press. Newspapers on the subcontinent speculated on corruption and industrial sabotage. The Indian parliament had to grapple with the issue of why India was having its banknotes produced abroad when it had its own note printers. Naturally the answer was that their modernization had not been completed. De La Rue and Giesecke & Devrient finally won the bid. But they had to deliver at a price lower than that of Bundesdruckerei. Giesecke & Devrient won a bid for 1.6 billion units of 500-rupee notes, initially printed in Leipzig, later in Munich. Reserve Bank of India did not want Bundesdruckerei to go away empty handed. It offered it a share of the note printing. But suddenly the word from Berlin was that it could print no more than 100 million units because of capacity limits, even though the new super printing facility was now in full operation. It was a refusal motivated by politics, and the Indians rightly believed they were having the wool pulled over their eyes. They backed out entirely. In the meantime, Menke had become embroiled in a huge argument with Hans Kabisch, his division director for banknote printing. The first attempt of Bundesdruckerei in twenty years to present itself to the export market as an outstanding supplier had foundered, said an internal report in Berlin. The reputation of Bundesdruckerei in the region had been badly damaged by the fiasco in India, it said.

That proved to be no exception. A year later, as mentioned earlier, the central bank of Nigeria was looking abroad for a printer for 4 billion new naira notes. There had been a government banknote printer for decades in Africa's biggest country by population. With eight installed printing machines from Koebau-Giori, the Nigerians really should have been in a position to cover their own annual requirement of 1.6 billion units at that time. Yet the supposed lack of foreign exchange for importing the replacement parts and the materials necessary for note printing, along with mismanagement in the printing facility – if not sabotage – had made Nigeria dependent upon additional imports of banknotes since 1990. They suddenly had the money for that. Since 1994 Nigeria had no longer printed any notes of its own. It was a given that De La Rue produced these notes. Yet Bundesdruckerei now also showed interest in the pending order, the largest export order for banknotes in history. It was represented by Walter Pohl, a paper engineer, who once had worked for Giesecke & Devrient and then for SICPA. He had had long experience on the ground in Nigeria. And this knowledge of local practices was urgently needed because the Nigerians had very particular wishes about billing. From the court reporting of a local newspaper, which quoted the evidence presented, it could be learned later that the central bank demanded that it be billed 47 dollars for every 1,000 units of naira notes but that it would pay only 24 dollars.[4] The difference – for the most part – was supposed to flow into the pockets of the Abacha clan and Pohl's Nigerian middlemen, who would arrange the order. Bundesdruckerei again put together an international consortium of banknote printers. In November 1998, in keeping with Nigerian wishes, it filed a structured bid, which had an expiration date. The competition dilly-dallied with similar bids in which even the transportation costs were included in the »net price.« Bundesdruckerei, as Pohl maintained, still stood the best chance of winning the auction. Yet just before the deadline was to expire, Pohl received a call from Harald Wendel, the second business manager for the technical side of Bundesdruckerei, instructing him that the »net price« could not be sustained. It had to be raised nearly to the level of the »gross price.« With this demand Bundesdruckerei had, in fact, deliberately thrown itself out of the running. In mid-January 1999, Giesecke & Devrient received the printing order for 4 billion naira notes from the Nigerian central bank. Of that, as already described, somewhat more than one half was passed along to De La Rue as a subcontractor. Capacity limitations at the printing works of Giesecke & Devrient were given as the official reason for this.

For Pohl, who had fought to the end for his order in Lagos, the matter came within a hair of taking an unhappy end. His enraged Nigerian business partner had him arrested on a trumped-up charge. German diplomats had to spring him from prison and escort him to the boarding ramp of the airplane that whisked him safely back to Germany. The German ambassador in Nigeria warned the foreign office in a telegram that the businessman's life was endangered in Nigeria. Pohl, who even had to leave behind his household effects in Lagos, never heard anything further from Berlin. The surprising retreat of Bundesdruckerei had been preceded by a meeting at Frankfurt airport. It was held between Wendel, accompanied by division director Kabisch, and Manfred Beck, who was in charge of paper and banknote printing at Giesecke & Devrient. There were things that a Federal Printer could not do, Wendel later said. That didn't sound entirely convincing, when one recalls the case of Venezuela. The consortium partners of Bundesdruckerei for the Nigerian order believed they were bamboozled. Not long after this episode, during the chaotic privatization of Bundesdruckerei, Wendel took early retirement, and Kabisch, who had spent most of his professional life at the complacent federal printing works in Berlin, surprisingly joined the private banknote printer Giesecke & Devrient in Munich.

Menke complained repeatedly about the penchant for »inertia« and also about »head-strong persons« in his own organization. A contributing factor was certainly bad chemistry between him and Wendel. But in a government operation that was suddenly being run by market principles and was supposed to work with market orientation and – *horribile dictu* – even profit orientation, two dozen bureaucrats could be a burden. And the obstructionists were not just in the bureaucracy. An influential group in the organization apparently had little sympathy for the reinforced quest for export orders. Whether this was pure complacency or second thoughts about the limited competitiveness of Bundesdruckerei must remain an open question. In the matter of complacency, the printing orders of Bundesbank, like everything else, had wafted down into the house automatically. In competition abroad it was not supposed to offer marginal costing. But it did not stand a chance if it had to bill all costs. Even after the expensive modernization one would keep hearing from the divisional director for note printing the familiar argument that no capacity was available for export printing. The attempted internal reorganization put an additional damper on the mood in the operation. One after another, technicians whose training had absorbed many years left the federal printing works. Their specialized knowledge could hardly be replaced. In the department for original production and the production of printing molds, director Heinz Kummer and deputy director Bertel Podoll took early retirement. This department plays a key role in the making of banknotes. Kummer and Podoll were regarded as top experts in their specialty and had developed important techniques for Bundesdruckerei, including an etching technique of particularly high value for microscript with variable depth. For the last D-mark note series, BBk III, Podoll had been responsible at the technical level, from drafting through proofs. Finally, the internationally renowned graphic artist Reinhold Gerstetter turned his back on Bundesdruckerei. Gerstetter had designed the last mark banknote series – and also the last series of Spanish peseta notes. To top it all off, personal dislike also caused tensions between Menke and the two great hopes in advanced technology: Maurer Electronics and Holographic Systems München. In the case of Maurer Electronics, this issue went to court, ending with the buyout of the remaining shares of development engineer and company founder Thomas Maurer. Bundesdruckerei was then the master of the house, but Maurer Electronics without its brain was worthless. In the case of Holographic Systems, on the other hand, the minority partner bought the shares back from Bundesdruckerei, which had already taken on board the hologram technology, however. Although two orders, one from Portugal and one from the Indian state of Gujarat for drivers' licenses on cards boosted the morale of the Bundesdruckerei group, their business impact was modest. The transition to privatization did not do Bundesdruckerei any good.

As a supplier, Bundesdruckerei had a tough time on the international market for note printing after India and Nigeria. The only foreign order it was finally able to book was a pipsqueak – 30 million units of Estonian 100-krooni notes. This is also the only banknote with the Elu security feature developed by Bundesdruckerei. And it was exactly this note that was the cause of another flap within the operation. As the debacle with the impending privatization offering of Deutsche Telekom shares showed, the supply of technicians in banknote and securities printing was threatening to dry up for the Berlin operation. The printing of Telekom's so-called T-share in 1996 had to be broken off ignominiously because of technical problems. Finally, the departure of important banknote technicians from Bundesdruckerei forced it to school a small service company in northern Germany in the highly secret manufacturing of intaglio printing molds for banknotes, stamps, and securities. At the end of a cooperation lasting months, during the course of which sensitive technology was transferred from Bundesdruckerei, this company made a complete printing plate for the aforementioned Estonian 100-krooni note »for trial purposes,« as it was said. Theoretically this small company, which had a subsidiary in Poland, could now copy every banknote in the world. The unusual occurrence, about which the business management had apparently not been informed but in which employees with the highest security clearances in Bundesdruckerei had been involved, became known by accident. It was determined to be a serious infraction of German securities regulations, rules that serve as the analog to banknote printing. And it was described as a breach of the honor code, according to which sensitive technical information is never allowed to make its way outside. The case caused a great dispute internally but remained without legal consequences.

... and the hard realities at home

The preparations for privatization were running along parallel to these dramatic events. In the meantime, Bundesdruckerei had been placed under the control of the finance minister. He now decided that 100 percent of it should be privatized, not just the 49 percent originally announced. Privatization was all the rage. Moreover, the new government, a coalition of Social Democrats and Greens, urgently needed funds. While the workforce of Bundesdruckerei protested the »sellout« with demonstrations and vigils, teams from Giesecke & Devrient and Bundesdruckerei were busy scrutinizing every detail of a possible merger. The Munich company was principally interested in rounding out its own businesses with the cards manufacturing at ORGA Kartensystems and the identification documents business, but not so much in note printing in which excessive capacity was starting to show. A takeover was a problem. Bundesdruckerei and Giesecke & Devrient were shaped by totally different corporate cultures. Moreover, Giesecke & Devrient had a strong position in the market. The unavoidable closing of overlapping parts of the operation, whether in Berlin or Munich, would be politically hard to carry out. And to boot, the impression would be made abroad that the Germans cooked up the privatization of such an attractive company among themselves again. Bundesdruckerei needed to be open to the world, it was said. The »German solution« was tossed out.

Also worth mentioning was the degree to which Menke personally supported the takeover sought by Giesecke & Devrient. After all, this would threaten his independence and perhaps even his job. Menke pushed for a management buyout, a takeover by the top managers supported by financial investors, with the aim of going on the exchange in five to seven years. On April 4, 2000, he made a final try with a personal visit to convince Manfred Overhaus, the assistant secretary of finance responsible for Bundesdruckerei. But he was rebuffed by this »grey eminence,« as a newspaper once described Overhaus. What he, Menke, sought demanded too much work and time. Exchange listings of privatized government companies were seldom successful, he was informed. Bundesdruckerei would have to be preserved as one concern, thereby becoming »international.« There was no fundamental objection to that. It was also the thinking and the stance of the chairman of Bundesdruckerei's supervisory board, Manfred Lahnstein. Overhaus, who was not a party member, had been Lahnstein's personal aide in their old days in Bonn when Lahnstein had had a ministerial post. Bankhaus B. Metzler seel. Sohn & Co. of Frankfurt, a private bank, received the coveted mandate to find a buyer. The bride was quickly dressed for the occasion. Bundesdruckerei was confirmed in a contract with the federal interior ministry for another five years as exclusive supplier of all German identification documents, with a renewal option for a further three years. Time was growing short. For budgetary reasons, the sale had to be settled in the current calendar year of 2000.

Industry insiders pegged the selling price at 350 million to 400 million euros. This seemed appropriate to the group sales of 440 million euros in the preceding business year – 45 percent from ORGA Kartensystems – and a net profit of 17 million euros – 75 percent of it from ORGA. Twelve bidders answered the calls for tenders; three made it to the final round. Avato, the industrial holding company of the Bertelsmann group, dropped out of the bidding early, as did British De La Rue. Strongly favored along with Giesecke & Devrient, Avato had been interested in the personal data bank of Bundesdruckerei. The Munich printer let its bid stand at 600 million. Francois Charles Oberthur Fiduciaire had gone as far as 750 million. Also in the final round was the bidding consortium of Schlumberger and Triton Fund. It filed the highest nominal bid but was only interested in ORGA, having said that it would sell the rest of the group. The seller rejected that offer. In this way, Apax Partners Private Equity of London won the auction in November 2000. The government had already worked with this private equity fund, which incidentally was ensconced in a Munich office building belonging to Yorck Otto, on the privatization of the autobahn filling station and rest stop chain »Tank & Rast.« Apax offered 1 billion euros plus a debtor warrant. Should the proceeds of a later public exchange offering exceed the corporate »goodwill value of 1.25 billion euros,« the seller would be entitled to a 25 percent share of the difference. Bundesdruckerei in its private form would be allowed to take along the coveted company emblem that suggested association with the government. This was a stylized half of the federal German eagle in the national colors.

The international high-security printing industry could not believe its eyes. True, Bundesdruckerei offered work of »German quality,« as Berlin had always stressed. But it made more then 95 percent of its sales in the »protected sector« of business with the government. There was no notable foreign distribution. Bundesdruckerei was only beginning to build up its own research and development. And Bundesdruckerei still owed 125 million to its retirement reserve. The purchasing price looked high. And there had been no lack of warnings before the gavel fell. Bundesbank went to Berlin to caution about taking care with the quality of the purchaser. Even the interior ministry had voiced strong concern for the security of its identification documents. All objections were shrugged off with comments about the budgetary problems of the federal government and the sales proceeds, which would exceed the most extravagant hopes. Assistant Finance Minister Overhaus was known for his energetic position before the budgetary committee, but there weren't any very serious objections there. The chair of this influential panel was traditionally filled by the opposition party. Nothing compelled this budget committee to give the award to the highest bidder. Panel Chairman Dietrich Austermann of the conservative Christian Democrats found the sale inappropriate to its purpose because »pearls in the field of security technology« would supposedly be lost to the federal government.[5] But the position paper of the committee, on the basis of which the sale was decided, praised the privatization »through which the concern is preserved, internationalization guaranteed, and the workforce offered a scheme for participation in the company.«[6] The corporate concept that was presented, read the record of the minutes, showed »sound growth and development possibilities for all important divisions of the company.« Everyone was transfixed by the manna of money. They were beholding a Fata Morgana.

Rescuers or robbers?

Private equity companies try to limit their own exposure. They attract financiers with the prospect of high returns. Apax liked to point out that it had showered its investors with an annual 40 percent growth in recent years. With that it whetted the appetite of the banks for strong yields. They too wanted to have their share in the gigantic returns that beckoned. The takeover of Bundesdruckerei was financed in this way. Around 225 million euros came from a ten-year loan from the seller at interest of 6.5 percent. About another 500 million was made available by Frankfurt's Landesbank Hessen-Thüringen Girozentrale (Helaba) as a loan with a mixed interest rate averaging 8.5 percent – a remarkable concentration of risk even for this powerful wholesale and clearing bank of the regional Sparkassen savings banks. Apax and its partners only put up the rest, most of it from a fund, Apax Euro IV, raised internationally. Among the investors subscribing to this fund were Chase Capital and the New York public pension fund for teachers. Some affiliated international investors also became directly engaged, among them Allianz Capital Partner and J.P. Morgan.

The financing model had a curve to it. All the loans were entered in the books as liabilities of Bundesdruckerei, which therefore must have financed its own purchase by Apax. This meant specifically that the Berlin company was supposed to come up with 106 million euros a year in interest and scheduled redemption payments, the latter fixed at 12.5 million euros a calendar quarter, as well as 15 million euros to replenish the company's own pension fund. But Bundesdruckerei was also supposed to finance its restructuring and expansion from its own resources. According to the business plan, 50 to 75 million euros a year were required for investment and acquisitions of companies over a period of five years. The ambitious growth objectives could only be achieved in this way. But Bundesdruckerei had just been made profitable again with great effort. It remained a mystery how these sizable funds could be earned by this weakly profitable company. Gabriele, the name of the holding company in which Apax parked its expensive new acquisition, was barely viable.

Nevertheless, Renate Krümmer, the Apax project director and architect of the takeover model, sketched a shining picture of the future of the holding company, Authentos, as the staid Bundesdruckerei was now registered. It would be built at a rapid pace into one of the world's leading authentication concerns, she soothed the employee's assembly in Berlin. Banknote printing would play only a subordinated role, she said. The future lay rather in high-tech ID systems, financed with earnings from the cards business. An internal Apax study concluded that sales of this Authentos concern by the end of 2005 would more than triple, compared with the actual 1999 result of the old Bundesdruckerei, to 1.4 billion euro for the group. Profit before interest and taxes was even supposed to multiply by 5 to 200 million euros. More than 5,000 workers were supposed to be engaged. Krümmer also foresaw the exchange debut – in about three years – probably as a double listing in Frankfurt and London.[7] Three months after the takeover of Bundesdruckerei Apax triumphantly reported the purchase of British Security Printing and Systems Ltd. (SPS) of Chadderton. There would be further acquisition in the near future, Apax announced triumphantly.

Only Apax negotiated for the purchase of this biggest of all passport producers in the British Isles – it even has a monopoly on British passports – and a company in which De La Rue was also interested. Not revealed was the purchase price, financed with another loan from Helaba. Menke assumed it was the equivalent of 61 million euros, which was already expensive. But Bundesdruckerei was charged the equivalent of 87 million by Apax. The difference was never explained. The Berlin company was also billed nearly 8 million euros in fees for just this purchase. The capital outflow from Berlin took on unsettling dimensions. Berlin had already had to pay 25 million in fees to auditors and lawyers of Apax for its own purchase. More millions fell due to Helaba as extraordinary repayments – for more favorable interest terms, it was said. On top of that came the scheduled redemption installment and interest in the first year, and finally the large loan for the promising ORGA. Apax also dipped in deeply. Every action and every study was billed to Berlin. And since naturally that was all done by highly qualified professionals, naturally the fees and commissions to Apax were also appropriate. Added all together, the amounts made a sum in the three-digit millions. Not a word leaked out about these »obscure transactions,« as *Manager Magazine* called them. And it was not the end of the blood-letting. Now the corporate consultants were taking turns trotting in and out of the Berlin company, all paid by Bundesdruckerei. This kind of consulting can render help. It can also help cover up one's own incompetence and perhaps evasion of responsibility. In Berlin, there was so much auditing, deliberation, and recommendation that it was a lark. Bundesdruckerei was managed to death, one prominent figure in the industry remarked. And it was squeezed financially dry. Insiders had long since been wondering who was revitalizing whom.

The programmed crash had begun. First the card business of ORGA collapsed. It was actually supposed to be the engine of the expansion. ORGA lived nearly entirely from deliveries of GSM telephone cards. As the fall of share prices on the New Market venture exchange accelerated in May 2001 and unsold devices by the millions were piling up in the warehouses of the cellular telephone manufacturers, Menke and Wendel, the two top managers in Berlin, were still assuming for ORGA »average sales growth of 35 percent in coming years.« They purported that the drop in sales was only a »dent in the market« in the current delivery crisis. A new plant was even completed in August in Flintbek in northern Germany for nearly 50 million euros. It more than doubled production capacity to 220 million chip cards a year. Second, the printing of the first batch of euro notes ended as scheduled, with no orders on hand to replace it. The gravity of the situation was shown in September 2001, when Helaba tried in vain to pass on part of the giant loan to other banks. About seventy bank representatives from abroad and from Germany traveled to Berlin. They politely declined to bite after they saw the company figures at close range.

The great management purge now began. This was naturally accompanied by ever more appealing salary terms for ever new brains at the top of Bundesdruckerei, which was now fighting for its life. And it was also accompanied by conciliatory severance packages – internally termed

»lump-sum removals« – for those who once again had to leave prematurely. Renate Krümmer was the first to leave Apax, after she had been stopped in the last moment by Siemens, the seller, from making her prepared takeover of MPM-Mannesmann Plastics Machinery AG. The drama swirling about Bundesdruckerei had played an important role in this, insiders from MPM reported. Then the entire leadership group at ORGA was replaced. And, finally, Menke and Wendel were shown the door.

With Menke, who was also director of labor relations, this solution only functioned on the second try, incidentally. Under the prevailing system of equal labor codetermination, half the members of the supervisory board were drawn from representatives of the employees, and this board initially balked at his firing. Menke and Wendel first had to withdraw from the business management of the holding company, Authentos. The departure from the operating direction of Bundesdruckerei came a few months later.

Apax dispatched Michael Pawlowski and Lando Zappei as the new duo to lead Authentos and Bundesdruckerei. Pawlowski had previously been the chief financial officer of the controversial Cinemaxx chain of motion picture theatres, which had made headlines with its exaggerated expansion and the crash of its share price on the New Market. Zappei came directly from Apax. He had previously worked for Boston Consulting. Both new business managers announced »sweeping measures« to put the group back on track. Their first official act was the formation of two working groups. The first Task Force had to examine the possibility of curtailing in stages the reporting of the group subsidiaries in order to eliminate the disclosure of company data after no more than three years. This was supposed to be done without damaging the group's international reputation, as it was phrased in its mission statement. The second Task Force examined the possibilities for restructuring the supervisory boards of both Authentos and Bundesdruckerei. The mission here was to circumvent the law of parity codetermination, enacted in 1967, with deliberate restructuring of subsidiaries or of the workforce in order to exclude the employees' representatives from all important decisions in the future.[8] While the Task Forces were meeting, incidentally, there were talks with Klaus-Dieter Langen about his entry into the business management as labor director. Langen had for years been the chairman of the works council of Bundesdruckerei. He accepted.

The movers and shakers in Berlin and Munich took refuge more and more in a public information policy that was right on the ragged edge of truth – often on the far side of this divide. In February 2002, Zappei was still denying any payments difficulties by citing equity, which was supposedly high. And he described the value of ORGA as »not permanently diminished.«[9] At this stage, the catastrophic condition of ORGA could no longer be overlooked, however hard one tried. The cards manufacturer was substantially responsible for the fact that Authentos closed its accounts with a loss of nearly half a billion euros in its first business year, the *FAZ* reported. The director general of Japan's state printing plant, Shizuharu Kubono, arrived in Berlin at the end of May 2002 to study the German experience in privatizing its government printer because the Japanese were planning the same step. He politely expressed his astonishment as to how the Bundesdruckerei group would be able to shoulder the financing. The 110 million in reserves, which Bundesdruckerei had brought along as a dowry to the pleasant surprise of Apax, had long since been spent, along with half of the 25 million in equity capital. Suppliers were being paid only with delay, with a corresponding impact on the group's credit rating. The hunt for the last financial reserves of Berlin had begun, which at least one Bavarian commercial bank noticed in time. It cancelled the company's credit line. There was a desire to tap into the British subsidiary SPS and Munich's Maurer Electronics. The British put up a fight and won. The pension reserve of Bundesdruckerei was less successful, because it had to assist with a fat loan at preferred interest. Shortly thereafter, the insurer Gerling Konzern terminated its special professional protection for the managers of Authentos, namely its »directors and officers liability insurance.« This was an unusual step and a dramatic warning signal by the insurer, but one which no one wished to heed. In retrospect, *Financial Times Deutschland* asked whether »rescuers or robbers« had been at work there.[10]

The rest of the tragedy is quickly told. At the start of August 2002, just eighteen months after the takeover, Apax parted ways with the Bundesdruckerei group for the symbolic price of one euro. The investment stake of the Apax partners of presumably one-quarter billion euros had to be written off as a total loss. JFVVG Neununddreißigste Vermögensverwaltung GmbH of Berlin and Dinos Vermögensverwaltung GmbH of Heidelberg stepped forward as buyers. JFVVG obtained 94 percent of the capital. The mysterious names front for Frankfurt attorneys of the law firm

Clifford Chance, which had originally prepared the contracts for Apax's purchase of Bundesdruckerei. Now these attorneys were playing the role of trustees for Helaba, which engaged them to look for a »real« buyer.[11] Pawlowski and Zappei cleared out their offices in Berlin after less than a year of vacillating crisis management. Lahnstein, the chairman of the supervisory board, surrendered his appointment, sensing fatigue in this office. Without the protection of Gerling's insurance coverage he would have become liable with his personal assets in the event that management lapses could be proven. The Social Democrat stuck in the memory of other members of the supervisory board for his persistent concern that an open conflict with the labor unions had to be avoided unconditionally because of the threat of bad press.

Only after Authentos closed its second business year with a new record loss and sales had plunged to 212 million euros did Helaba concede that write-downs of unspecified magnitude would have to be taken. A spokeswoman dismissed this belated admission with her comment that the »prudent businessman« had a duty to do this. This remark about prudent businessmen will have appeased many a Hessian and Thuringian savings bank director. Their Sparkassen are the ones that have to pony up financially in the end for the disaster of their central bank's jumbo loan. The collapse of the Bundesdruckerei group could have been avoided only if Helaba had waived some of its claim. Shortly thereafter, the new owners precipitately dumped ORGA Kartensystems. It was given for one euro to GW Card Holding of Bamberg, a company of a southern Germany lottery owner. The divestment was naturally touted as an important step in getting Authentos back on its feet, even though ORGA Systemhaus was lost again in this one move. Its business with ID systems had been built up with the great effort expended on its development capacity. For Authentos, this also meant that ORGA's corporate goodwill and all the credit extended to ORGA had to be written out of the books as a total loss. That added up to an amount on the low end of the triple-digit millions of euros. As a condition for this divestment, though, Helaba again had to advance another amount in the high two-digit millions of euros to ORGA.

Under a two-year contract, Ulrich Wöhr now took charge as chairman of the business management of what was left of the proud Bundesdruckerei. Helaba had recruited out of retirement this former member of the managing board of Frankfurt's Metallgesellschaft AG. Wöhr was supposed to restructure Bundesdruckerei and prepare it for a new sale because business consultant Roland Berger believed that the group could be returned to profitability in two years. But with which products and at what price? Bundesdruckerei had been permanently weakened in banknote printing. No sooner had they arrived in Berlin, Pawlowski and Zappei, the two managers dispatched by Apax, had exercised a put option to sell back a Super-Intaglio machine and a Super-Simultan machine to the manufacturer, Koebau-Giori. They did this at the last possible moment under the contract and accepted considerable losses, too. This action deprived Bundesdruckerei of its required flexibility in production and took it once and for all out of the international competition in banknote printing. The surprising departure of Kabisch was an additional sign that Berlin was regarded as a loser in the race for banknote printing. The printing demand for replacement euro notes is small. The share of this allotted to Bundesdruckerei was just two denominations of 100 million notes each in 2004. This is too much to die with but too little to live with. The fact that cost-efficient printing is scarcely possible anymore with such small order lots can be mentioned in passing. Berlin had long since come to depend upon the tacit assistance of Giesecke & Devrient. This printer occasionally passes along a printing order, say, a couple of million units for Yemen, Tanzania, or Estonia. The stamp business was also declining because Deutsche Post had turned to printers from abroad in order to suppress costs. Much capacity also lies fallow for passports and for drivers' licenses in card form because the movement of the market was wrongly gauged. Great hopes have been pinned to identity cards, but the money for appropriate research is lacking. The divestment of ORGA has weakened the position of Bundesdruckerei in the hotly contested market for identification cards of all types. Be it for biometrics or the development of a surveillance system for border crossing points and major programs of border control management, Berlin today depends entirely upon suppliers for software and hardware. The major order for a chip card for truck drivers, which is supposed to be employed in the digital tachograph within the EU, was lost to a foreign consortium. And the system of electronic filings of tax declarations and applications they and other suppliers have in stock pose some serious uncertainties: to what extent will citizens use it and what will it bring Bundesdruckerei in terms of sales and profits?

Since Bundesdruckerei was converted into a limited company in order to prepare it for privatization, two-thirds of the workforce - altogether more than 2,000 men and women – has been made redundant, not to mention the lost apprenticeships. Bundesdruckerei had been, after all, one of the largest trainers of apprentices in Berlin's printing industry. The rollback of staff was necessary, no doubt. But the haste with which it was done was not the result of deliberate rationalization but rather the result of dilettantish business planning. And that still hasn't ceased. An employment and qualifying organization (BQG) has been called into being to take charge of hundreds of employees of Bundesdruckerei for retraining during a transition period. The whole workforce was supposed to be reduced to well below 1,000 employees by the end of 2005.[12] Yet BQG turned out to be a rather useless instrument of employment policy, and a more expensive instrument for the taxpayers, as was to be expected. At the end of 2005, Bundesdruckerei still had 1,200 employees, which is regarded in the industry as plenty.

The rehabilitation approach taken by Wöhr seemed to make sense, even though the forecasts he expressed to the media seemed somewhat too optimistic to many observers. But the unresolved financial crisis of Authentos was simmering below the surface. Wöhr unexpectedly threw in the towel in February 2004, leaving Berlin on just a few days' notice. He had never felt at home there. His financial director had departed before him. This post remained vacant for twenty months thereafter, incidentally. No one wanted that thankless job. Wöhr's relationship to business attorney Heinz-Günter Gondert, Helaba's paladin at Authentos, had not been free of tensions. As chairman of the supervisory board, Gondert tried to exert too much influence on daily operations, Wöhr had often complained.

The subdued celebration of the 125th year of Bundesdruckerei's existence was arranged by Wöhr's successor, Ulrich Hamann, in late summer 2004. Shortly before that, the much younger Hamann had left chip manufacturer Infineon AG, not entirely of his own volition. He took on a nearly hopeless task as business manager of both the Authentos holding company and the operating company, Bundesdruckerei. The finance minister had, however, agreed to a ten-year moratorium on payments of principal and interest on his whole seller's loan of nearly 300 million euros. And Helaba had accepted an interest moratorium along with the subordination of one-third of its major loan of 455 million euros. For the remaining part of the loan, still around 330 million euros, only scheduled redemption installments were waived. But Authentos was not even able to scrape up the reduced interest burden for this. The group financial statement for 2004, the first presented by Hamann, highlighted this aspect. Sales had shrunk to 181 million euros. Banknote printing contributed only 24 million euros to the sales. Profitable British passport producer SPS, which answers directly to the holding company, steered its 70 million euros of sales into the group figures. But that didn't make an iota of difference to the misery of Authentos. It is technically bankrupt, with cumulative debt of about 1.2 billion euros, which has not been covered by equity for some time. Only the patience of the creditors, who have no choice, is holding Berlin above water – for the moment, anyway.

So, in the short term, Bundesdruckerei, in the tried and true manner, again is counting on the government-protected home market. To begin, Hamann is assuming steeply rising replacement printing of euro notes starting 2006. These contracts will still be assigned to printers by the respective central bank. Berlin will print a respectable 700 million notes, and euro notes are known for being well paid. Also, there is the new German electronic passport. Germans will need around 2.5 million to 3 million such passports a year, Hamann projects. Bundesdruckerei will be able to make all of them, thanks to its exclusive contract with the interior ministry. With its price-tag of 59 euros as a consequence of this politically sanctioned supplier monopoly, of course, the German electronic passport promises to be one of Europe's most expensive biometric passports. As a precaution, the taxpayer was not asked what he might think of this additional – and now concealed – payout of subsidies to Authentos.

But Hamann has to shape the group up for a sale by 2007. After all, the federal finance minister and Helaba would like to see their money again. In order to prepare for this deadline, Hamann wants to make the desiccated state printer into an internationally active group for high security products and services. The slogan is »secure identification,« meaning ID systems, electronic passports, border control, and government communications down to the municipal level. This goal, incidentally, has been announced repeatedly since the unfortunate privatization. It has been missed again and again. Now, with little money for R&D, it will be even harder to achieve. The disposal of ORGA has further weakened Bundesdruckerei, while the buildup of effective foreign marketing is still pending. In trying to become a company internationally active in the field of secure identification, Hamann seems to be ready to shed most of the traditional businesses of Bundesdruckerei. The electronic printing of patent documentation has already been farmed out to Poland. The ailing stamp printing and the printing of excise tax wrappers on merchandise are up for sale. Hamann would also like to sell SPS, which makes the British passport and will most likely produce the planned British identity card. At the end of 2005 a British newspaper reported that SPS was up for sale for 150 million British pounds (222 million euros) – about three times the price Apax had paid for the company.[13] And in the long term, even in banknote printing Hamann seems to see little future for Bundesdruckerei once the market for printing euro banknotes is effectively liberalized (in 2012). So all that disinvestment, will leave an even weaker Authentos. This misery, however, is not Hamann's fault; he only inherited it. Not often had a privatization been handled with such short-sightedness and cynicism.

9 How Ciccone Calcográfica wasted its fiduciary capital

The worldwide battle on the market for the printing orders of central banks is waged so ruthlessly that it does not always comport with the elitist claims of this industry. Representatives of the industry like to emphasize the great store of confidence that the central banks must place in their note printers and that this trust must be earned every day. Trust is, indeed, the most valuable capital of the banknote printer, more valuable than any technical prowess. The printed note becomes money only when a simple administrative act of the issuing institution confers the aura of legal tender upon what merely is a slip of colored paper. No one is able to observe whether the note has properly undergone this procedure because it entails just one simple entry in a computer: the registration of the denomination at the moment of its issuance. Absolutely nothing about the appearance of the note is changed by the issuing institution with this. Herein lurks the danger of abuse, for it is not just criminals who forge banknotes.

Secure printing without security

In the years 1999 and 2000, PT. Pura Barutama Indonesia, a paper maker and printer from Kudus in central Java, delivered several million Somali shilling banknotes to »Colonel Ahmed,« a Somali rebel leader. They were earmarked for circulation in the »autonomous territory of Puntland« in northeast Somalia. PT. Pura's owners were ambitious and they had influential friends. The family of the toppled Indonesian president, Suharto, held a stake for a time in the company. Thanks to this political protection, the company had succeeded in doing business with Bank Indonesia. PT. Pura had produced Indonesian 100-rupee notes in simple

Moneymakers, Klaus W. Bender

ISBN: 3-527-50236-X

offset mode without official authorization. Thereafter, it had even received an order for the delivery of security paper for Indonesian rupees. These transactions came to pass against the will of those responsible at the National Bank. The Indonesian foreign ministry had heard of the Somali contract and had advised the printer against taking it. Pura made its delivery to the Somali rebel chieftain in spite of that and the *Asian Wall Street Journal* chronicled the case in great detail.[1] PT. Pura cited the fact that it had not been alone in this deal. British American Banknote (BABN) of Ottawa had printed for the same warlord shortly before. BABN, which was struggling with numerous problems, belonged to the Canadian media concern Quebecor. Its business contacts with the warlord were terminated only when Giesecke & Devrient in early 1999 began negotiating to buy the Canadian outfit.

It was not the most spectacular case of this nature, nor was it the first to raise the international issue of a legal framework for banknote printing. Controversy about the delivery of banknotes had arisen at the end of 1966. It had roiled emotions and now has become part of the standard history of banknote printing. A year before that, Ian Douglas Smith had unilaterally proclaimed the independence of Rhodesia, the former British colony called South Rhodesia, today Zimbabwe. Great Britain had not recognized the unilateral declaration of independence of South Rhodesia. In April of the following year Reserve Bank of Rhodesia, headquartered in Salisbury, ordered new banknotes from Giesecke & Devrient. The British banknote printer Bradbury, Wilkinson had for years printed for South Rhodesia. But the Labour government in London had forbidden Bradbury, Wilkinson to deliver its printed new Rhodesian banknotes. A trade embargo had not yet been imposed, and when the United Nations finally imposed one, expressly banknotes did not fall under the boycott measures. It was arguable, however, whether a note printer could make itself liable by printing for a national bank that was legally empowered by its own government, although this government was not recognized by the UN members. Giesecke & Devrient had the issue researched – East Germany was cited as a comparable case – and its attorneys saw no problems. Munich wanted to start delivering the banknotes at the end of 1966 and the beginning of 1967. Wanting to set a political example, the British crown had the freight confiscated at Frankfurt airport, saying that it was »counterfeit money.« A heated diplomatic row ensued, during which the West German government asked the Rhodesian government in Salisbury to waive fulfillment of the contract for the sake of peace among nations. Rhodesia finally pulled out of the contract and agreed to the destruction of nearly 30 metric tons of banknotes. But it refused to pay for the notes.[2] The case was treated in the press around the world. The British government then filed a suit against Giesecke & Devrient and against Siegfried Otto personally. The criminal case of counterfeiting was dropped and a civil lawsuit for damages ended in a compromise. The British government accepted a damage settlement amounting to 3 million marks. The penalty was not paid by the British government, however, but by a hitherto unknown »Reserve Bank of Rhodesia, London,« which didn't even have an address. It was assumed that the Labour government had paid itself the money from the reserves held in London for Reserve Bank of Rhodesia of Salisbury.

Part of this story was leaked to the British press. But then the affair took a turn with which the public is less familiar. Reserve Bank of Rhodesia in Salisbury promptly arranged for Giesecke & Devrient to build for it a banknote printing facility. As a precaution, an impeccable South African company was used as a middleman. Siegfried Otto sold this company two old two-plate Intagliocolor printing machines from his own printing works for a good price. Before the British secret service even noticed, the machines were shipped to South Africa and taken northward from there to neighboring Rhodesia. Within a few months the government of Ian Smith had its own banknote printing plant, installed in the basement of a government building, while Giesecke & Devrient at home bought two more efficient machines as replacements. Munich then delivered the backup materials for Rhodesian production for a long time, although there was no shortage of attempts via diplomatic channels by De La Rue to disrupt this, especially after the regime change in Rhodesia. Today's Reserve Bank of Zimbabwe is still among the customers of Giesecke & Devrient.

Now back to the questions: Who may place a printing order for banknotes, who may print them, and under what circumstances? What happens, for example, when Chechen separatists see their independence from a dissolving Soviet empire within reach and approach a banknote printer about printing their own currency? What should a printer do if, as happened in Somalia, rebel leader Mohammed Farah Aidit, who had also collaborated with Osama bin Laden, wants his own banknotes? Or when the Northern Alliance or Taliban want to have notes printed for Afghanistan in order to pay their soldiers and buy weapons? To pre-empt the inquiry: there is in this industry a voluntary obligation assumed by the suppliers that no machines, no materials, and no knowledge of techniques may be passed on to unauthorized persons. For example, Voith GmbH of Heidenheim, the German specialist in the manufacture of cylinder-mold plants for security paper, will deliver only upon presentation of an authorization from the national bank that is affected. Since PT. Pura could not produce such an authorization, Claus Jung, the representative of Voith-Heidenheim, refused to render any technical backup for the cylinder-mold paper machine. But for neither the production of banknote paper nor for banknote printing is there any legally binding regulation that is enforced at the national or the international level through the surveillance of a national bank or the International Monetary Fund. And IMF actually seemed predestined to fill such a role. In Germany, Giesecke & Devrient must renew its permit for manufacturing security paper every two years at the Bundesbank. Other countries do not even observe such a minimal requirement. Therefore, every paper manufacturer or commercial printer can try his luck as a producer of banknotes, as the case of PT. Pura shows. This is not without risk for the printer. When Croatia wanted to have its new kuna notes printed by Giesecke & Devrient shortly after securing its independence, the similarity of the 10-kuna note drawn by a Croatian graphic artist to the 10-Deutschmark note was striking. Bundesbank was asked about this as a precaution, but it raised no objection. The excitement was then all the greater when 10-kuna notes were fraudulently passed in German grocery markets in lieu of 10-mark notes. The Croatian 10-kuna note had to be withdrawn and printed anew with different colors.

The serious manufacturers of banknotes have therefore adopted ground rules for themselves. First, an order for the printing of banknotes may in principle be issued only by the issuing institution established by law. That is usually the central bank or a currency board. Second, the notes have to be delivered to this issuing institution. Third, the payment for the banknotes may come only from this institution. This self-control is well meaning. But it does not protect against abuse when political interests come into play. Printing for warring factions in a civil war is frowned upon in this industry. The Chechens went away empty-handed in their desire for their own banknotes, which they presented to several private printers. One can imagine that it would not have been easy to brush off their rabid agents. Yet, it comported with Moscow's political stance that its state printer, Gosnak, printed extensively for the Afghan Northern Alliance, while the state printer of friendly Pakistan helped out the Taliban. By their behavior, both banknote printers contributed to the collapse of the Afghan economy after the end of hostilities – which was perhaps their intent. But private printers can also lose their bearings in the gray area of missing guidelines – with striking results.

Sole note printer in the Southern Hemisphere

The growth of the available market for banknotes has come for years, as previously mentioned, primarily from the countries of the so-called Third World. The printing of their notes has been done with few exceptions, however, by high-security printers of the so-called First World. The Ciccone brothers of Buenos Aires weighed their chances of tapping into this profitable market. They wanted to break the dominance of the private printers of the industrialized countries with the pointed reference that they had the only private banknote printing plant in the Southern Hemisphere. It was a seductive idea – and a case of serious overreaching. In the end this was to cost both brothers their life's work.

Héctor Hugo and Nicolás Tadeo Ciccone were the sons of immigrants from southern Italy, persons with impeccable reputation and cultivated demeanor. They built up a small printing company in Buenos Aires with much diligence and boldness. Pictures from the 1950s show the two as young men in shirt-sleeves at their printing press. At the end of the 1960s they invested, expanding into secure printing with the making of lottery chances, check forms, securities, and stamps. In their heyday they printed up to 300 million personalized check forms a year, sometimes done with expensive steelplate engraving. The new business niche was a success and stirred ambitions. The driving force behind the idea was Nicolás, the younger and more ambitious of the two brothers.

At the end of the 1970s the brothers bought a large industrial tract on the outskirts of Buenos Aires, next to Ruta Panamericana, the Pan-American Highway. Here they began building a high-security printing plant. The centerpiece was a 600-square-meter vault with meter-thick ferroconcrete walls. It was built below the water table of the nearby Rio de la Plata. Even the representatives of Interpol were impressed when they inspected it. Giorgio Coen, who looked after Latin America for DLR Giori, benevolently followed the ambitions of the two brothers. Coen had lived several years in Argentina in the 1950s and had family ties to Buenos Aires. The Ciccones had already purchased from him a used standard line for printing lottery chances and check forms.[3] As high-security printers of banknotes and identification documents, the brothers promised to become still more important customers for used machines. This, in turn, would make it easier to deliver new machinery elsewhere. The Ciccone brothers did indeed buy machinery freely, investing around 40 million Swiss francs in two other complete lines of printing machinery. These were used machines that had been given a general overhaul by Ormag.[4] Finally, at the start of the 1990s they even purchased a Super-Orlof-Intaglio right off the factory line. This new high-performance machine was expensive. Giorgio Coen, who might then have had bittersweet recollections of his interlude as an owner of the former family company in Milan, Calcografia e Cartevalori, gladly helped the two daring brothers. He arranged favorable payment terms for the machinery and introduced them to international contacts; but he never had a stake in the private Argentine printer, he says.

The ambitious project stood from the start on shaky ground. Construction stretched out over a decade. The situation in Argentina was catastrophic. First came the Falkland War with Britain that was launched by the military junta. Then there was hyperinflation, this time with two currency devaluations in as many years. Roberto T. Alemann, the publisher of the German-language weekly *Argentinische Tageszeitung* in Buenos Aires, has served briefly as finance minister twice. He calculated during an interview with the author that a peso of 1899 was worth 10 trillion pesos of 1969, but that a peso of 1970 was the equivalent of 100 billion pesos of 1983. After another currency revaluation, Argentina's »new peso« devalued within two years to only one-ten-millionth of its original value. The »austral,« which was then introduced, had to be replaced by another new peso in 1991 in a ratio of 10,000 australs for the new one. This was followed by pegging to the dollar, which has been abandoned in the interim. One might suppose that hyperinflation is an integral part of Argentine economic policy. It would have been a great challenge for any entrepreneur.

Argentina's mismanagement of monetary policy hit the Ciccone brothers especially hard. The capital squeeze finally drove them into the arms of a shady but influential businessman of Lebanese extraction, Alfredo Yabran.[5] Don Alfredo belonged to the so-called Arab Mafia, a coterie of persons of Arab ancestry who were friends of Carlos Saúl Menem, the head of the government. The unknown and impoverished Yabran, who later committed suicide under mysterious circumstances, built up the country's largest company for secure transport with methods reminiscent of U.S. business practices during the era of Prohibition. Secure transport plays an important role in the economic life of Argentina because business transactions there are settled whenever possible in cash, even with amounts in the millions. Yabran had already helped the brothers purchase a lucrative second license for the lottery chances, and he had big plans for them.[6] He envisaged that he could channel the printing of the planned new Argentine passports and personal identifications to the Ciccone brothers, thanks to his close contacts to the government, and that his armored car company would then take over the distribution of those documents exclusively. That promised to be strong business because the possession of a special personal identification, called *cedula de identidad*, is a prerequisite for exercising the right to vote in Argentina. Every citizen must have one. Yabran opened the door to banks for the financially strapped brothers.[7] Banca Svizzera Italiana among others granted a 25-million-dollar, three-year loan for the completion of the printing plant, for which credit the brothers had to surrender to the bank all of their shares as collateral. Yet the Ciccones had difficulty earning the money to service the bank loan. Their cashflow could not even cover the payment for the used machines. Payment schedules were aborted, acceptance credit went into arrears. Giorgio Coen was called to account by the supervisory board of DLR Giori and had to explain. It was only too evident that the Ciccones had overextended themselves financially.

Only with difficulty were the Ciccone brothers accepted for full membership in AIIF, the association of private security printers. They needed someone to vouch for them. Lausanne obliged. From then on the brothers strongly stressed in their promotions their membership in this exclusive body as the »only high-security printer in the Southern Hemisphere.« They also changed the name of their family joint-stock company to Ciccone Calcográfica S.A., Ciccone intaglio printing, to emphasize their new business field. Yet the business with banknotes never really took off. Ciccone was allowed only in exceptional cases to print for Argentina, namely whenever the chaotic Argentine state printer, Casa de Moneda, was no longer able to cover the need for the inflating paper money. On the other hand, Ciccone was totally unknown abroad as a banknote printer. A list prepared in 2000 on the countries for which Ciccone Calográfica had already printed notes named only seven countries. For any banknote printer, that was too little to live on and too much to die with.[8] The established printers – De La Rue, American Banknote, Giesecke & Devrient, Francois Charles Oberthur Fiduciaire – knew only too well how to defend their market.

Banknotes for kleptocrats

The market breakthrough for which Ciccone yearned seemed within reach in mid-1993, however. Ciccone Calcográfica had received an inquiry on whether it was interested in printing banknotes for Zaire. As the third-largest African country by population this was an attractive market, and its population was growing extraordinarily fast.[9] Moreover, the country was suffering from galloping inflation.[10] Banknote printers love this mixture because it signifies a steadily rising need for banknotes. For years Zaire had been exclusively a customer of Giesecke & Devrient. Ludwig »Lutz« Devrient had been invited by Banque de Zaire to visit the country in 1970, when he was the technical director of Giesecke & Devrient and had signed it up as a customer. There had been tension over prices and quality between Banque de Zaire and De La Rue, which had long printed Zaire's notes.

During the hyperinflation Zaire required more than 800 million notes a year. The country had a banknote printer, Hôtel des Monnaies de Zaire. This printer had been set up by Giesecke & Devrient as part of a long-term agreement, and a group of technicians from Munich even had the technical direction. The planning and construction, however, had meandered for half an eternity. The expensive printing machines, therefore, had to be kept in storage for years. When the printing facility was finally christened in 1987, after thirteen years of planning and building, the capacity was totally inadequate for the ballooning requirement for inflationary banknotes. The two standard machinery lines together were set up to produce only 250 million notes. Munich was certainly not responsible for the ubiquitous mismanagement in Zaire. But it was not exactly unhappy about the problems of Hôtel des Monnaies, either. The number of banknotes that had to be printed abroad rose in this way. And they were delivered exclusively by Giesecke & Devrient. »One of the most important events of the company's recent history,« was what a statement of Giesecke & Devrient modestly called the cooperation with Zaire. The central African country was indeed the most important of all Munich's customers in the business with banknotes. Cumulative sales made there over the years came to the equivalent of 250 million euros. It was a highly profitable business, even though the rising tide of notes on order finally confronted even Munich with capacity problems. For this reason part of the notes earmarked for Zaire were produced by Giesecke & Devrient on printing presses rented for the purpose in Burma. These notes were then issued in Zaire as banknotes from its own domestic printing facility. It was a closely guarded secret that these banknotes, billed at the world market price, actually came from the low-wage country of Burma. Even at Banque de Zaire only the top management knew of this.

Nearly three decades of the Mobutu dictatorship had run Zaire's economy into the ground.[11] Mark Pieth, a Swiss attorney and chairman of the OECD Working Group on Bribery, described the country as the »epitome of corruption.« Its dictator was fighting prostate cancer and his star was falling. Signs of the disintegration of his regime abounded in plain view. In the eastern part of Zaire Laurent Kabila and his rebel forces were steadily gaining ground, threatening to take over important provincial centers. Kabila was backed by America. Mobutu was a Francophile and the darling of the Belgians and the French, the former colonial powers in the region. There was the danger of losing their hold on this poor country, so immensely rich in precious metals and diamonds. In order to stop Kabila's advance and preserve Belgian and French influence in Zaire, Mobutu's troops would have to put up a more energetic fight. But there was no money to pay them. So the »kleptocracy,« as a report of the UN Security Council later dubbed the clique around Mobutu, rallied for a final coup. They had the tacit blessings of influential circles in Brussels and Paris, and Banque de Zaire was their willing instrument.

In mid-1993, while the finishing touches were being made to a plan for currency reform, interim Premier Faustin Birindwa sought a new printer for his planned »nouveau zaire.« It was not the first time. A year before, the British Harrison & Sons Ltd., part of the Lonrho group, had printed new banknotes of a denomination of 5 million zaires. Harrison was never paid for this, however. Others were also fighting to collect their receivables. Zaire was officially insolvent. The new push for diversification was billed as a response to the capacity bottleneck at Hôtel des Monnaies and as a desire to secure lower printing costs. There had indeed been complaints about the banknote price of Giesecke & Devrient and about excessively expensive imports of supporting materials for the note printing at Zaire's own state printing works. IMF even had to take up this question later. It soon became clear that lower printing costs had nothing to do with this newest gambit.

»Confidants of the head of government« placed calls to several European banknote printers. They said they had a »strictly secret printing order« to offer, so secret that it could not even be discussed with Banque de Zaire. All the printers thus contacted begged off. Finally the president of the Brazilian-Zairean Chamber of Commerce, Josefino Hernani de Freitas Viegas, and the owner of the Egimex trading company of Antwerp, a Lebanon-born man named Naim Khanaffer, were entrusted with the quest. Khanaffer had advanced a few million dollars to the premier of Zaire, supposedly for the printing of the new notes. The Brazilian-Lebanese duo was unknown in the international banknote business. Viegas and Khanaffer were separately given executive power, conferred by two different interim governors of Zaire's national bank. There was method in this confusion. Both men contacted the Brazilian government printing facility, Casa da Moneda do Brasil. But it turned down the contract, pleading capacity bottlenecks. The true motive for the rejection was the demand of Egimex to print parallel banknote series that were exact duplicates in numbering, it was later said in the investigative dossier of Interpol. The Brazilians had apparently seen through this questionable deal. This contract finally landed at Ciccone Calcográfica after making a detour through the Argentine state printer, which was also approached.[12] The boss of the Argentine Casa de Moneda, Armando Gostanian, was another colorful character from the clique of Menem, the head of state. Gostanian had worked together with the Ciccone brothers several times in opaque ways.

These doings did not go unnoticed. In mid-1993 Giesecke & Devrient received an inquiry from the Anglo-French paper group Arjo Wiggins concerning the delivery of Zaire's security threads through Papierfabrik Louisenthal. Arjo Wiggins did not name its customer, which is normal in the industry. When Giesecke & Devrient as a routine inquired of the Banque de Zaire about the validity of this request it was informed that nothing stood in the way of this delivery. There was also a highly unusual letter from Zaire's embassy in Brussels to Giesecke & Devrient, asking the Munich company to comply. Shortly thereafter Banque de Zaire asked Hôtel des Monnaies to turn over the supporting materials in its custody because they would be needed for the production of printing plates. Munich learned of this from its team of technicians on the scene. When the company again questioned Banque de Zaire about this, it was informed that it should let the matter rest or risk losing all its business in Zaire.

It soon became known that the printer was Ciccone. It was diligently printing the zaires *and* nouveaux zaires. In the beginning the Argentine private printer asked Banque de Zaire to confirm the order. Thereafter, it was initially Viegas and later only Khanaffer who furnished the printing documents and the definitive order confirmations. Ciccone received no further direct confirmations from Banque de Zaire, although this would have been the usual procedure. The treasury of the central bank was empty. But the ringleaders of the counterfeiting plot had discovered a marvelous way of financing the banknote printing – a *perpetuum mobile* of creating money. The first banknotes delivered to the national bank, as Interpol later discovered, were exchanged for dollars. And these dollars were used to order further banknotes from Ciccone. These additional notes then went directly into circulation without passing through Banque de Zaire. New ACS Airfreight (Air Charter Service), a Belgium-Zaire company, handled the transportation at the wish of those who placed the orders. Ciccone never obtained a confirmation that its consignment of banknotes actually arrived at Banque de Zaire. The airlifts of banknotes in this way went to Mobutu's jungle residence at Gbadolite, where the money was used to pay his praetorian guard. Or the money was routed to the regions where his generals controlled the mining of diamonds, gold, and columbite-tantalite (coltan) a rare mineral, mostly used in small electronic devices. A small mishap occurred at the start of September 1994. Thirty metric tons of banknotes arrived at Kinshasa airport, a delivery about which Banque de Zaire had no knowledge. The cargo was confiscated. When the national bank got wind of another delivery to Kinshasa, the alerted military temporarily sealed off the airport and routed the plane into the hinterland, where Banque de Zaire could no longer intervene. Nevertheless, as the press reported, a delivery of 50 million banknotes was still able to be confiscated in Mbandaka. In another instance, 20 million notes were intercepted.

Although Banque de Zaire was responsible for the production and issuance of banknotes, it had no idea how many notes had entered the country. It knew neither where nor when. And it determined that there was extensive duplication in numbering. Sometimes, as police records revealed, the same numbers appeared on three different banknotes, especially those with high denominations. Combinations of letters and numbers, the so-called numbering sequences used there, had previously been employed by Hôtel des Monnaies. The numbering sequences of Giesecke & Devrient, which also continued to print for Zaire, were not affected, however. Notes turned up in the same denomination but with slight variations of background printing. The local newspapers were full of reports on the shower of banknotes.

When the security features of the zaire banknotes were improved, illegal counterfeit notes with improvements in exactly these features promptly turned up. They had been manufactured on the basis of originals and were identical with notes authorized for circulation. This made them scarcely distinguishable even by experts. There was no longer any doubt about the illegality of this operation. And it was apparent that, apart from the high levels within the central bank, even the military was involved in the case. The logistical effort for transporting hundreds of tons of banknotes is considerable. Meanwhile, there was again a new prime minister, Kengo wa Dondo, and a new governor of Banque de Zaire, »Patrice« Djamboleka Loma Okitongono. Following the incident at Kinshasa airport, they immediately revoked the executive signatory powers of Viegas and Khanaffer. At the same time, in a telex message to Interpol the high command of the police of Zaire officially identified Ciccone Calcográfica as the printer of the illegal banknotes. The »mystery« was not that much of a secret after all. Ciccone was ordered to stop printing forthwith. In spite of that, another 50 million notes of the 500-nouveaux zaires denomination left Buenos Aires for Zaire. A printing order from Banque de Zaire did not exist for this shipment either. The illegal flood of notes simply continued.

After Mobutu was ousted from government, the Argentine printer began preparations for printing another batch of counterfeit zaire banknotes, this time for the new head of state, Laurent Kabila. Now Banque de Zaire and Interpol intervened directly in Buenos Aires and found another 52 million banknotes and more than 240 metric tons of paper with the Mobutu portrait as watermark in the vault of Ciccone. This paper would have sufficed for the production of another 185 million notes. Banque de Zaire had to buy the 52 million notes to prevent them from going into circulation illegally in Zaire as well. No trace was found of the remaining stock of around 270 million printed banknotes delivered to Zaire.Ciccone finally had to oblige itself officially to cease further printing of unauthorized banknotes for Zaire. An investigation assisted by Interpol and the national police authorities later revealed that Ciccone Calográfica had obtained around 1,200 metric tons of banknote paper between October 1993 and November 1994 from Portals, for which Ciccone served as Latin American agent. In the same period, more than 100 tons had also been purchased from Arjo Wiggins. That paper was fitted out with the security threads of Papierfabrik Louisenthal. Its delivery had been authorized by Banque de Zaire. The total amount of paper would have sufficed for the production of far more than 800 million banknotes. Of this amount, 370 million notes were actually delivered to Banque de Zaire – or its representatives. These alone were covered by the printing order of the national bank, regardless of the intention behind the placement of the order.

The approximately 820 million banknotes that were printed had a theoretical face value of 1.25 billion dollars when converted at the exchange rate of the day. Gold as well as the rare metals coltan, cobalt and niobium and especially diamonds were purchased with the zaire notes. All of this was flown out and sold for dollars in Western capitals. The diamonds went to Antwerp, the international center of diamond polishing. Belgium's Egimex, which specialized in the trade with diamonds and gold, played a key role in this.[13] All this signified a gigantic creation of liquidity with disastrous consequences for the already heavily damaged national economy of Zaire. The inflation rate, which had been running near 3,000 percent in 1993, quickened in 1994 – despite currency reform – to 10,000 percent. The exchange rate of the national currency against the dollar plunged in the same period from 3 nouveaux zaires to 4,400 nouveaux zaires. It was the death blow for Zaire's economy. And it was the beginning of the end of the terror regime of Mobutu Sésé Seko. He was toppled in 1997 and died shortly thereafter.

Association Internationale des Imprimeurs Fiduciaires had been keeping tabs on the Ciccone case for some time. AIIF's president was Manfred Beck, the man responsible for banknotes and security paper at Giesecke & Devrient. He had been informed of the suspected phony money in August 1994 by the new governor of the national bank. This information responded to Munich's inquiry in Kinshasa about a new order from Arjo Wiggins for security threads, which were no longer authorized. Shortly thereafter, Giesecke & Devrient was approached by Bavaria's state police agents at the behest of the German federal police and Interpol. As the responsible member of the management of Giesecke & Devrient,

Beck had more than one reason to be angry at the competitor, Ciccone. As AIIF president, however, he saw that the conduct of Ciccone Calcográfica could threaten the reputation of all private high-security printers. In the traditional rivalry between state printers and private printers, the accusation is repeatedly leveled that the private printers as profit-oriented companies might play fast and loose with banknote printing. And Ciccone Calcográfica had broken several of the usual commandments of this industry simultaneously.

The AIIF president hoped for a swift agreement between Banque de Zaire and Ciccone so that the matter could be laid to rest without brouhaha. At the behest of the AIIF president there was a meeting on October 1995 at the premises of Giesecke & Devrient between several representatives of Banque de Zaire and Ciccone Calcográfica. In a »procès verbal« signed by both Banque de Zaire and Ciccone Calcográfica, Ciccone obliged itself to surrender within a week all correspondence about printing orders, shipping tickets for paper purchases, documents on note printing and paper consumption, details of the printed denominations, all bills of lading of the banknote shipments with certification of receipt, bookkeeping entries on payments, etc. In short, this covered all those things which the Argentine banknote printer had been holding back in clear violation of the practices of the high-security printing industry. Ciccone was also supposed to destroy the remaining 240 metric tons of banknote paper. This had not yet been run through customs because Ciccone had been hoping to re-export it.

The meeting in Munich was to have unexpected repercussions. The representatives of Ciccone later maintained that they had not been informed in advance of the purpose of this meeting and who would attend it. They said Beck had steamrolled them, thereby spicing his own business interests with that of his AIIF office. These two allegations served Ciccone as justification for failing to fulfill the obligations to which it had agreed in writing. During a state visit to Germany in November 1995, Prime Minister Kengo wa Dondo asked AIIF for help. He did this at a meeting with Beck in Bonn in the presence of representatives of the German government and the German ambassador to Zaire. Perhaps it was not an entirely convincing appeal for help, since the answers to most of the questions raised by this scandal were to be found in Kinshasa. The conspirators at Banque de Zaire feared for their lives and preferred to keep silent, however. It was revealing that neither the government of Zaire nor its national bank ever filed charges against Ciccone Calcográfica.

AIIF was quite a loose-knit association. Its by-laws were vaguely formulated and included no possibilities for taking disciplinary action against a member. There was a heated debate about this at the annual meeting of AIIF in Amsterdam in autumn 1996. Some members didn't want to rule out the possibility that this was really about just the exclusion of one difficult competitor from the so-called Third World. Ciccone therefore stubbornly – and successfully – refused to turn over the documentation and to destroy the paper. In lieu of that, Ciccone demanded of Banque de Zaire and Giesecke & Devrient that they purchase the 240 metric tons of paper for its value of 3.7 million dollars. The exclusion of Ciccone from AIIF had not yet come up for discussion at this point. In a tediously long brief peppered with legal niceties, a German attorney engaged by Ciccone tried to demonstrate unfair competitive practices by Giesecke & Devrient and abuse of office by the AIIF president. This wrecked the effort of AIIF to prevent the case from being aired in public. In the middle of this impending showdown exploded a fresh printing scandal that was to seal the fate of Ciccone Calcográfica as a note printer.

›Real-phony‹ Bahrain dinars

In April 1997 Ciccone Calcográfica was offered the possibility to print banknotes for the tiny emirate of Bahrain, which has 630,000 residents. The printing of 7 million 20-dinar notes at a price of 54 dollars per 1,000 notes would bring in exactly 375,000 dollars. The order was rather insignificant. But it gave Ciccone the chance to crack into the lucrative market of the rich Gulf states, a market previously dominated by De La Rue. Bahrain's inquiry had again been mediated by Josefino Viegas, the man already known from the Zaire scam. Viegas had grabbed an order from France's Francois Charles Oberthur Fiduciaire for 1.2 billion kwanzas reajustados banknotes for Angola, and he had been made the representative of Ciccone Calcográfica in Africa. The idea for the Bahrain coup came from (Richard) Nozy Mwamba Munanga, then president of the Congolese FIFA soccer association. According to newspaper reports, he had been involved in diamond deals until the toppling of Mobutu. The term »plundering« would have been more appropriate. Mwamba's name had already come up in connection with the note scandal in Zaire. When the

30 metric tons of banknotes were confiscated at the airport of Kinshasa, Mwamba was on the spot, awaiting the shipment. He briefly went to prison, but Mobutu had him set free.

There followed a sting operation, such a minutely prepared fraud that Hollywood could not have thought up a better one. The French newspaper *Le Monde* has thoroughly described this in numerous articles for which the Swiss police probably allowed it to take a look into the investigation dossier.[14] The unfolding of this scam was strongly reminiscent of the previously mentioned fraud scandal in Portugal in the mid-1920s. In that instance, Artur Virgilio Alves Reis, a Portuguese who represented himself as a special envoy of Banco de Portugal, had several million 500-escudos notes printed by the British Waterlow & Sons by presenting forged documents. These notes were supposedly earmarked for the Portuguese colony of Angola. The perfectly imitated notes, which could hardly be distinguished from the authentic banknotes of Banco de Portugal, were no problem to circulate and gained wide distribution. When the fraud was finally revealed by coincidence – a cashier discovered a counterfeit note with numbering that corresponded to a real one – the country was brought to the edge of bankruptcy. High-security printer Waterlow & Sons, one of the world's leading note printers at that time, never again recovered from this loss of trust and was finally taken over by De La Rue.[15] This counterfeiting scandal could have provided the script for the Bahrain coup.

The ball got rolling with the formation of two delegations under the leadership of Mwamba and Viegas. They showed up in Buenos Aires in autumn 1997, identifying themselves as proxies of His Royal Highness, Prince Faisal bin Moshari bin Abdul Aziz al-Saud. They demanded to tour the banknote printing plant on behalf of the Bahrain Monetary Agency. The delegation was impressed by the level of technical proficiency of Ciccone Calcográfica. Shortly thereafter, the prince announced a personal visit. With a facsimile message, he reserved a whole wing of Alvear Palace Hotel, the top hotel in Buenos Aires. For, as is customary among oil sheikhs, he would be traveling with a great entourage of bodyguards and private secretaries as well as a maid for his accompanying spouse. The reservation attracted attention because it was twice subjected to elaborate changes and finally was cancelled completely. A »secretary« of the prince excused himself politely to the hotel management by fax, saying he was only »carrying out orders.« The imposing royal letterhead, incidentally, gave the address as merely a post office box in Riad. Instead of the prince, a written power of attorney of the Bahrain Monetary Agency arrived at the start of December. It was supposedly signed by the premier of the emirate, who was also the chairman of the Bahrain Monetary Agency. And it directed a certain Sheikh Mohamed bin Saad al-Ajimi, director of the secretariat of the executive board, to seal the contract with Ciccone for the printing of the notes. The contract signing by Héctor Ciccone and Sheikh Saad al-Ajimi then took place at the customer's wish in the Johannesburg Hilton in Johannesburg in mid-January 1998. The meeting place dovetailed well with the travel itinerary of both partners, an explanation given by Mwamba said. At this meeting the sheikh identified himself with the »original« of the executive power of attorney. Héctor Ciccone and Franco Lago, the director of printing who traveled with him, later had to concede that no one from their company had ever before met the person who was supposedly a director of the Bahrain Monetary Agency. Yet, at that moment everyone was impressed by the gaunt, distinguished figure in the white burnoose, who didn't smoke and took no alcohol. The hotel service staff seemed to know the sheikh, since he was given red-carpet treatment, as Ciccone and Lago were reassured to observe.

The Argentineans began their printing preparations. They ordered nearly 8 metric tons of secure paper with Bahrain's watermark from the Anglo-French Arjo Wiggins and the ink from the Swiss SICPA. The numbering scheme with Arabic numerals – as specified by the customer – was ordered from Atlantic Zeiser, which was then still a U.S. company. The originals department at Ciccone began its workup of the printing plates. A 20-dinar note printed by De La Rue served as the model. Such plagiarism is actually frowned upon in the branch, since it is somewhat of an assault on professional pride. But the company bowed to the customer's wish. During this period all contacts and coordination of the printer with the Bahrain Monetary Agency were passing through Viegas and Mwamba. No one at Ciccone made an effort to obtain an independent written comment from the Agency, nor did any representative of Ciccone ever pay a visit to Manama. Robert Molina, Ciccone's sales chief, and Viegas and Mwamba did set out for the emirate with the printing plates in March of the same year in order to obtain the printing approval and the order confirmation. At the obligatory stopover in the Saudi capital of Riad they were informed in the VIP lounge that they would not need to travel on to Manama. His Royal Highness was off for a pilgrimage to Mecca and would receive them here. The meeting took place in the royal palace of

Riad. There the Ciccone sales director met not only Sheikh Saad al-Aljimi, the supposed director of the Bahrain agency. There was also a brief meeting with another person, introduced as Prince Aziz al-Saud – the same prince who had not been able to come to Buenos Aires. The group made a professional inspection of the note proof sheets and took them along. They were returned to the representative of Ciccone the next day by Viegas and Mwamba with the required seal of approval.

Ciccone could now let the banknote presses roll. As security, however, Buenos Aires still wanted to have the signatures of Sheikh Saad al-Ajimi and the mandate of his Agency officially notarized, including the signatures of his executive board. But the Saudi embassy, which represented the interests of Bahrain in Buenos Aires, was not in possession of any official signatures as samples. Instead of that, a letter arrived from the Agency at the start of April, again signed by the executive board and adorned on the reverse side with numerous seals and stamps of Saudi authorities This was supposed to confirm the authenticity of the signatures of the Agency's executive body. In the letter His Highness said that Bahrain did not wish to transmit instructions through the embassies of other countries because of the strong confidentiality of the printing order. He also said that other countries would not be requested to notarize signatures. »Much work awaits you,« the letter ended. Yet Ciccone had the translated letter and mandate notarized by the Argentine foreign ministry. A futile effort, as it would later turn out.

Five weeks later everything was ready for shipment. Nearly 8 metric tons of banknotes were sent on the way to Manama in a Boeing 707 in three consignments: May 18, May 25, and June 8, 1998. A Belgian-Zaire air carrier registered in Kinshasa again handled the transportation at the wish of the customer. This time it was called Espace Aviation Services. The transport security detail was composed entirely of persons who had been previously identified by Bahrain with names and passport numbers as supposed representatives of its Agency. Payment came promptly, albeit in installments, and partially in cash.

Three weeks elapsed between the first and last shipments, plenty of time to place an inquiry with the customer. But no one at Ciccone ever once deemed it necessary to call up the Agency for reassurance that the three consignments had been properly transported. Moreover, none of the printing plates were returned by Ciccone to the customer, squandering another opportunity for at least indirect control. The Argentineans later pretended they were not aware of the fact that their deliveries had not arrived at all in Manama, that they had learned of it only later. Actually, it would have been easy for them to find out because it was the Lebanese gentleman who accompanied the flights out of Buenos Aires – the same Monsieur Khanaffer who had helped set up the Zaire scheme. The first shipment of 40 million Bahrain dinars went to Niamey, the capital of the Republic of Niger. And the two others, worth 100 million Bahrain dinars together, were unloaded in N'Djamena, the capital of Chad. All these airports were controlled by French military, and in all three instances the shipments of banknotes were awaited by French nationals. On one flight there was also a light aircraft among the cargo, a gift for the local potentate. The last act of the drama began.

Bahrain's dinar is pegged to the dollar and is freely convertible. At that time 20 dinars of the emirate of Bahrain corresponded to 55.20 dollars. The seven million »real-counterfeit dinar« notes, as they soon came to be called, had a value of nearly 367 million dollars. They quickly found their way to Europe and back to the Near East. Before Ciccone had even sent its last consignment on its way, a middleman succeeded without problem in exchanging 75,000 of the notes at CPR Billets in Paris. Three suitcases would have been needed to carry them. The exchange value was 4 million dollars. And the exchange was made, although the notes were in virgin condition and had sequential numbering. The unobtrusive currency exchange office in a mall on the Champs-Elysées was well known for offering a more favorable exchange rate than the competition when clients wanted to sell their dollars. Long lines of tourists at the counter testify to this reputation. Serving as the cash courier for the Bahrain notes was a Moroccan, who bragged about having been a special adviser to the late King Hassan II. To legitimize the exchange of notes he presented a letter of recommendation from a high government official in Bahrain, who supposedly wanted to invest money in France. The assiduous Moroccan exchanged another portion for more than 7 million dollars in Lebanon shortly thereafter.

Initially, the flight crew that accompanied the transport was not aware of what their cargo was. When during one flight Khanaffer was absent they found out and quickly helped themselves to a couple of bundles of fresh, crisp notes. They got away with a considerable sum. But precisely this was their undoing. When they presented their stack of freshly printed Bahrain dinars with perfect sequential numbering at a private bank in Geneva, the bank clerks became suspicious. They promised to proceed with the exchange operation, but called the police instead. Since the flight crew had already left Switzerland, they were lured back into the country under the pretext that the bank wanted to discuss with them various possibilities for investments. Upon their return they were promptly arrested. It was rotten luck for the whole scam because the attempt of other middlemen to exchange more money in Paris then went sour. Two high officials from Chad were involved in that attempt, according to press reports. The police sprang their trap on a group wanting to pick up the hot »goods« at the airport in Brussels in preparation for an exchange operation. On two other occasions diplomats arriving from Chad were arrested in Dubai after large volumes of virgin »real-counterfeit« 20-dinar notes were found in their luggage. Exchange attempts were also foiled in Syria and Singapore.

One million of the 1.5 million dinar worth of notes exchanged in Paris embarked upon a remarkable odyssey through various banks until they were offered by foreign banks for exchange to the Agency in Bahrain. The Agency suspected they were counterfeits. It bought them in spite of that before the departure of the last note shipment from Buenos Aires. A French newspaper later reported that the Agency had agreed to the exchange purchase on the condition that the cash must be exchanged in small amounts – in order to avoid disclosure. Then nearly a week passed when practically nothing happened. It was said later that this time was needed in order to determine beyond doubt that these were counterfeits. Not until two days after the departure of the last note shipment did the Bahrain Monetary Agency place a call to Ciccone Calcográfica. The female caller, Ciccone asserted, was a former employee of De La Rue, who had taken a job with the Agency. She informed the Argentineans that they were under suspicion of having counterfeited dinar notes. Even the lawyers, who were then brought in by the Bahrain Monetary Authority, usually worked for the British banknote printer, said Ciccone.[16] The 7 million 20-dinar notes with a face value of nearly 138 million dinars exceeded the total value of the 20-dinar notes officially in circulation in the emirate. Since the »real-counterfeit« dinar notes could hardly be distinguished from the legally issued notes, the Agency recalled all 20-dinar banknotes and had new ones printed – this time by De La Rue.

Ciccone Calcográfica found that offense was the best defense. In Buenos Aires it filed charges against Sheikh al-Ajimi and others. Investigations of Interpol, the U.S. Secret Service, and national police authorities were in progress around the globe. The range of speculation extended from a purely criminal counterfeiting ring to a politically motivated attempt to destabilize the Emirate of Bahrain. Bahrain is populated by a Shiite majority but is ruled with an iron hand by the Sunni clan of the al-Khalifa. Internal unrest is no rarity. And Bahrain serves as a base of the U.S. Fifth Fleet. Neighboring Iran has a Shiite majority. Its secret service could, as suspected, have been interested in destabilizing the emirate in concert with an opposition group in Bahrain. Whatever the motives of the instigators, they made one serious miscalculation: they knew that the Emirate of Bahrain was not yet a signatory to the Geneva Convention of 1929 on counterfeiting. They therefore hoped that Interpol would not get involved, and they would get away with their sting operation. They were wrong. French judges took over all cases connected with the »real-phony« Bahrain dinars and a few French nationals were recalled from Africa in a hurry. But the judges did not get far. Although Mwamba was arrested in Switzerland and extradited to Belgium, he was able to flee house arrest to South Africa. And the Moroccan middleman, Hicham Mandari, had promptly gone to Florida, and he was not extradited to France until early 2002.[17] The emirate proved to be no big help in the search for the ringleaders of this spectacular affair either. It refrained from placing charges against Ciccone but demanded an apology and damages of 10 million dollars. From the moment the plot was uncovered, Bahrain Monetary Agency had strenuously resisted letting the case become publicly known. Nevertheless, the ringleaders must have had helpers in the Bahrain Monetary Agency in order to draw the mighty Saudi Arabian neighbor into the matter. The embassy of Bahrain in Paris emphatically denied any involvement of the functionaries of the emirate or its Agency in a letter to the newspaper *Le Monde*, parts of which were published. Yet the Arabian princes suspected of involvement in the case refused to be questioned by official foreign investigators. But Interpol Buenos Aires informed the presiding judge in the Argentine investigation that a cellular telephone handset repeatedly used in the counterfeiting case had the number of a prominent member of the ruling family of Bahrain. It cited a corresponding report of April 7, 2000, from Interpol Bahrain.

At AIIF, where the secretariat has since been taken over by the respected Swiss private printer Orell Füssli, the new scandal involving Ciccone struck like lightening. Concern that the reputation of the whole industry could be damaged was widespread. Representatives of the Argentine note printer defended themselves against accusations of counterfeiting with the threadbare argument that their dinar note differed in seven respects from the 20-dinar note printed by De La Rue and legally issued by the Agency. The watermark especially was different. No one who had intended to counterfeit would do that, they said. There was never any secret made of the order, they pointed out. The Bahrain Monetary Agency was expressly named as the customer when paper was ordered from Arjo-Wiggins. Legal counsel of the Argentineans looked for vulnerable spots in the by-laws of AIIF, which had its headquarters in Zurich and was subject to Swiss law on associations. It discovered something. Discussion at the annual meeting of AIIF in October 1998 waxed emotional on both sides, although the Argentineans were unable to convince the membership. All the members in attendance voted unanimously for the expulsion of Ciccone Calcográfica from AIIF. Nevertheless, the expulsion – or the examined alternative of a voluntarily dissolution of AIIF – threatened to cause a legal imbroglio of many years with the Argentineans. Therefore, another approach was decided upon. At an extraordinary meeting of AIIF held in London in early 1999, nearly all members of this once-so-prestigious organization withdrew from membership – without dissolving AIIF. It was a radical decision. Left behind in an AIIF doomed to insignificance were Ciccone Calcográfica, Milan's Calcografia e Cartevalori, and American Banknote. This made a hash of the matter, participants in the dramatic AIIF meeting said in retrospect. It was a classical example of »banknote printing on call,« as industry insiders later confirmed. In such a grave case of misconduct, one could have expected that the guilty would draw the consequences and pull out of AIIF voluntarily. Yet Ciccone had not done this. The split decision did little for the Argentineans. Despite bitter opposition, Interpol shortly thereafter crossed Ciccone Calcográfica off its invitation list. Ciccone was also no longer welcome at the professional gatherings of the high-security printing industry. In short order, Ciccone was no longer even admitted to public biddings on contracts for banknote printing in Uruguay. This country is on the opposite bank of the Rio de la Plata, practically in view of Ciccone Calcográfica's printing works.

The Argentine printer has in the meantime had to seek court protection from its creditors. The severing of the peso's link to the dollar had finally forced Ciccone Calcográfica to its knees. Despite all evidence, the Ciccone brothers regard themselves and their company as victims of a conspiracy instigated by the three greats of banknote printing, for whom the matter was merely the preservation of their monopolistic grip on the market. Not even all Argentinean observers familiar with this drama agree on that. An adviser to Menem, who had often taken part in the discussions of the former head of government with the two brothers, looks at the facts critically. The two had succumbed to the temptation of power, he said. They squandered the greatest capital of the high-security printer, its trustworthiness, he concluded in a conversation in Buenos Aires.

The investigation of the scandal of the »real-phony« Bahrain notes continues. A complete picture will probably never be pieced together, or at least will not be made public. Saudi Arabia and Bahrain have cleaned up the mess internally, it is said. Somewhere on the continent of Africa around 250,000 of these »real-phony« Bahrain dinar notes are still mildewing in a garage. In the summer of 2005 a middleman offered to sell them, presenting a bundle of virgin notes as credentials. The notes were sequentially numbered and still sealed in their original packing: once hot merchandise that has not entirely cooled off. This is but a trifle for the high-security printing industry. It has other worries. And those worries are linked to the deal of the century, the introduction of euro notes. In ten years it may be determined that nothing has shaken the foundation of this elite industry so much and changed it so greatly as this common currency. It is time for a closer look at the common European currency.

Money Jitters

10
Why the euro became a bonanza for moneymakers

There aren't too many industrial products nowadays for which the Europeans can still claim a role of world leadership. Banknote printing in its broadest sense is one of the private industries that has secured this success. So one might have anticipated that the production of Europe's new common currency would have yielded a model for a banknote that would be modern in design, technically perfect in security, and also reasonable in price. Despite colossal efforts, this mammoth task has not been accomplished. True, the currency conversion was prepared down to the last detail. This was handled in general-staff style by the designated member of the directorate of the European Central Bank (ECB), Spain's Eugenio Domingo Solans, and his Finnish director for banknotes, Antti Heinonen, together with the affected national central banks. It ran smoothly and »in the buoyant spirits« of New Year's revelers, as newspapers across Europe reported the day afterward. The three hundred million Europeans knew little of the efforts and demands that went into the ten-year technical preparation for this grand monetary experiment. But there had been no lack of national vanities and ambitions poured into this economically and psychologically challenging project. Ever present and well understood, egoism had extracted compromises calling for the least common denominator all along the way. The euro, the »calling card« of the unified Europe, morphed successively in this way into a »political banknote« – that occasionally took its toll on the usually strict standards of the security industry. Little of these affaires seeped into public discourse, of course. For a complete gag order on publicity had been imposed by the participating central banks and the European Monetary Institute (EMI), as the forerunner of the ECB, right from the early phase of the planning. Those in the boardrooms of the high-security branch who were concerned with the

Moneymakers, Klaus W. Bender

ISBN: 3-527-50236-X

preparations had to commit themselves in writing to absolute secrecy. Even their workforces, right down to apprentices, were sworn to silence. »Whoever chats about this over a drink after hours, risks his job,« it was clearly understood. The development of new weapons systems hardly could have been conducted under greater confidentiality.

The precautions were taken for good reasons. All those foreign ministers and finance ministers who put their signature to the project of a European common currency at Maastricht in Holland in February 1992 were well aware that this would be not only an expensive undertaking, but also an unprecedented political and technical one.[1] The then European Community consisted of twelve countries. Central banks are normally accustomed to a great degree of autonomy in the design and printing of their national banknotes. Apart from the national flag, the national currency with its banknotes is the primary symbol of national sovereignty in any country. Now this symbol of national character was supposed to be taken away to make room for a common currency that was to be a joint project of twelve central banks in its production and use. National prestige was at stake and so was money. Wim Duisenberg, the first president of the ECB, once estimated the cost of all the measures associated with the currency conversion at as much as 0.8 percent of the aggregate gross domestic product of the twelve countries that made the euro. That was 52 billion euros. Naturally only a few percentage points of this involved mere printing of banknotes. Yet this particular euro pie was still appetizing and everyone wanted to have a piece if he could. This could not be handled without conflicts.

Just pinning down the various euro denominations and then determining the total number of notes needed in each denomination by each member state separately for the initial cash supply caused endless discussions and had to be held in abeyance for years. Sound experience on which one could fall back in a pinch was lacking. The traditions of cash circulation in the euro countries varied. EMI determined in its examination that the Finns held only 21 banknotes per capita at the end of 1996, while the Italians and Austrians held on average 51 bills per person. It is no accident that both of these countries are preferred tourist destinations. The number of issued denominations, the distribution of cash and credit cards, the scope of cash hoarding that is quite commonplace in rural regions, the stray money that tourists take home with them, the extent of the moonlighting economy, and many other things were responsible for the differences. In Finland, for example, one can pay for a taxi with a credit card even on the Arctic Circle while on the Iberian Peninsula or in the Peloponnesus it is advisable to have cash in one's pocket, especially in small denominations. Equally difficult were the estimates of the EMI currencies held abroad, particularly for the Deutschmark as the world's most important reserve currency after the dollar.

Finally, toward the end of the 1990s the order was given for 15 billion banknotes for the initial conversion issue, of which around 40 percent was designated as a »logistics reserve« to be withheld from immediate issuance (see Table II). These notes were supposed to replace the 12.7 billion »old notes« – a generously proportioned initial complement, if one considers that the euro notes had a considerably higher value than the banknotes they were supposed to replace, for example the French franc, Italian lira, and Austrian schilling notes. Counting ECB's strategic emergency reserve of 1.8 billion notes, which was also ordered in 2001 as a complete surprise, along with the initial issuing requirement of 4.8 billion notes in 2002, the whole batch came to 21.6 billion banknotes. That corresponded to nearly one quarter of the worldwide requirement for notes for one year. Laid end to end, these euro notes would form a paper chain that would stretch four times to the moon and back. One could also wrap them as a belt around the Earth's equator seventy-five times.

Concealed behind this number of notes was a gigantic requirement for materials to produce banknotes. It was the largest printing order in the history of paper money. And it was supposed to be settled according to the advantageous formula of »proven costs plus appropriate profit.« The price for banknotes on the world market was under pressure. Euro banknotes promised juicy earnings again, for »proven« can mean many things. Talk of the »euro bonanza« in which one could name one's price soon was making the rounds in this industry.[2] The euro notes – and much the same applied to the coins – required great investment for printing machinery, for sensors in quality control of production, inspection machines for the authenticity checks as well as for the sorting of the old bills by the banks. And finally it also called for special, highly secure machines, insulated from human intervention, for the destruction of the old notes removed from circulation, namely the so-called shredder. The fight over who would be allowed to deliver was programmed.

Table II: Euro printing for initial supply by country and denomination

Country	Final printing volume for initial issue (in millions of notes)							Total volume
	5 €	10 €	20 €	50 €	100 €	200 €	500 €	
Belgium	125	110	140	100	50	10	15	550,0
Germany	1 158,7	1 027,2	771,9	1 144	362,9	99,6	218,6	4 782,9
Finland	40	60	66	30	20	7	2	225,0
France	350	625	710	360	150	20	50	2 265,0
Greece	158	183	178	67	26	4	1	617,0
Ireland	60	45	130	50	8,3	0,2	0,2	293,7
Italy	540,5	516	441,2	525	361	32	24	2 439,7
Luxembourg	6	3	13	11	3	2	8	46,0
Netherlands	135	130	105	223	35	15	16	659,0
Austria	150	150	45	60	105	20	20	550,0
Portugal	123	90	259	58	6	1	0,5	537,5
Spain	308,9	281,5	547,2	655	103,3	12,8	15,4	1 924,1
Total	3 155,1	3 220,7	3 406,3	3 283,0	1 230,5	223,6	370,7	14 889,9

Source: ECB

Friendly enemies

The situation was confused and fraught with conflict. Measured by the population figure, printing capacity in no other part of the planet is as high as on the Old Continent. Eight of the eleven currency-union countries had their own state-owned printing works at the time of the euro's christening in 1995. There were exceptions, though. Since the time of Napoleon the Netherlands has had its technically excellent guilder notes made exclusively by the private printer Joh. Enschedé. In Germany as well, neither the Reichsbank nor Bundesbank had ever owned its own printing plant. Bundesbank obtained half of its D-mark notes from the government-owned Bundesdruckerei, the other half from Giesecke & Devrient. This benefited the quality and manufacturing costs of the Deutschmark. And the people of Luxembourg, known for counting their pennies, did without their own printing, preferring to have their modest volumes of »Letzebuerger frang« produced by assorted private and public printers abroad. Portugal did the same, albeit for other reasons, as will be treated in greater depth below. As though the market situation were not already complicated enough, Europe still had the largest private security printers in the world: De La Rue, Francois Charles Oberthur Fiduciaire and Giesecke & Devrient. The British and French private printers were traditionally excluded from the printing of their own national currencies, however.

Government printers and private printers are united in a genuine dislike for one another. Comments about »shocking inefficiency« of government printers and their rejoinders about »roughshod business methods« of private printers are routine. The rising demands on secure technology for banknotes in the struggle against technically advancing counterfeits actually force both camps to work together. They remain »friendly enemies,« as once was said. The government printers were little inclined to include private rivals in the production of the euro. Early on, the national bank governors activated a special task force, Banknote Working Group (BNWG). It was supposed to deal in subcommittees with the development of the euro, its quality of paper and printing, its security features, and the fight against counterfeiters in general. The chair of this panel was given to Alex Jarvis, then the director general of the Debden printing works of Bank of England. The participation of Britain in the euro was still undecided at that time. The directors of the treasuries of all the national banks and the representatives of the government printing facilities belonged to this influential body, which is known today as the Banknote Committee (Banco). One would search in vain for a private printer as a full member of it, however. The efforts of some influential central banks to circumscribe the role of private printers in the euro production as much as possible were clearly at work. It was suggested by influential members of the Banknote Working Group that Bundesdruckerei forgo full membership in this body for that reason. The official explanation was its impending privatization. Unofficially, the reason was to avoid creating a precedent for other private printers. They were probably thinking of Giesecke & Devrient.

The central banks used their close government contacts for their own vigorous lobbying of ministries, parliaments and committees with the argument that the jobs, technical knowledge, and capital invested in the state printing works had to be protected. This intent was clear. Carrying it out was more difficult, for it was apparent that no banknote printer in Europe would be technically and logistically capable of mastering this gigantic task alone. In addition to the new euro notes, the need for national notes still had to be considered. These would be necessary until the time of the currency conversion. For the common-currency countries this requirement was, after all, around 3 billion notes a year. For the period between the end of the printing of national currencies and the issuance of the euro, an inventory of these had to be produced.

The establishment of central banknote printing works, as there are in the United States, could be ruled out in Europe for political reasons. Even the pooling of printing orders, in which a printer is assigned a certain note denomination for one or more countries, initially proved too difficult for the common-currency countries. This would have eased harmonization and saved money. Too many bidders, too divergent costs, it was said. Thus it was determined that each national bank would have to take care of the initial complement of euro banknotes for its own country. Public contract solicitations were waived, although auctions were envisaged for the replacement requirements for the euro. Still in its formative phase, ECB resigned itself of necessity to the role of coordinator and supervisor of quality control, which under the given circumstances was extremely difficult.

The technical qualification of the personnel of the government printing facilities was as a rule not in question. The quality of the banknote took priority and, at some of them, was the best in the world. Yet the realization that cost also played a role in banknote printing made headway only with difficulty against the self-esteem of the government printers. Some of them even worked without cost calculations. They were, with exceptions that prove the rule, clumsy organizations with huge staffs, paid above scale and often immune to dismissal. Expensive machinery ran on a single shift and too many employees stood idle around the plants that were long since fully controlled with electronics. The government printers were not exactly the embodiment of industrial efficiency.

Euro investment rapture

Measures to raise the efficiency of the state printing works were unavoidable in the prelude to euro printing. But no one was eager to cross swords with the workforce, which could hit the economic nerve of every country with its protests, putting the government in a bind. To promote a dialogue among unions, central banks, and government printers, a round table was initiated. But measures to thin the workforces or improve machinery operating rates were hard to carry out. The national labor unions and their European federation in Brussels jealously guarded privileges that had been won. In this way the central banks embarked along the political line of least resistance, driving modernization primarily by expanding capacity. The issue of whether this capacity would be needed later received short shrift. The bulging need for euro notes in the short term served as an excuse. In the beauty contest among government printers, money was no object. Those who can practically print their own equity capital need not concern themselves about money. The Olympian principle prevailed: printing alone is everything.

Bundesdruckerei opened this lively roundelay with its new security printing center right adjacent the former Berlin Wall. This industrial gem of steel and glass cost at least 100 million euros without the property. It was financed from Bundesdruckerei's retained earnings, which the finance ministry and Bundestag's parliamentary budget committee had generously made possible over the years. With a new line of machinery that revved up its capability with additional presses – in addition to the old ones – the new Bundesdruckerei was not exactly modest in scope. One hoped to land additional euro printing orders from other countries. Italy, which was supposed to print the largest number of euro notes after Germany, had scarcely less extravagant plans. The banknote printer of Banca d'Italia had two modern lines, which would have sufficed to cover the current as well as any future Italian requirement for euro banknotes if the capacity were used sensibly. Yet the unions of the government printer, which were known for their militancy, successfully blocked more flexibility in manning shifts and using machinery capacity. The central bank therefore had a complete third line of machinery installed there. The smaller member countries naturally did not want to be left behind. Ireland, with an annual need of banknotes for its 4 million people, a need undercut only by Finland and Luxembourg, raised its printing works technically to the (Super) state of the art. Generous assistance from Brussels helped to create printing capacity that far exceeded its own requirements. This transpired in what was celebrated in professional circles as the world's prettiest banknote printing facility. Greece and Portugal, two more countries with moderate note requirements and structurally weak economies, were also slurping from the EU trough in order to make their note printers fit for euro production. That wasn't necessary either.

The booby prize, however, went to Oesterreichische Nationalbank (OeNB). In pricey downtown Vienna, a compact space that is architecturally protected, it set up a truly imposing printing plant. All the conditions for cost-driving construction were cheerfully met. Opened after eight years of planning and building, this money center swallowed around 330 million euros – the building alone cost 225 million euro before tax – according to official statements. That made it three times as dear as the already expensive new buildings of the Berlin printer, not even counting the renovations that followed. The Viennese received for this – recalling shades of *The Third Man* film from director Orson Welles – a 100-meter-long underground tunnel connecting the printing facility with the headquarters of the national bank. The inspiration for this again was exaggerated security considerations with respect to flexible production and no less exalted hopes of export orders. Investment far exceeded need. The two installed printing lines could theoretically have produced as many as two billion banknotes a year. In the age of the shilling, the country's annual replacement requirement had been somewhat more than 150 million notes, because of the high replacement need for low denominated 20-schilling notes, today worth less than 1.5 euros. Banknotes of Austrian production are highly respected in the professional world for their graphics, printing, and security characteristics. But Oesterreichische Banknoten- und Sicherheitsdruckerei GmbH (OeBS) – assuming realistic pricing – now threatens to fall through the cracks of any international solicitation for banknote printing merely because of its fixed costs. OeNB's extravagant ways with its resources also caused a domestic political row. Viktor Klima, then the federal chancellor and a member of the Social Democratic Party of Austria, dispensed with a tour of the plant for »lack of time« during the opening celebration for this gorgeous project. He was upset about the amount of money invested in the new printing works. After the initial euro print the workforce of 340 men on average produced about 200 million banknotes per year. Sometimes the annual losses of this high-security printer exceeded its annual turnover. OeNB has repeatedly sought foreign capital participation in its money center. There have been no takers.

The private high-security printing companies observed the spending rapture of the government competitors with lips buttoned. It could be anticipated, for one thing, that this capacity could hardly be used in the long term and would soon ram its way onto the free market. Obviously the common currency would be very interesting from a technical security standpoint, and therefore the participation in euro printing would be indispensable for the private printers in their own subsequent efforts on the export markets. As things then stood, Joh. Enschedé and Giesecke & Devrient could expect to participate. This was less certain for De La Rue and

Francois Charles Oberthur. Both had to try to get their foot in the door somewhere. Portugal offered a possibility. It traditionally had its notes printed abroad. The Portuguese had been the victims of an international counterfeiting plot in the 1920s, a scandal that drove the country to the edge of bankruptcy.[3] Thereafter, Lisbon switched to having its notes printed normally by De La Rue or Joh. Enschedé. But for security reasons it then imported the sheets uncut and without the banknote numbering. The final touches were handled by a small local printer, which was controlled by the finance ministry. Francois Charles Oberthur lobbied the finance ministry in Lisbon for two years with the proposal to build a banknote printer jointly. It pulled out all stops in cost and effort. Yet the talks dragged on without a result, particularly since other interested parties turned up, including Bundesdruckerei. Suddenly the representatives of De La Rue and machinery supplier DLR Giori showed up in Lisbon and negotiated briefly with the national bank. And they soon departed with the contract for a new high-security printing plant in hand. Apart from a respectable capital stake of 50 percent, the British offered especially to fill any available capacity in Portugal with own orders. In the industry people spoke respectfully of a »cavalry raid« and »excellent contacts« in Lisbon.

Afterwards, the British no longer recollected the agreement to occupy the unused capacity at the Portuguese printing works. Yet the contract won De La Rue a minority participation of 25 percent in the new printing works of the Portuguese national bank, Valora-Servicos de Apoio a Emissao Monitaria S.A. of Carregado. Friends in Lausanne had warned the Portuguese that they should not make any more than this available. And the British private banknote printer through this cooperation had access to euro production. De La Rue was even able to see that the Portuguese would not become too independent despite their new printing facility. De La Rue convinced the Portuguese national bank it was not worthwhile for Portugal to buy expensive special machinery for the technically complicated addition of selected security features to the new euro notes. The British kindly offered to handle that, and Lisbon accepted. Since then Portugal's banknotes are no longer taken to Lisbon from Gateshead, De La Rue's note printing plant, but to Gateshead from Lisbon. Francois Charles Oberthur drew the short straw. After its merger with the Dutch Joh. Enschedé collapsed, the French were in danger of being the only private printer in Euroland excluded from euro printing. Thanks to continuing difficulties with banknote printing at Banque de France, however, it still had a chance in the end.

The equipment makers, especially DLR Giori, naturally got a big kick out of the investment derby. In the late 1980s, before the start of the euro marathon, Lausanne went on the market with its Superline, a version enhanced by souped-up printing capability. Now with fully electronic controls, this line of printing machinery combines in its standard variant a Super-Simultan for background printing, one or two Super-Intaglios for the steelplate engraved printing, a Nota Check for controlling the quality of the printing, a Super-Numerota for numbering banknotes in sequence, and a Cutpak packing machine for the final cutting, inspection, and packaging. In the case of euro production, accessories were required for the technically difficult job of affixing the hologram films and patches or for the silk screen. Just the standard configuration, six machines in this Super line, cost around 50 million Swiss francs (35 million euros). In spite of this price, Lausanne had already been able to book a bundle of orders, especially from the former Soviet republics, from the People's Republic of China, and from India. The euro gave this boom another powerful boost (see Table III). Between 1994 and 2001 Lausanne sold around 400 of its expensive printing machines around the world. Sales at one point notched a record of nearly half a billion Swiss francs.

Other companies benefited from this, principally Koenig & Bauer as the exclusive manufacturer of DLR-Giori printing presses. But there were smaller and lessknown suppliers who were also getting pieces of the big pie. There was, for example, Atlantic Zeiser, a maker of special equipment for printing the obligatory numbers on banknotes. Few outside the security industry have ever heard of Atlantic Zeiser based in the small Swabian town of Emmingen-Liptingen, yet it leads the world market in technology for numbering machines with a market share of 95 percent. There are only a few banknotes in the world today for which Atlantic Zeiser is not involved in the sequential printing of numbers. Notes produced on Japanese printing presses of Komori are an exception. The numbering of banknotes uses typefaces that cannot be obtained freely in commerce. The numbering equipment is a technical wonder, which is appropriately expensive. Although only one numbering machine per printing line is needed in note printing, a unique set of numbers has to be printed on each note. For anyone it is difficult to imagine the number of installed lines of machinery for euro printing or to envisage the underlying investment required merely for this small detail of banknote numbering. In the case of the 5-euro note, for example, 54

Table III: Printing capacity and euro printing needs, early 2003 (in millions of notes)

Country	Printer	Status	Machinery	Printing capacity	Readjusted euro printing volume
Belgium	Belg. NB	SPW	1	200	550 (460)
Germany	BDR	CPW	1	300	4 783 (4 000)
	G&D Munich	CPW	1	300	
	G&D Leipzig	CPW	1 1/2	300	
Finland	Setec OY	SPW	1	200	225 (124)
France	BdF	SPW	2*	700	2 540 (2 265)
	BdF	SPW	1	200	
	FCOF	CPW	2	600	
Greece	GNB	SPW	1	200	617 (---)
Ireland	INB	SPW	1	200	294 (150)
Italy	BdI	SPW	3	600	2 440 (2 200)
Luxembourg	LNB	nil	nil	nil	48 (---)
Netherlands	Enschedé	CPW	2	600	659 (600)
Austria	OeNB	SPW	2	400	550 (460)
Portugal	PNB/DLR-JV	SPW/CPW	1	200	538 (400)
Spain	SNB	SPW	4	800	1 924 (1 900)
Britain (outside euro zone)	DLR-Gateshead	CPW	1	300	(500)**
	BoE/DLR Debden	CPW	2	500	nil

Sources: Industry and own research

Notes: The amounts reflect the average printing capacity calculated for a one-shift operation. Amounts in ( ) indicate the original volume planned for.
Capacity calculations incorporate many parameters: how often the note type to be printed is changed (machinery reconfiguration), the size of note being printed (notes per sheet), how involved the intaglio printing part is, etc. Throughput of 200 million notes per Super line in one-shift operation is not regarded as very ambitious, especially since the government printers produce rather long-running series, with correspondingly little loss of time in reconfiguring. For the private printers the throughput is at least 300 million notes on a line per year. They also work more often in two shifts. The U.S. government's Bureau of Engraving and Printing even runs its machines basically around the clock – with corresponding savings. The capacity figures for web printing by BdF are regarded as high-range estimates.

Abbreviations:
SPW state printing works
CPW commercial printing works

*web printing, all other sheet-fed printing
**printing share only for ECB emergency reserve

units are on one sheet. By doubling the numbering sequence for the reverse side, 108 different numbering sets are needed. And each set costs several thousand euros.[4]

The French patient

With its demands on graphics and quality in printing, ink, and paper, banknote printing is regarded as the crown jewel of graphic art. It demands extreme precision. Color coordination, especially when one color grades smoothly into the next, is painstakingly controlled. Deviations in the depth of the steelplate engraving are measured down to the thousandth of a millimeter. A printer who tries his luck in this challenging market segment need not apply to some commission, pass a test of some panel of masters, or enroll in some trade guild. He must only convince the central bank of his choice that he has the required tools and techniques in order to work up the originals for making a printing plate. And then he has to show that he can produce this institution's banknotes while adhering to the highest standard of quality, security in production, and security in storing the finished notes in his vault. For the euro as well, interested printers who were so qualified had only to list themselves with the European Central Bank. To do so they had to specify their existing – or planned – technical equipment and guarantee in writing that they could carry out the printing order within the allotted time and according to the technical specifications. These declarations were then scrutinized. All printing plants had to produce a »test note« in which were incorporated all the demands that could ever come into question for the euro. This test note revealed to the experts all the technical weaknesses in printing. One episode here illustrated the contradictory stance of the Eurocrats, who true in their search for the lowest common denominator would readily jettison what was tried and true and at the same time bureaucratically puzzle over trifles. The test note for the preparation of euro printing was a fictitious note with a yellowish tint and with the placement of the denomination number and the name of the printer exactly in the middle of the banknote on a crossing of two thick bars. It had absolutely nothing to do with the concrete appearance of the euro notes that came later. Nevertheless, the unusual denomination of »seven« was proposed for it in order to head off abuse. This idea was then scrapped. Yet the outcome of the printing test revealed, as had to have been anticipated, enormous differences among printing plants, and the results required many months of tedious coordination. The quality of a banknote simply does not depend upon machinery alone.

No printer was spared criticism, but in the case of France the test result was devastating, although Banque de France had previously wrested concessions from ECB on the quality specifications. A technical digression is needed to grasp why this was to have far-reaching consequences for the euro. For fear of another German invasion, Banque de France had relocated its entire banknote production to the area of Clermont-Ferrand in central France after the First World War. There it did not use the usual cotton combings, a by-product of yarn production, in its paper mill at Vic-le-Comte for the making of security paper. Used instead was a type of thistle (ramie) also known as China grass, which was obtained from the former Asian colonies. This paper pulp is so hard to drain and dry that only a comparatively thin paper can be made. For this reason the franc notes of ramie paper were always a bit reminiscent of rice paper.

Even in note printing Banque de France went its own way. Its printing plant in Chamalières worked with web printing instead of the commonly used sheet-fed printing. With sheet-fed printing the sheets of paper are individually drawn into the machine and the banknotes are printed on it in a separate step. With the web printing commonplace in newspaper printing, banknotes are printed in a sequence of steps on an endless roll of paper passings channeled into the press as though it were a roll of toilet paper. Web printing was developed in the 1950s by technicians of the state printing works of Bank of England, together with Sweden's Reichsbank and Maschinenfabrik Goebel GmbH of Darmstadt, Germany. It was employed on a grand scale after 1962 for the printing of a new 1-pound note.[5] From the standpoint of productivity, the idea was obvious. But web printing of banknotes had considerable weaknesses and was a commercial flop in the end. Apart from France, only the Algerians, Danes, Norwegians, and Swedes still use it.[6] The English had long since scrapped their last web press by 1989 when the French surprisingly installed two machines of this type.

Banque de France looks back on a brilliant tradition of banknotes that were successful both in graphics and technical security.[7] It had earlier printed its banknotes in the sheet-fed method, too, on machines from Lambert of Paris. But these were regarded as outmoded. Banque de France risked the changeover in order to compensate for the frequent disruptions of production by the militant unions at Vic-le-Comte and Chamalières with the enormous throughput of the web printing presses. Work stoppages, often mere political sympathy strikes, had repeatedly caused embarrassing bottlenecks in supplying France with banknotes. Yet the hope was an illusion. While the web achieves higher speed of production, it is feared for its susceptibility to disruptions and is notorious for its great waste of security paper, which is costly. Moreover, the entire banknote production automatically comes to a halt in an outage, while other production steps can be done during a disruption with sheet-fed printing. In other words, web printing not only causes high additional costs; it can also make a royal mess of the time schedules. Banque de France was about to get a taste of this with the precise deadlines associated with euro printing.

The perfect matching of the printed image on both sides of the banknote in sheet-fed printing can be achieved only with difficulty in the web method. The steelplate engraving is also considerably shallower, losing its tangible relief. Important security characteristics are lost in this way. When the erosion of quality through web printing became too apparent, Chamalières simply set up a steelplate intaglio printing machine from DLR Giori alongside, even in the era of the franc. Web and sheet-fed presses do not go together at all, but cost seemed to be of no concern. Banque de France stubbornly refused to retool completely for sheet-fed printing for the euro. This meant that the imprint of the intaglio was very greatly flattened, sharply diminishing its worth as a security feature. Under pressure from the other national banks, the French did, however, convert Vic-le-Comte to cotton as a raw material, however. For years this paper mill had been marked for closing, a fate circumvented by the resistance of the labor unions. For this reason there was no interest in investing in it. In the interest of homogeneity, therefore, all the other participants had to make do with considerably lighter – and therefore thinner – paper than was universally accepted. For the quality and security of the euro banknotes, this was not without its ramifications. The thin paper had a particularly disturbing effect on the 5-euro note, later causing complaints from the citizens.

The view of the experts of Bundesbank carried great weight in these discussions as well as in the outfitting of the notes with security features. Yet Frankfurt mostly held its tongue. These were hard times for the representatives of Bundesbank. The tug-o-war over the headquarters of the European Central Bank was in full swing. Bundesbank wanted it to be Frankfurt, unconditionally. And on the table there was the application of France's Jean-Claude Trichet to be the first ECB president. Bundesbank was rather reserved about his candidacy. It was not just German representatives of the industry who occasionally had the feeling that Deutsche Bundesbank was exercising »political tolerance« in the discussion of the outfitting of the euro.

The political note

The euro is a political currency. It also became a »political banknote.« It gained this reputation among experts no later than the decision on the design of the banknote. Robert Kalina, the graphic artist of Oesterreichische Nationalbank, was commissioned in December 1996 to design all seven euro denominations. He was singled out for his »windows, gates, and bridges,« symbolizing an open Europe oriented toward the future with its peoples reaching out to one another. For its philosophy it was certainly an original idea, and the drawing of these fanciful images took considerable effort. The symbols could not be classified as somehow national under any circumstances. Nevertheless, the majority of a special selection commission took only days before speaking out for portraits on the euro bills – with good reason. Over the millennia the human being has learned to recognize a face quickly and accurately. He immediately notices anything wrong with a portrait on a banknote. A portrait finely etched in the palpable relief of steelplate engraving on the front of a banknote and the repetitive shading worked into the paper as a fine, multi-toned watermark are still regarded as efficient safeguards against copying, despite the great advances in making reproductions. Only staunchly Islamic countries forgo this proven security characteristic for religious reasons.[8]

European banknotes are known around the world for their outstandingly executed portraits and graphics. One can say without exaggeration that this portrait art of European banknote printers – which improved the security of the note by making it more difficult to copy – is unique. In consideration of national sentiments, the panel that made the award probably could not have chosen any historical personality. For example, instead of the head of Leonardo da Vinci, Columbus, Voltaire, or Martin Luther, an idealized one of a typical but fictitious person was supposed to be reproduced. And this head was supposed to reflect the morphological characteristics of European peoples. A Finnish woman in Salla was supposed to recognize herself in it just as much as a Sicilian man from Trapani. The portrait studies of the graphic artists filled file binders. Some series of drafts were expressly innovative and could have set a trend for modern design of banknotes in graphics and technical security. Instead of this, an historic opportunity was buried in timidity. A guest commentary in the French daily newspaper *Le Monde* later made a point of just this »void and facelessness« of the euro notes as proof for the current crisis of purpose and identity in the EU.[9] The prize jury did not just amaze the whole security industry with its abrupt change of mind in favor of abstract, sterile architectural symbols. It raised the suspicion that maybe there was not so much anonymity at all in the prelude to the »anonymous« design competition conducted under the supervision of a notary. The suspicion that political pressure brought to bear on the panelists in order to orchestrate stronger involvement of even the smaller members of the currency union has still not been laid to rest. After all, the members of the award panel had been nominated by the governors of the national banks.

Whatever the political background of this decision by the award panel may have been, the vote on the graphic design of the euro cleared the way for fixing the security features of the euro. Only now could one decide what would be positioned where in the limited space on the bill. The security features played a key role because the euro was supposed to be secure from counterfeiting to the highest degree. Security features have various functions. They are supposed to protect the public from fraud. And they are supposed to enable machine recognition, inspection, and sorting of the notes – fully mechanized processes absolutely necessary because of the gigantic quantities of paper money that collect daily for inspection of authenticity and condition. These security features are divided into three categories.[10] On the lowest level are those features recognizable by the broadest public – steelplate engraved printing, watermarks, hologram, color-changing ink effect, guilloche border patterns, security threads, transparency spectrum, and so forth. Next come the characteristics that can be checked with special equipment by retailers, banks, and centers with high cash turnover – electronically coded security threads, ultraviolet and infrared features, and magnetism. At the third and highest level are the invisible chemicals and physical properties incorporated into the banknote, including the M feature exclusively offered by Giesecke & Devrient. This last family of security features is covered by absolute secrecy. It allows the central bank to identify its own banknotes beyond doubt. In the matter of the right mixture of security characteristics, money is also the arbiter. Nowadays the most money in the production of banknotes is no longer earned on pure printing. More attractive profit margins come from the business with security features, such as highly secure paper and the diverse characteristics in the printing ink or those placed on the paper or worked into it. Thanks to its special attributes, the paper alone is an important security feature. These characteristics are the domain of private suppliers that are on the cutting edge of security technology because of their continuously high outlays for research and development. Naturally the government printers also develop and improve security features. Yet that is a rather spotty occurrence. Many government printers don't even have their own research departments.

This spelled a further, scarcely acknowledged complication for the national banks in their euro planning. There was an uncommonly high number of potential suppliers for this multinational currency project and all of them had to be considered. Favorable prices and uninterrupted resupply called for avoiding dependency upon certain suppliers. On the other hand the close alignment of the euro notes for protection against counterfeiting demanded the standardization of supporting materials and raw materials. There was agreement that there would have to be at least two sources of supply. But only suppliers within the EU were supposed to be considered and no license fees would be paid. The formulas, even for the most secret of substances, all had to be registered with the European Central Bank. This was not exactly a testimonial to open competition. Yet the limitation to the EU region was not at all inconvenient for the private suppliers, either. Arguing that there was no dearth of intervention to skew competition in the world market for banknotes anyway, some would have preferred having competition narrowed to Euroland only. But private printers and suppliers, which had worked hard for their technological edge, also detected in the specifications an attempt by some national banks to hitch a free ride on their technology. Giesecke & Devrient especially complained out loud.

Ruining competitors with an equipment binge

A lively tug-o-war ensued over the security attributes of the euro. It involved issues of whether there would be steelplate engraved printing on one or both sides and whether the security threads should be mechanical or electronic. There was also infighting over a latent image, color-shifting ink, holograms, and other things. While one player had a feeling that his security features were being deliberately rejected, another would grumble that the new banknotes ought not to be festooned like a Christmas tree. On these choices politicians often had the upper hand over the advice of the experts, those professionals complained. But their advice was not always unbiased, either. Paper and security threads provided an illustrative example of this. Within the euro zone at that time, only France, Italy, and Spain afforded themselves the luxury of a government paper factory. The Spanish plant was the most efficient, while the Italian factory has since been privatized. The other countries bought their banknote paper on the market, mostly from Portals, Louisenthal, and Arjo-Wiggins. For the 15 billion notes of the initial euro issue alone – namely, two-thirds of the total requirement – much more than 12,000 metric tons of secure paper were needed, not counting losses from cutting and misprints. The government paper mills of Europe just could not deliver all of that. One had to fall back on the private manufacturers.

For decades Louisenthal had exclusively delivered the very special paper for all D-mark notes. But it had never had a binding, long-term supply contract with Bundesbank. The Frankfurt central bank had stubbornly refused this. The specifications for the paper for euro production are uniform and the purchase of this paper is open. So, Louisenthal had to assume that its privileged supplier relationship with Bundesbank would end some time. A similar fate would threaten Portals, the exclusive paper maker for pound sterling notes since 1724, if Britain adopts the euro at some point. Both these paper mills are locked in tough competition on the world market. But neither one had an interest in making life difficult for the other with the euro. Portals was therefore always a trifle more expensive than Louisenthal in the bidding for the specific German paper requirement in the euro denominations. And that was not all. Both suppliers attempted to shut less capable competitors out of the market by building high technological hurdles into the paper specifications. Both papermakers suggested incorporating into the euro an extremely wide security thread, imbedded in the paper.[11] This security thread is a polyester thread of 0.9 to 4.0 millimeters in width, cut with extreme accuracy. A coating of precious metal or aluminum is sweated onto it. Information, such as the denomination of the banknote, then is printed on this in precisely placed microscopic script. The wider the thread and more legible the microscript beneath the paper coating, the harder it is for counterfeiters to copy, at least at manageable costs. The introduction of the thread into the paper pulp is complicated, and Louisenthal and Portals had developed a special technique for it. Two layers of wet paper of different thicknesses are put together for this – the technician would say »couched« – and the secure threads are simultaneously included while the fibers of both paper layers are mingled inseparably. No one else had this special forming technology at that time. The competition was supposed to be challenged to death, which is a legitimate strategy for a supplier of a superior technology. Some government and private paper mills, especially France's, saw through this intention and reacted by rejecting the proposal. The euro went with a tiny thread in thin paper instead of a wide security thread. None of this was advantageous for the security of the euro.

Euro bonanza

The wish of many national banks to handle especially the printing of banknotes alone, if possible, and to assign private industry only a bit part in euro production, if necessary, looked more and more divorced from reality as the euro planning advanced. There was no way around the private players, whether as printers, as security paper manufacturers, or as suppliers of supporting materials. And sometimes one of them would be both. Naturally, the private suppliers permitted themselves to be royally compensated for this, as is the case with the private supplier of banknote paper. Although there are no official numbers for paper, one can assume for the German allocation a price in the vicinity of 12,500 euros a metric ton, including M feature and security threads. If this euro paper were then also delivered with kinegram strips, as used in the 5, 10, and 20-euro notes, the price would even double. Gauged by the prices commanded at the same time by Switzerland's Landqart as the paper supplier for both the Swiss franc, which is scarcely less challenging in technical security, and the Austrian schilling, this was a fat premium. And America's Bureau of Engraving and Printing pays only 10,500 Dollars (8,750 euros) per ton of dollar-paper, although it lacks the expensive M feature.

The new family of kinegram and hologram security features that seem to move when viewed from different angles was developed in the late 1980s by Swiss note printer Orell Füssli, optics specialist Landis & Gyr, and Leonhard Kurz GmbH & Co. of Fürth, Germany. Research had been supported financially by Swiss National Bank (SNB). These fixed and moving kinegram or holograms are extremely thin metal films on which respectively two and three-dimensional images are engraved with computer-controlled instruments so that the images change their appearance and color with the angle of incident of light or of viewing. Even before the Swiss, the Austrians became the first to use this new feature for their 5,000-schilling »Mozart« note. Deutsche Bundesbank also equipped its last 50-mark »Balthasar Neumann«, the 100-mark »Clara Schumann,« and 200-mark »Paul Ehrlich« notes with two-dimensional kinegrams.

The market for this family of security features is still developing. Until the introduction of the euro, less than 5 percent of all issued banknotes were fitted with a kinegram. Since these films can be used in all three stages of security bulwark for a banknote – from the citizen to the central bank – the growth of this market is regarded as particularly promising. Dutch experts even regarded these metal films as the ultimate security characteristic.[12] The making of kinegrams is technically demanding. A clean room absolutely free of dust is required for production. Moreover, the glistening, silvery, and extremely thin strips and patches must not react chemically with the paper and may not come loose from the banknote, even if the paper is stretched or shrunk. This partly explains their high price. ECB and the central banks decided that this image on edge – as a strip or a patch – should play a prominent role as a security feature of the euro. Encouraged by its good experience with this in its last Deutschmark series, Bundesbank became a strong proponent of the metal films. This was also justified by the desire for savings. These cost savings, however, were never actually realized because of the technical difficulties in integrating them and the enormous losses this implied. Hologram Industries of Paris actually had hopes of getting into this business. But during the pilot phase it sent a highly secret imprinting die for a kinegram patch to the Kurz company in Nuremberg by normal air freight. It was promptly stolen during the air transport and never turned up again. That did not advance the market entry of Hologram Industries. Kurz, the German specialist for imprinting films, benefited from this. It had already delivered the glistening metallic kinegram patches for the last Deutschmark series. The foil, which was usually introduced during the manufacture of the paper, had been patented by Louisenthal under the designation of »long-lasting economical anticopy device« (LEAD). It had developed these to the serial production stage and had already placed them in the currencies of several African and Asian countries.

Leonhard Kurz and Giesecke & Devrient divided the manufacturing of this »obscenely expensive stuff,« as one expert dubbed the kinegrams. As the supplier of the patches, the Fürth company took over the Swiss patent owner, OVD Kinegram Corp. of Zurich, which was previously a subsidiary of Landis & Gyr. It began producing on a huge scale in the Upper Palatinate. Giesecke & Devrient with Hueck Folien of Weiden entered into a joint venture called High Security Films (HSF) and began producing the strips of film in nearby Baumgartenberg, Austria. These efforts paid off handsomely. The strips are used in the lower euro denominations with high replacement volume. The neat part of this business is that the mounting of the strips of film is usually integrated into the paper production – doubling the already lofty price for secure euro paper, as previously mentioned. As for the patches, their mounting in a difficult hot stamping process can be associated with considerable losses. More than 5 billion of them were needed for denominations starting with 50 euros. They are likely to have cost nearly 7 euros for 1,000 units. Louisenthal, realizing how much money could be made with kinegrams and holograms, suddenly lost interest in the joint venture with Hueck Folien. It set up its own production of film strips at its paper factory compound in Gmund. That was explained by the necessity of having a continually uniform quality. Other suppliers barely got rolling with metal films for the initial euro supply, sometimes because of technical problems.

Finally, the business with special inks also deserves to be classified as a euro bonanza. The cost share of all the inks used on a banknote easily makes up 15 percent of the total manufacturing cost of the note, sometimes even more. Calculations of the ink requirement in banknote printing depend upon the size of the banknote, its design, and the proportion of intaglio printing involved. The intaglio printing weighs especially heavily here because the special intaglio printing ink must be laid on comparatively thickly in order to achieve the tactile effect. As a result of the procedure of wiping the plate cylinders – extraneous ink is wiped off here – about one-third of the intaglio printing ink is lost. There is a similar ratio for the OVI ink with the color-shifting effect. It also has to be laid on thickly for relief so that an optimal color shift is achieved. Because of the cost its use was restricted to denominations starting with the 50-euro note and applied sparingly with a silkscreen.[13] For the 15 billion euro notes of the first supply alone, about 1,500 metric tons of various secure inks were needed, of which more than 80 percent were inks for intaglio printing and nearly 6 percent for the expensive OVI ink. Apart from the small amounts that Gleitsmann was permitted to deliver, this business went exclusively to Switzerland's SICPA.

There were also heated discussions about the use of the M feature exclusively offered by Munich for determining beyond doubt the authenticity of notes by their central banks. Bundesbank saw to it that the M feature was adopted in a special version reserved exclusively for the common currency. Giesecke & Devrient remained the exclusive supplier, of course. The completely invisible M feature is mixed into a special ink color, called »cool gray,« for the euro.[14] But usually the M feature is blown onto a still moist paper layer, leaving a different marker for each denomination. Most of the powder is used for the paper. Naturally, there is no concrete data on the amounts involved, but one can risk a hypothesis. Assuming a requirement of three grams per 1,000 banknotes – in the case of the euro a pure assumption, but realistic in banknotes of other countries – 15 billion notes would take around 45 metric tons of this highly secret powder. The price per kilogram of this powder is no less secret than its composition. But it does permit comparison with quotes from the market for precious metals. And since the M feature is worthless without special sensors, the central banks of Euroland also had to tool up their testing devices with these sensors – another exclusive supplied by Giesecke & Devrient. The price for a single sensor – not a complete testing system – is the equivalent of that for a small car.

Mistakes, mishaps, and misprints

Agreement on the details of the euro's security characteristics cleared the way for the manufacture of printing plates. In order to achieve the desired homogeneity, it was decided that all euro notes of a specific denomination would be printed from an original printing plate, which would be duplicated and used by all printers. Government and private euro printers were supposed to be included in the plate production to the extent that they were technically capable. This division of labor was bound to cause trouble. The production of the so-called originals is complicated. And the specifications of the European Central Bank further complicated the process. For the background printing of the banknote, which is done in indirect relief printing, the printed image is copied from a film to a light-sensitive printing plate. But the original plate is engraved or etched by hand for the steelpate intaglio printing with its tactile relief. In that process the engraver has to carve in a mirror image. The production of printing plates is a highly complex working procedure that calls for much experience. Many a printing plant was in over its head here. Many had to engage help, often even handing over the production of their printing plate entirely to some friendly printer, which is actually strongly frowned upon in this industry. Months of coordination and corrections elapsed before the printing of the test series of real euro banknotes could be risked. Debden, the printer of Bank of England, took part in this dress rehearsal with a few million notes.

The degree of harmonization achieved in this process was very impressive, when one considers the large number of printers and how well the production ran, even though conditions were not quite up to industrial production, as ECB proudly asserted. Some printers probably had turned in hand-picked notes for inspection. Nevertheless, the laboratory of Bundesdruckerei, which scrutinized all notes of the test series from top to bottom, detected deviations. In production norms, quality control, equipment, and capability, the differences among the participating countries were too great. More months of closer coordination between Europe's capitals were required before the traditional »ready to print« was pronounced for every single euro denomination and this clearance could be notarized on the proof sheet of notes with the signature of the printer and the customer. During this period the infant euro became »the most traveled currency in the world,« as one expert joked. The proofs, in fact, were delayed so much that this made a colossal mess, for example, of the planning of Bundesdruckerei for the year 2000.

Still, the number of misprints was shockingly high in the run-up phase to industrial production of the euro banknotes. Some of the specifications set at the planning table were alien to standard practice, people in the printing halls fumed. Even the best of the lot initially reported printing discards in the double-digit percentage range, multiples of the commonplace error rates for regular production. Visitors to France's Chamalières reported a still more dramatic error ratio, just because of the problems described with web printing. Not an official word was said about this. These observations were, however, indirectly confirmed by deliveries received there of supporting materials; ink, for example, which far exceeded the normal requirement for France's national euro printing allocation. There were many outages, mistaken color settings, inadequate tolerances on the facing and reverse sides, ink spots on the notes, and more problems of this nature. There were larger failures, too. Giesecke & Devrient, of all addresses, made a mistake on the 100-euro bill. The production mishap was related to an anti-copying device developed in the mid-1990s by a team of specialists from various central banks in collaboration with the Japanese Business Machine Association. The so-called Omron Effect prevented the reproduction of notes by means of a color copier. For this to work, a large number of little yellow spots are printed on the banknote in seemingly random order. Only an exactly prescribed number of these dots actually have a function. Some of these spots, which appear on both sides of the euro banknote, were missing on the 100-euro banknotes printed in Munich. A change in the computer program, presumably while upgrading this security device, had not been properly stored. There had been a lapse in control. The incident was unpleasant for Giesecke & Devrient. The private printer had already made headlines in autumn 1997 with banknotes of the 100-Deutschemark denomination that were printed on only one side. Static electricity had caused four sheets to stick together so that each was printed on just one side in that incident. This was not discovered until Bundesbank had put the notes in circulation. It had been amusing then. Now no one was laughing.

When Bundesbank learned of this new mistake, the Munich company had already printed and shipped most of the 363 million 100-euro notes that had been ordered. The efficiency of the copying block was not diminished. Bundesbank would like to have laid the matter quietly to rest, but the misprint was made public by a deliberate indiscretion.[15] The report went around the world. The competitors were gleeful. In a statement, ECB announced the destruction of the defective notes and their new printing. This would have meant not only a large financial loss for Giesecke & Devrient; it would also have made the private printer unable to meet the deadlines for its other obligations for euro printing. The printing capacity was lacking for that. The Munich company put up a stiff fight, pointing to hardly less serious mistakes that had been accepted from other euro printers. Giesecke & Devrient prevailed in the end with a proposal that it would fix all the defective notes. Since this involved banknotes already cut and ready for issue, the security precautions needed for the recall were highly complex and highly expensive. The operation was to keep the printer busy until shortly before the euro was issued. This »gnat shit,« as a company spokesman cavalierly dismissed the error, cost the Munich company at least an extra 15 million euros, according to industry estimates.

The euro's series of gaffes and goofs went on. Next hit was a small Italian family company, Mantegazza Antonio Arti Grafiche near Milan. It is a special supplier of security threads, of which more than 1.1 million kilometers were required for the initial euro issue alone. Mantegazza said it was supposed to deliver 60 percent of all the security thread needed for the euro production. Giesecke & Devrient had received the contract for the other 40 percent. A lot of advanced technology is packed into this extremely thin little thread, which one can hardly see. Just the cutting of the minute thread requires the greatest precision. Given the euro pricing logic, this in turn justified a delivery price far above the world market price. Mantegazza is supposed to have calculated nearly 15 euros a kilometer of security thread and was still not happy with its nice order. Giesecke & Devrient was even more expensive. The euro security thread was technically »overloaded.« Too many wishes had to be fulfilled in one item. The polyester thread was too thick. And the microscript printed on it began to flake off after some time in the paper substrate. The flaking also contributed to problems with the paste of the paper after the security thread was embedded in it. One was reminded of the exclusive paper technology of Louisenthal and Portals, which had been turned down. The problem was actually already noticed in autumn 2000 by technicians of the still state-owned Italian paper factory, Cartiere Miliani di Fabriano. And it is hard to believe that the European Central Bank had not gotten wind of this matter soon afterward. But it sat on its hands for a long time. Perhaps it was the horror that paralyzed it. Mantegazza supplied primarily the government paper mills of France, Italy, and Spain, and private papermaker Arjo-Wiggins along with its subsidiary, Van Houtum & Palm. Initial estimates spoke of as many as 4 billion defective notes. The deadline for the introduction of the common currency seemed in danger. When the error became public, the assumed damage was no longer quite so extensive.[16] There was talk in industry circles of as many as 500 million affected banknotes, including some already printed. The error ratio was then reduced with gentle arm-twisting to around 100 million banknotes. Some countries still had to have their allotted denominations printed again, however. Only insurance coverage saved Mantegazza from ruin. But Mantegazza was sold in April 2004 to the Fedrigoni paper company of Verona, which had already taken over the government's security paper plant, Cartiere Miliani di Fabriano. These were not at all the only bloopers. Five-euro notes from Austrian production turned up with printing only on the facing side. In Germany a large number of 50-euro bills from Bundesdruckerei went into circulation with the wrong numbering, and other 50-euro notes were lacking the large denomination numerals on the top right-hand corner. The kinegram film was missing from euro banknotes in Finland. And in Italy the inspection system refused to function because the security thread was defective.

All these things were no trifles, certainly not in the world of high-security printers that are accustomed to the greatest precision. But these mistakes no longer stirred great interest. There had also been printing errors with the national currencies of Europe in the past, and the public had become accustomed to the reports of euro bungling. One probably could have supposed that something like this was no longer possible. Right after the printing mistake of Giesecke & Devrient, additional electronic systems for quality control were installed by some printers to intercept such production mistakes. Yet, one couldn't even speak of an alignment of quality control. The quality standards and the necessary degree of harmonization became perennial topics.

The unloved rescuers

On balance, the euro's printing was no less of a test of nerves than its planning. The Portuguese central bank had problems with its new printing plant and had to call upon the help of De La Rue – and others – more and more frequently, although it had waived the printing of the highest euro notes entirely. The Greeks, the last to join the currency union, needed assistance because their printing plant was not equal to the task. Luckily, those two countries are small. The more serious problems proved to be in Italy, where 2.5 billion notes had to be printed, the second-largest volume of euro notes anywhere, as mentioned. It was apparent that this could hardly be accomplished in time. Banca d'Italia asked Giesecke & Devrient about helping out, practically triggering a revolt of the labor unions in its Roman note-printing plant. Among insiders, this plant was a notorious »viper's lair.« Since not all the euro notes were needed on deadline, Rome chose to be »flexible.« It stuck to its guns that it would print all its euros itself, but decided simply to catch up in the following year on the printing of the portion of notes that could not be done on time. In the end this was the entire logistical and strategic reserve, which had to be delivered after the introduction of the euro during 2002.[17] The Spanish, who had waived their own printing of the 200- and 500-euro notes anyway, also had to resort to the »Italian solution« despite their generously proportioned capacity. Disquieting was also the situation at the printing plant of Banque de France, where management and union officials fought to the bitter end about measures for restructuring and modernization. There were several strikes, sometimes lasting weeks. On top of this came the aforementioned problems with the web presses. Practically the entire management was changed in Chamalières. After that, Chamalières concentrated on the printing of the 5, 10, 20, and 50-euro notes, without even entirely managing just that. It transferred the printing of higher denominations to other banknote printers. The Belgian state printing works and François Charles Oberthur Fiduciaire had to be asked for help. Also requested to help was Giesecke & Devrient, with whom there had been such a big dispute over the French desire for lower standards of quality. This request was an admission of failure. The cost went on the tab of the French taxpayers.

Now the idea of pooling certain denominations for production by assigned printers unexpectedly regained respectability. Under deadline pressure for the approaching introduction, printers who had previously eschewed any cooperation joined hands. Above all, the higher euro denominations with their comparatively small volumes were found to be too labor-intensive and technically too complicated. A lively swapping of printing allocations suddenly set in. The Dutch and Austrians bundled some volumes and both together printed for Greece. The Belgians printed for France and Spain; Bundesdruckerei for Greece and Luxembourg. De La Rue not only assisted Portugal but also printed for Finland and Ireland. The Irish also finally printed for Portugal, while Giesecke & Devrient printed for France, Greece, the Netherlands, Portugal, and Spain. This became a lively European roundelay. European Central Bank became nervous and decided upon an additional printing of an ECB emergency reserve that was supposed to bridge bottlenecks in banknote supply on the deadline day. The government printers had no capacity to spare but fought bitterly for the order. After protracted negotiations, the printing order went to a consortium of private printers consisting of Giesecke & Devrient, De La Rue, Joh. Enschedé, and Bundesdruckerei, which had been privatized in the meantime. This quartet produced the nearly 1.8 billion notes, with Giesecke & Devrient garnering the lion's share as consortium leader. Switzerland's Orell Füssli was not allowed to print, despite fallow capacity – and an attractive price.

At the end of the day, the nine government printers accomplished only with difficulty the printing of 52 percent of the euro notes despite their gigantic combined capacity. The rest had to be printed by five private printers.[18] If there were in this euro marathon a winner by default, it would probably be Giesecke & Devrient. It alone printed more than 25 percent of all the euro notes. Munich had imposed forceful rationalization for this challenge, and it had risked just that expansion of printing capacity from which any private printer would have refrained in fear for its future operating rates. The overriding conditions – handsomely paid euro printing and the publicly subsidized formation of jobs in the new eastern German states – were too tempting. In this way the company's original plant at Leipzig, bought back from the government trust set up for the industrial holdings of what had been East Germany, was modernized and equipped with printing capacity aligned to the euro. The full vertical integration of this high-security corporation printed not just notes, however. Giesecke & Devrient delivered nearly everything, from paper and supporting material to machinery for banknote processing, sensors for production control, and shredding equipment. It was this euro effect that was responsible for the highest group sales in the company's history in the 2001 business year – just in time for the company's 150th birthday.

Euro quality

The manufacture of euro notes progressed under extraordinary conditions. In the course of its difficult inception, the common currency of the twelve countries mutated into a true mutual enterprise, such as the fathers of the euro had scarcely anticipated. Nine paper mills, fifteen note printers, and more than twenty other suppliers finally had become involved in the production. For the experts this was a nightmare of work and technical security precautions. This fragmentation violated a basic rule of high-security printing, namely that the handling of all stages of the work must be concentrated as much as possible in order to discourage the abuse of original materials. Moreover, too many cooks spoil the broth, even in banknote printing. The requirement that the notes look and feel alike, that they are absolutely identical in both optical and tactile characteristics, could hardly be fulfilled with this fragmentation of production. Naturally, there have been discrepancies in the production of smaller series of banknotes, even in the time of the Deutschmark in Germany. How much greater is the number of potential sources of error when 15 billion notes have to be printed in one go? The inhabitants of Pantelleria or Lampedusa might take umbrage that some Italian islands are missing from the map of Europe on the reverse side of all euro banknotes. Even so, this was not a catastrophe. There are precedents with other currencies. Even the missing title under the illegible signature of the president of the European Central Bank has a less disturbing effect, when one considers how many languages there are in the common currency sphere and how little room there is on a banknote. The same consideration applies to the Braille writing, found only on the 200 and 500-euro notes. This writing is in dispute among associations of the blind, anyway. They fear that the threshold of deference toward sightless persons and those with impaired vision might be lowered. Counterfeiters usually shrink from frauds against such persons.

Because banknotes are a governmental promise of value, especially high standards of manufacturing quality are imposed on them. The euro leaves something to be desired here. A glaring weakness of the euro notes is without a doubt the far too flat intaglio printing that is also done only on the facing side. More than that was not possible because of the French web printing. Some of the watermarks are of great simplicity and many are inadequate in their gradation from bright to dark. Why the watermark of the 5-euro note is of so much better quality than that of the 50-euro note, which is much more vulnerable to counterfeiting, must remain the secret of the Eurocrats. Although demonstratively expensive, the security features of kinegram strips or patches were decided upon, and they were positioned on the unprinted spaces of the banknote. And to top it off, the Eurocrats even dispensed with the important steelplate intaglio overprint on the kinegram patches. For German, Finnish, Dutch, and Austrian banknotes, a colored background *under* the kinegram and steelplate engraved printing *on* the patch had been the norm. That was not done with the euro because most of the government printing works were technically incapable of doing this, especially the French with their web presses. Therefore, despite the explicit warnings of counterfeiting experts, this important security feature against copying had to be set aside, with grave consequences for the security of the higher euro denominations, as we now know. And if that were not enough, there were also color deviations. For example, in the denominating numerals at the bottom left of the front side of the 10-euro note, the precisely prescribed share of red to brown coloring actually deviated considerably on some euro notes. Or there were sometimes bright and sometimes dark green tints on the reverse side of the 100-euro note, depending upon which country and producer was involved. Euro notes initially even react differently under ultraviolet light, depending upon the country of their manufacture. And, while the OVI effect of the color-shifting ink changed as specified for the higher euro denominations, the effect was often different. Rounding this out, the microprint has to be mentioned briefly. At the request of some printers it had to be enlarged so much that the term »micro« hardly applies anymore on these euro notes.

Table IV: Country code (verso)

Z: Belgium	S: Italy
X: Germany	R: Luxembourg
L: Finland	P: Netherlands
U: France	N: Austria
Y: Greece	M: Portugal
T: Ireland	V: Spain

Country codes reserved for later entries: W – Denmark; J – England; K – Sweden.

Note: The Internet website of the European Central Bank uses for Luxembourg also the country codes of the national banks that the country engaged for its printing, namely Belgium – Z; Germany – X; Netherlands – P, etc.

Table V: Printing plant code (recto)

T: Imprimerie de la Banque Nationale de Belgique, Belgium
R: Bundesdruckerei (private), Germany
P: Giesecke & Devrient (private), Germany
D: Setec OY (semi-public), Finland
L: Imprimerie de la Banque de France, France
E: Francois Charles Oberthur Fiduciaire (private), France
N: printing works of the Greek central bank, Greece
H: De La Rue (private), Britain
K: Bank of Ireland printing works, Ireland
J: Officina Cartevalori della Banca d'Italia, Italy
G: Joh. Enschedé en Zonen (private), Netherlands
F: printing works of Oesterreichische Nationalbank, Austria
U: printing works of Banco do Portugal, Portugal
M: Fábrica Nazional de Moneda y Timbre, Spain
Codes reserved for later entry:
A: Bank of England printing works, England
C: Tumba (private), Sweden
S: printing plant of the Danish central bank

Perhaps the layman did not notice all of these deficiencies and discrepancies on the initial series of euro banknotes. For professionals they were unacceptable. Yet, that subject is taboo to this very day. With respect to the euro's printing quality, European Central Bank has pursued a systematic and critical review but takes the position that the public should not be upset. Individual producers are not supposed to be identified. For fear of endangering the acceptance of certain euro notes, for example, only a country code of euro bills was published. It tells which national bank issued which euro note. The country code is on the (verso) reverse side of the banknote in the twelve-digit serial number in which the starting letter identifies the national bank of issue. For example, U stands for France and S for Italy. But the euro note of any Euroland country can only be traced to its printer through a secret printer code on the (recto) facing side. Of course, the significance of the combinations of numbers on the facing and reverse sides of the euro banknotes or the details of who printed for whom can be found in detail on the Internet[19] (see also Tables IV and V). The information on the printer comes in a so-called short code, which is hidden in various places on the face of the note, depending upon its denomination. The suggestion of the police to print the code on the same spot on all notes was rejected, incidentally, with the argument that this would infringe on the creativity of the graphic artist. The short code identifies the banknote printer and contains various coding for the printing plate employed, the series, and the position of the unit on the sheet. Accordingly, the country code U on the reverse side together with the printer code L on the face would say that this banknote is part of France's initial supply and was printed by its own state printing works. The same country code in combination with the printer code T on the face would reveal that this was in fact a note from Banque de France but that it had been printed by the state printing works of Belgium. And the short code F002C2 on a euro note reveals the printer Oesterreichische Banknoten- und Sicherheitsdruck GmbH, indicates the banknote series 2002, and gives the precise position of this unit on the sheet.

Not even ECB would assert that the euro banknotes, with their bland and borderless images partly in rather dull colors, represent the graphic or technical level of banknote printing in Europe. Europe's banknote printers could have done better – had they been allowed. The notes are the least common denominator of countless compromises – a product perhaps unavoidable for the start of such an ambitious project. But what a damaging start. It caters very considerably to the nefarious craft of the counterfeiter.

11
Why there is a problem with the euro's security

Money has probably been counterfeited ever since this abstract medium of payment has existed. Certainly this applies to coins, and it applies even more to banknotes. They are so easy to copy because it takes only a rectangular piece of paper, a small quantity of four basic colors of ink – magenta red, yellow, cyanide blue, black – and a bit of technical skill with photography and printing. Presto, a worthless slip of blank paper becomes a valuable banknote! The facility of copying paper money poses a unique threat: there is no absolute safeguard against counterfeiting it. »The human hand can copy all that the human hand creates,« Baron von Eichthal observed in 1843, when he was the director in charge of note issuing for Bayerische Hypotheken- und Wechsel-Bank.[1] Without reservation and despite all the new security precautions, these words still ring true.

Ever since French painter Louis J. Daguerre introduced his first photograph in 1837, the rapid development of graphic arts, often in leaps and bounds, has condemned the central banks and their banknote printers to an unrelenting race with counterfeiters. With their state-of-the-art printing capability, they strive to stay a nose ahead. Because the counterfeiters have their own continually improving possibilities for reproduction, the central banks have tried to make the copying of their notes as technically complicated as they possibly can by using special paper that is not optically brightened, complex graphic designs, multicolored printed images with smooth transitions of coloring and composition, and many other security features. The intention, of course, is ideally to make copying so expensive that the counterfeiter's effort is no longer worthwhile. For apart from the production of his copy, he must also consider the cost of its distribution. And distribution is often the

Moneymakers, Klaus W. Bender

ISBN: 3-527-50236-X

most risky part of the business. If he engages a middleman for this, he sometimes has to grant a large discount from the face value of the counterfeit note.

The most effective protection against copying is the raised, intaglio printing that can be recognized at a touch of the finger. Ever since Gualtiero Giori's development of his new intaglio printing machines and the gradual adoption of his new technique after the Second World War, not a single instance of a counterfeiter copying this intaglio characteristic has become known. The production of intaglio printing plates is much too complicated and expensive for counterfeiters. Of course, the counterfeiter is not striving for a 100 percent copy of the real banknote. The *impression* of authenticity suffices for him. His deception only has to work once. He does not care what happens thereafter with his »dud,« as policemen call counterfeit notes.

Digifeiting, the new copying quality

The traditional counterfeiter was a single perpetrator – often a loner – and therefore hard to detect. But his elaborate work with the camera and offset press left traces. The counterfeiter needed a workshop and materials. For example, the French police sought the master counterfeiter Czeslaw Bojarski in vain for fourteen years. When they finally apprehended Bojarski in Paris in January 1964, this loner, who was known for his elegant and unobtrusive appearance, had spread among the people phony money worth several hundred million old and new French francs (*anciens et nouveaux francs*). The damage done was the equivalent of several million euros today, if one takes into consideration the purchasing power of the fifties and early sixties. Bojarski's counterfeits, in fact, were so perfect that Banque de France felt compelled to compensate the cheated citizenry for the damage, a highly unusual step. It did not do this out of compassion; public criticism of the inadequate security of its franc notes from counterfeiting had simply become too loud.

The art of counterfeiting has changed fundamentally since the 1980s.[2] It is increasingly hard for the central banks to stay ahead because many of their weapons have become blunt. The quantum leap in the quality of banknote copying began when the color copier replaced the camera as a tool. One could prevent the danger posed by color copiers with the Omron copying safeguard, already mentioned, which had been introduced in the nineties, provided the counterfeiter was not using one of the old machines or knew how to manipulate the image-processing program of a new copying machine. With advances in digital reproduction technology, even the Omron hurdle was finally vaulted by counterfeiters. No automatic blocking device stands in the way of digital reproduction anymore. With these digital systems, moreover, the close matching of lines and colors and the filtering out of gray tones and blurring colors in the image of a counterfeit bill are possible. Even the special typeface of banknote numbering, which is not commercially available, can be imitated on a personal computer with deceptive authenticity and with sequential numbering. Combined with a flatbed scanner and a laser or ink-jet printer, a PC easily allows copying with »acceptable quality« – a double entendre – in any volume and at any time. This way of counterfeiting leaves no traces. Anyone can buy such equipment for a reasonable price, tailored to individual requirements, at a local store and install it at home. This new, computerized reproduction technology attached to a printer has even blazed the trail for a new type of counterfeiter, the amateur, and partly explains the strikingly high proportion of youthful perpetrators of money copying offenses. To date, the youngest PC counterfeiter caught by police was seven years old. Now another threat is posed by the spread of digital, offset printing machines, distinguished by an unprecedented printing quality and high printing performance, but they are comparatively expensive and not easily obtained. The anonymity desired by counterfeiters cannot be preserved in the purchase. Yet, this lack of anonymity is no guarantee against abuse. That was shown, for example, by the discovery of a printing plant for counterfeit euros in Lithuania. By day, this printer produced printed literature and documents for the Lithuanian government; by night, it produced phony euro notes on the same machines. The fact that this printing establishment was serving the government also hindered the police investigation considerably. Digital reproduction and printing technology have finally caused counterfeiting gangs to replace the lone counterfeiter. These gangs pursue this business on a large scale and operate across borders. Not only can all data needed for the printing process be stored safely until it is needed next but also transmitted through the Internet. In 2004, when a printing establishment for counterfeit money was broken up in Bulgaria, the joy of the police over this successful crackdown on copiers was short lived. It turned out that the complex printing procedure, from the design of banknotes to the color of the inks, was burned on a compact memory disc. Stored on the CD was even a list of suppliers on the world market from whom the counterfeiters could obtain their required supplies; for example, copied security threads, imitated kinegrams, and duplicated color-shifting ink. And then it was discovered that this highly professional gang of counterfeiters had done a brisk business selling copies of this disk. They had marketed their technological knowledge. While there were once ten thousand counterfeiters for every five phony bills, today five counterfeiters can easily make tens of thousands of false notes, warns a film from the Bureau of Engraving and Printing.

The central banks, the counterfeiting experts of the national police authorities, and the international police agency ICPO-Interpol in Lyon, which is commissioned by an international convention to combat counterfeit money, speak of a new quality of banknote copying with the so-called *digifeiting*. Statistics confirm this. According to data presented at the seventh Interpol Conference on Currency Counterfeiting in 1987 in Lyon, half of all the counterfeit notes removed from circulation had been made with cameras. Only ten percent had come from color copiers, and the rest, from so-called nuisance counterfeits. As reported a decade later, at the ninth Interpol conference in Helsinki, the proportion of banknotes copied with electronic equipment – most of it digital – had surged to nearly 90 percent. Of that 90 percent, Interpol estimated only a third had involved color copiers. The remaining 10 percent were allotted to camera copying and an almost insignificant amount of nuisance counterfeiting. This increased use of digifeiting could be observed, according to the message of the conference, around the world in Europe, Africa, Asia, and the two Americas.

Under the aegis of the Bank for International Settlements (BIS) in Basel, the central banks have been following the development of reproduction technology with an Argus eye. In 2000, the central-bank governors in the Group of Ten leading industrialized countries created a special working group to seek technological answers to the growing threat of digifeiting and to work together with the industry. Given the internationalization of counterfeiting gangs, the development of deterrent weapons also has to be pursued across borders. This working group, called the Central Bank Counterfeit Deterrence Group (CBCDG), includes central banks and their government banknote printers. Because there are too many equipment manufacturers in the world for the Deterrence Group to watch effectively, it focuses its guard primarily on the less numerous producers of picture-processing software. In response to this special working group's requests, the Japanese electronics company Canon has come on the market with an innovative security feature called bitmap. The technologically outmoded Omron recognizes the banknote and triggers a copying block, whereas bitmap recognizes not only the banknote but also registers the date, time, and running number of copies, as well as the encoded serial number of the device, when a banknote is reproduced. Using bitmap, the counterfeiter practically delivers his calling card along with the copied bill. This assumes, however, that the devices are actually registered when sold by the dealer. In early 2004, the BIS working group reported the successful development of bitmap for the computer and other digital reproduction devices. The new system has been voluntarily adopted by some leading manufacturers of computer hardware and software, it said.[3] Bitmap has been placed on the dollar and euro banknotes. Now it is regarded as rather effective protection. But how long will this technique stand in the way of professional counterfeiters of banknotes? Toward the end of 2005 the international media, particularly the English service of the Arabic Aljazeera.net, reported that computer experts of the U.S. Electronic Frontier Foundation (EFF) had succeeded in cracking this secret code for the devices of a number of manufacturers. The police were not happy about the publicity. The decoding information has not yet helped the counterfeiters. But this is the first step toward neutralizing this security feature someday. More than ever in the age of information technology the before-mentioned maxim applies: »That which can be wrought by human agency can also be destroyed by it.« A small indication of how seriously Interpol now takes this situation is seen in the frequency with which it holds its conferences on counterfeiting of banknotes – and identification documents. They were previously held every ten years, then every five years. Interpol now issues its invitations every four years. In the struggle against digifeiting the exchange of information must be intensified because the threatening conditions are constantly changing.

The professional bands of counterfeiters react with incredible speed to changing techniques, using the latest developments for their copying. For example, forged Swiss franc notes are now almost exclusively counterfeits from personal computers. Swiss banknotes have a very complex design that is easier to copy than to engrave, although the distribution possibilities of counterfeited Swiss banknotes in that small country are limited. But another reason is that the current note series, which has been in circulation for a decade and was once a model of secure composition, is now lacking the latest security features and is therefore partly outmoded. In contrast, the vast majority of counterfeit dollar and euro notes that are turning up in Europe are printed. Why? Because both note series are comparatively young and their up-to-date security features make duplication by copier more difficult.

Icon in distress

Europe's common currency has fundamentally changed the world map of monetary policy. For the first time in recent history there are two currency blocks, dollar and euro. For the first time central banks and private entities have a free choice in their investment decisions between two currencies of global importance. The continuing twin deficits in the U.S. budget and current account have made the dollar a topic of discussion. The flood of this paper is rising. During the last twenty-five years the Bureau of Engraving and Printing has increased the number of dollar notes printed each year by a factor of 2.5 to around 9 billion notes, while its printing of the 50-dollar note increased by a factor of 4, and of the 100-dollar note by 5. The »icon« in the fight against inflationary mismanagement and monetary policy caprice, as financial expert Wilhelm Hankel of the Bologna center of Johns Hopkins University years ago called the dollar, has shed some of its luster. Many European observers foresee an important role for the euro on the globalized financial market. In keeping with those expectations and in an effort to spread their risk, more and more private investors are deciding for investments booked in the euro rather than in the dollar. Central banks are likely to do the same, making the euro a global reserve currency.[4] Naturally the euro optimists know that the confederation of loosely affiliated Euroland countries cannot lay claim to the same political weight as the United States of America, not to mention the military might of this last remaining superpower. But measured by the mere size of its market, they argue, the euro zone of 309 million consumers, excluding Britain, Denmark, and Sweden, can certainly measure up to the United States. And including the 75 million residents of the ten new EU member countries, all wanting to have the euro as well, this market will soon far outweigh the United States.[5] Moreover, the pool of potential investors has widened, compared with that of the twelve national currencies the euro has replaced. In the three years since its inception as a printed currency, in 2002, the euro has taken over the role of a parallel currency in many countries of eastern Europe. On the southern littoral of the Mediterranean and in Africa its importance as a store of value is rising. ECB estimates that 15 percent of the issued euro notes, valued at 501 billion euros at the end of 2004, are being held outside the euro zone.[6] The euro's share of global currency reserves, which was 25 percent at the end of 2004 according to IMF, is rising too.[7] This share is more than the twelve national currencies ever achieved together. Among the twelve, only the Deutschmark played a certain role as an international reserve currency. When the euro was adopted in 1999 as an accounting currency, the Deutsche Bundesbank had estimated that between 30 and 40 percent of all D-marks circulating were held abroad. But the total volume of D-marks issued then was only 274 billion (140 billion euros).

In the passionate discussion on the future of the dollar, not everyone shares this euro optimism – not everyone in Europe, and especially not everyone in the United States. There is no shortage of rebuttals. The gross domestic product of the twelve euro countries amounts to only 75 percent of the U.S. GDP. And the U.S. economy is growing strongly, while Euroland has stagnated for years. Moreover, Euroland traditionally has been earning a small surplus on the current account or has at least had a current account that is roughly in balance. Large euro positions are therefore difficult to amass abroad. The United States remains the biggest importing country in the world, and nearly half of the international commercial transactions are still priced in dollars. This applies especially for crude oil. Iran has plans to build its own derivatives exchange for oil, the Iranian Oil Exchange, and to convert its crude oil transactions simultaneously to the euro. But those are still just plans. In fact, the strongly diverging ratios for the euro and the dollar are easily overlooked. The dollar's share of global currency reserves was still an impressive 66 percent at the end of 2004. And the moderate decline of 5 percentage points in this share since 1999 might be attributable to exchange-rate fluctuations. Conversely, the calculation of the euro's share in global currency reserves was made in nominal terms and could therefore be the result of the strong euro exchange rate on the day the statistic was compiled at the end of 2004.

According to an estimate by the Federal Reserve, 66 percent of the banknotes it had issued by the end of 2002 for a value of 620 million dollars were held abroad. That Fed estimate may be a bit high. Currency expert Ed Feige of the University of Wisconsin assumes the foreign holdings to be less than 50 percent. Still, this remains a volume of dollars for which an investment alternative is nowhere to be seen. Mieczyslaw Karczmar, the New York economic adviser of Deutsche Bank, has focused the discussion: The true cause of the twin deficits lies in the boundless momentum of the U.S. economy. If America is really living beyond its means, it has been doing this with impunity for quite a long time and will continue to do this without incurring damage, he predicts. There really is no investment alternative to the dollar, Karczmar and his colleague Robert Solomon from the Brookings Institution insist .[8]

This discussion about the future of the dollar and the euro is not simply prompted by national vanities. It is hard-headed business. A high proportion of a given currency held abroad improves the liquidity of the capital market in this currency. And it raises the revenue of the issuing country by means of *seigniorage*, an ancient term with a modern sense. This term is little known, but it plays an important role in a country's financing. It comes from the Middle Ages and describes the value added by minting coins, namely the difference between the precious metal in the coin and the face value of the coin. This added value was a tribute to the ruler, the *seigneur*. Today it is used to mean, among other things, the difference between the cost of the production and provision of a banknote and its buying power. This difference is due the government. But when a commercial bank obtains money (banknotes and coins) from its central bank, it must put up securities as collateral. The interest accrued by these securities flows to the central bank. The central bank in turn surrenders its profit to the government, which includes these funds in its budget. That can add up to a considerable sum. In 2000, when interest rates were still comparatively high, the Fed said that it had received 32.7 billion dollars in seigniorage.[9] As a hypothetical numbers game, taking just the share of dollar notes voluntarily held abroad, foreigners then had to pay the Fed 21.6 billion dollars in seigniorage that year alone. Comparing this interest income with the half a billion dollars the Fed spends each year for printing notes, one could say this is a splendid business.

A global reserve and repository currency is considerably more exposed to the danger of counterfeiting than a currency of limited circulation abroad. The battle against counterfeiters becomes especially acute, and Americans and Europeans traditionally have used different tactics because they pursue divergent philosophies on banknotes.[10] Like the majority of all countries, the Europeans bank on *prevention*; copying is supposed to be made as difficult, and therefore as expensive, as possible. The Americans count on *repression*; the counterfeiter is supposed to be rigorously punished. That has direct repercussions for the design and security composition of the banknotes. For European notes – even the national notes before the euro – the dimensions of the banknote increases with its face value. This is also supposed to help persons with impaired vision. The printed image is multicolored and various colors are reserved for each denomination. In addition, the paper is slightly tinted in keeping with the particular background color of each denomination. The dollar notes issued by the Federal Reserve System are strictly identical in their dimensions. The slight coloration of the paper is uniformly greenish white. The printed images are colored strictly in black on the facing side and in green on the reverse side. In any event, this was how it had been until recently. At all three steps of authentication, European notes are chock full of visible and invisible features as protection against counterfeiting. Until the start of the 1990s, dollar notes had no security features at all, no multi-tone, localized watermark, no security thread, and no chemical or physical markers in the printing ink. The robust dollar paper and the raised intaglio printing had to suffice as authentication. This intaglio-engraved printing on both sides was originally even prescribed by the Federal Reserve Act of 1913, but it was modified by regulation in 1981.

It is easy to understand why all banknotes in Europe have to be taken out of circulation after a certain scheduled period and replaced by a new series: their security composition is outmoded. In the United States, no series of greenback has ever been declared invalid since 1863! The 500-dollar note remains legal tender, although it was issued by the Fed for the last time in 1934 and has completely disappeared from circulation today. Whoever so desires can even pay with one of those decorative silver-certificate dollar notes of the late 19th century – this assumes, of course, that he is undisturbed that the collector's value of this bill is much higher than its face value. The United States deliberately places prime importance on the unlimited validity and the nearly unchanged appearance of its dollar notes as confidence-building factors at home and abroad. Success has proven the Fed right. And when a change in banknote design occurs, this can impose bizarre strictures. When the Fed finally wanted to introduce new banknotes in the 1990s, for example, it introduced the new series abroad in only one place: Moscow. The stash of hoarded dollar notes is especially large in post-Soviet Russia.

The organization of the Americans and the Europeans in the fight against counterfeiters and counterfeiting is also different. In America the law enforcement is centralized; almost since the birth of the greenback, it has been entrusted to the U.S. Secret Service. The towering distinction of this secret service is underscored by the fact that its second exclusive mission – its first, some insiders might say – is the physical protection of the U.S. president. In the battle against counterfeiters, however, the Secret Service concentrates on the U.S. homeland, and as a result, the frequency of bogus dollar notes in the United States has been comparatively low for decades. Behind this strategy is the thought that only counterfeit dollar notes placed in circulation within the United States can cause economic damage to America. Of the 173 million dollars worth of bogus dollar notes reported by the Fed for the year 2001, only 60 million dollars worth were traced to the U.S. homeland. The main damage occurred abroad. According to experts, the amount of undetected dollar counterfeits abroad is even larger, because many counterfeit dollars are not recognized as such or are simply not reported to Interpol by the respective central bank. For many years fighting dollar counterfeits abroad was of no real interest to the Secret Service. Even today the U.S. Secret Service owes its zeal for the international hunt for counterfeiters more to the U.S. global war against terrorism than to the conviction that the citizens of the world have to be protected against bogus dollar notes. All the information concerning counterfeit banknotes that is gathered abroad by the Secret Service is automatically passed on to the CIA.

Mysterious supernote

The American policy of »benign neglect« has not necessarily done the dollar any good. Over the years the »almighty greenback« has been far and away the most counterfeited currency in the world. Its worldwide distribution and its inadequate security composition practically invited this. For years the increase of dollar counterfeits disturbed no one in Washington. A counterfeit 100-dollar note that turned up in 1989 in a Philippine bank in Manila was the first to make headlines. Everything about this perfectly copied counterfeit note was correct. Its perfection began with the special dollar paper, for which one needs a Fourdrinier machine not used by any other country. Topping that off was the raised intaglio printing so typical of the dollar. Strictly speaking, this was no counterfeit note in the classical sense, but rather an illegal parallel print done on an original intaglio printing machine from DLR Giori, such as those used by the Bureau of Engraving and Printing. The bogus bill was only detected by chance. No lone counterfeiter could afford such technical and financial outlays. A government had to be been behind it. Respectfully christened »supernote« or »superdollar,« more of these bogus 100-dollar bills soon were detected in other parts of the world. Sixty percent by value of the aforementioned 620 billion dollars worth of notes issued by the Fed are held in the 100-dollar denomination. The potential threat seemed enormous, and the excitement was great. Special agents of the Secret Service swarmed out of their American borders into the world like bees from a shaken hive. Estimates were soon making the rounds that the supernote could have been printed in a press run of millions of bogus notes. Congressmen and experts of the Fed as well as the Bureau of Engraving and Printing expressed the suspicion during a congressional hearing that this could be economic warfare against the United States with the aim of destabilizing the dollar. This suspicion was hardly hyperbole. There are enough examples of such things in history.[11]

The supernote created an uproar among police investigators around the globe. And it gave the high-security industry many a restless night. Printing presses for banknotes have their special printing idiosyncrasies. Moreover, the origin of the security ink on a banknote can be precisely determined with the help of chemical analysis, right down to a particular batch of production. Machinery supplier De La Rue Giori and security ink manufacturer SICPA had to suffer through pointed interrogation by the Secret Service. Initial suspicion devolved upon North Korea as a customer of DLR Giori and SICPA. A hot trail seemed to lead to Berlin. After the Berlin Wall fell in 1989, a special printing plant of the Stasi State Security Agency of defunct East Germany was found in East Berlin. Protected by barbed wire and spotlights behind a double wall in the Hohenschönhausen district of the city, a high-security printing plant with modern equipment was discovered on a plot of 2.5 hectares. It even had a small paper machine on which a few hundred sheets per hour of security paper of either cylinder mold or Fourdrinier process could be manufactured as needed. About a hundred highly qualified specialists from this counterfeiting factory gave assurances that only personal identifications and other documents had been counterfeited there. They said banknotes had never been counterfeited. Representatives of the West German police and technicians from high-security printer Giesecke & Devrient turned the plant inside out. Not only did they discover that all Stasi employees had carefully obliterated any clue to their military rank before the arrival of the West Germans, but that incriminating materials and machines had been systematically carried off from the plant – perhaps to Russia. Missing from such a perfectly equipped counterfeiting factory, for example, was an intaglio printing machine, which is indispensable even for counterfeiting passports. And Fourdrinier paper is not needed for printing a passport, but rather for printing the dollar. Indeed, large batches of supernotes have turned up again and again in Berlin, often in the baggage of visiting North Korean diplomats or businessmen, even long after the Iron Curtain fell. Had the Stasi perhaps instructed the North Koreans in the high art of engraving printing plates and printing notes, perhaps at the request of the Russian KGB? Experts are certain today that the Stasi men had at least schooled technicians of friendly countries in the counterfeiting of banknotes. But the German sleuths and the allied European services were unable to show a trail to Pyongyang. Even a delegation from the U.S. Secret Service inspected the special printing plant before it was dismantled and closed. The Americans compared notes continually with their West German colleagues and even traveled to Munich to Giesecke & Devrient. The Secret Service seemed convinced of the East Berlin-Pyongyang axis but later refused to provide any information on the progress of its investigation. Through informal channels it was learned only that an unusually high concentration of heavy metals was detected in the paper of the supernotes and that this information could point to a paper factory in the former Soviet empire as the supplier. But which one?

The Iranians and Syrians were next to be accused of printing the supernote and of having put it into circulation through the Hizbollah in Libanon's Bekaa Valley. Damascus, however, has its note printing done abroad in Pakistan and could have only figured into this at best as a distributor. Hardly more convincing was the accusation against Iran. An internationally recognized expert with an intimate knowledge of the Iranian security printing plant is convinced that such an ambitious counterfeiting operation, with all its logistics, could not have been concealed from him during his repeated visits to Teheran. Naturally, both governments denied the accusations. In the summer of 2004, the British BBC warmed up the assertion in its *Panorama* television program that the supernote was made in North Korea and that its distribution was supported by secret Russian agents of the former KGB. The television film specifically dealt with a large batch of supernotes brought to western Europe by a radical wing of the underground Irish Republican Army. Named as a person possibly involved was Sean Garland, president of the Irish Workers' Party. Apart from British and U.S. agents, a high-ranking defector from North Korea was trotted out as the star witness for supposedly having worked on the counterfeiting of the money in North Korea. However, the case described by *Panorama* had unfolded some years ago; it had long since been settled before British courts. And Panorama did not report that this was not the only IRA shipment of supernotes to be exposed. The Germans and Dutch had observed or intercepted such consignments several times, and they continually informed the British and the American authorities – who blocked further investigations by their colleagues from the continent. It was not until late autumn of 2005 that, according to media reports, the U.S. government formally accused North Korea of printing the supernote and brought charges against Garland.

The longer Europe's anti-counterfeiting experts delve into this superdollar counterfeiting, the more riddles they churn up. This begins with the print quality of the supernote. Experts regard it as simply superb. In certain ways the supernotes are even better than the authentic 100-dollar bills of the Bureau of Engraving and Printing. Under the microscope, for example, the supernote shows an especially fine execution of lines on the facing side, which cannot even be found on the real note. The complicated seal of the Department of the Treasury on the facing side is copied with absolute perfection, but just below it, one finds in the banknote numbering a marking compound that should not be there. And then, missing from this excellently copied supernote, of all things, are the magnetic and infrared security features that would prevent banknote examining systems from bouncing it. Every surveillance device of an American bank or the Fed recognizes the supernote immediately as a counterfeit and spits it out. Do the counterfeiters perhaps intend that the supernote be recognized immediately in the United States? Further, why would they have chosen the 100-dollar note if they really want to do economic warfare against the United States? True, every year the Fed has between 600 million und 850 million 100-dollar notes printed. But they are earmarked mostly for foreign countries. For example, the Fed itself assumes that all the newly issued 100-dollar notes in California soon leave the country. The 20-dollar and 50-dollar notes are much more popular in the States because amounts in the range of 100 dollars are usually paid with a credit card. And, to round out the list of open questions: experts on printing machinery have grave doubts that the North Koreans could have printed the supernote at all with their antiquated DLR Giori machinery. With that machinery, experts say, they could never have printed the 100-dollar bills issued starting in 1996. North Korea is even having difficulties with the printing of its own won notes, as the miserable quality shows. But precisely 100-dollar bills of the post-1996 series keep turning up in supernote quality.

So-called clearing houses serve as intermediaries in international trading in banknotes. One of the largest in the world can be found in Zurich. Banknotes worth the equivalent of 5 billion dollars are delivered there every day. Huge volumes of notes, often stacked on palettes, are checked here for their authenticity with high-precision banknote examining machines from Giesecke & Devrient and then shipped out again. Such clearing points allow an unusually deep insight into the secret world of the international flow of banknotes. Thus, one notices that the supernotes always turn up in small, well-measured quantities, as though their volume were controlled. The only exception is the period of the fasting month, Ramadan, and the traveling of pilgrims to Mecca. Then the number of supernotes climbs noticeably. Normal gangs of counterfeiters do not behave like that. They want to unload their hot goods as quickly as possible. Further, experts believe they have determined that the supernotes regularly crop up in those regions in which U.S. foreign policy is just encountering problems: the Near and Middle East, certain African countries, and especially East Africa. Active in these places are opposition politicians, rebelling tribes, and private armies of diverse warlords doing the bidding of the CIA. Could it be that they are being paid for their services in counterfeit dollar notes? It would not be the first case of this nature in history. Have these groups perhaps used the money to buy weapons in East Germany and, after the Wall in Berlin had come down, in North Korea? Is this counterfeit money then making its way back from North Korea to the West, preferably to western Europe? The Secret Service is keeping mum and official inquiries routinely go unanswered. The Geneva Convention of 1929 that was mentioned earlier also bears the signature of the United States of America. This convention obliges the signatory powers to work actively together and to cooperate internationally in the struggle against counterfeit money. But it is not clear how much the U.S. Secret Service knows itself, or how much it is allowed to know. In its search for the masterminds of this mysterious counterfeiting affair, perhaps the Secret Service ought to take a look just north of Washington D.C. There, it is said, the CIA has a printing plant in which there are precisely the same modern DLR Giori machines installed that are used for printing banknotes. In this top-secret printing plant, of course, only passports and IDs are forged, it is said.

Whatever might be behind the supernote, the Bureau of Engraving and Printing finally seized the occasion of the general excitement to issue new dollar notes. Within just four years, an unusual rush, it produced two new dollar series: 1992 and 1996. This was the first change in the appearance of the greenback since 1928! Only the second series, however, can be considered a real overhaul and improvement in technical security. The Bureau decided to do that after the issuance of the first new notes in 1992 because the number of phony dollar notes being detected had leaped again. In addition to security threads and microprint, both first employed in 1992, the dollar notes now received a much more detailed portrait with still finer microscript as well as OVI color-shifting ink in the denominating numerals on the facing side. For the first time they also received a multi-tone, localized watermark. This was the security feature without which a European banknote would be unimaginable, but which the Americans had long rejected. On the long fibers of the paper from the Fourdrinier machine, obtaining adequate quality in a precisely placed watermark with bright-to-dark gradation of tone is hard to do. Crane & Co. had not mastered the technique of the watermark and had, therefore, opposed the adoption of this security feature in the dollar paper. At the end of the 1980s Crane finally hired an expert in Italy, the country of origin of the watermark. Luigi Casoni was supposed to initiate the young employees of Crane & Co. in the difficult craft of scraping wax into a watermark pattern. Casoni had worked for decades for Cartiere Miliani di Fabriano and later as an engraver for Banca d'Italia. Never in his life had he set foot outside of Italy. This made his introductory visit to Dalton a special occasion even for the person who accompanied him on the journey. As though he had personally just explored the headwaters of the Amazon, Casoni reported home of his safe arrival in New York with fifty-two postcards. The old gentleman was quite set in his ways and managed in short order to quarrel with every one of his apprentices. After several working years replete with tensions, there was a parting of the ways. Casoni's craft was no longer needed, anyway. By this time watermark patterns could be scratched with the help of the computer. What had once required month of artistic craftsmanship takes shape today fully automatically in a matter of a week. The affluent and childless Italian, by the way, had negotiated royal compensation for himself and fought with the Americans over every penny of it. With this respectable sum of money he built a mausoleum for himself and his wife in the cemetery of his hometown of Pioraco, near his beloved Adriatic Sea.

At the end of 2003, the Bureau of Engraving and Printing again began issuing a new dollar series, the third within ten years. The new 20-dollar bill was put in circulation first, followed a year later by a new 50-dollar bill. The Bureau also showed its colors then. For the first time in the history of the U.S. dollar the Fed resorted to the printing of a colored background, albeit in a demonstratively muted coloration. Congress, which has the ultimate say, and the Fed, which is charged with designing the notes, were not ready to add more color. They feared that citizens would be made even more insecure by abrupt changes in the appearance of the dollar. Yet the new 20 and 50-dollar bills are already diligently counterfeited just as were all the 100-dollar notes put into circulation since 1992. Copies exist of all the new 100-dollar series without exception in supernote quality. Experts have made bets on how long it will take before the 100-dollar note of the new series slated for 2006 also comes out as a supernote.

Euro frailties

When the twelve European central banks devised their common currency, they had, of course, studied the problems of the dollar. The sheer size of the euro market would offer money counterfeiters a potential for distribution and profit far beyond any extent that the twelve national currencies subsumed in the euro had known. It was also to be expected that the international counterfeiting operators in their choice between dollar and euro would concentrate henceforth on the currency that was easier to copy. With its multiple and complex security devices the euro was supposed to be more secure than the dollar. And therefore the euro was equipped with the most modern security features. No fewer than twenty-six security features were packed into the notes. The euro was declared the »world's most secure currency.« Only the Swiss franc notes are more heavily equipped, namely with thirty-two characteristics, but a part of these is now outmoded.

Four years after the euro's introduction as legal tender, the ECB officially says it is satisfied with its work. The phony euro notes taken out of circulation and analyzed in the first half of 2005 show in their number and their value only a minimal increase from the first half of 2004 (see Table VI). In ECB's opinion, the problem of counterfeiting has stabilized, following the admittedly high rate of increase in the incipient period. Measured against the 9.7 billion euro notes issued by the end of June 2005, the 600,000 counterfeit notes intercepted per year are regarded as a number that indicates an acceptable result in their attempts at prevention. With its ratio of 63 bogus notes for every 1 million good notes in circulation, the euro seems to be in good shape by international comparison. For the 22 billion issued dollar notes in circulation, the estimates assume 200 counterfeits for every 1 million dollar notes. The exact figures, of course, are strictly secret. With respect to the euro, chances of winning a lottery are actually greater than the danger of being handed a bogus note. With »feel, see, tilt,» the advertising slogan of ECB in the campaign against phony euro notes, the consumer can unmask any false euro note. So goes the comforting message.

ECB's counterfeiting statistics cannot be verified by consulting national data. ECB has left up to each Euroland country the extent to which it will reveal its national figures on counterfeiting. It explained this by saying that the twelve had previously also applied different policies for counterfeiting statistics. In the era of the franc, France had had the biggest counterfeit-money problem in Europe, a fact that was always concealed from the public. Even today, Banque de France likes to exercise its right to deny information. Italy and Spain are also silent on this matter. Deutsche Bundesbank is more open. The number of bogus euro notes – 81,000 in 2004 – is now twice as high as it had been in the time of the last Deutschmark series. But Germany had traditionally been only fourth on the target list of the volume of counterfeit money. Police statistics indicate that the numbers of counterfeit euro notes intercepted in France, Italy, and Spain are two or three times higher than that in Germany. Such small countries as Finland, Ireland, and Austria saw hardly any counterfeits during the time of their national currencies. Nor was there much of a problem in Belgium and the Netherlands. Today, all of these countries are battling with rapidly rising euro counterfeits. Throughout Europe, also outside the euro zone, false euro notes have now taken the place of counterfeit dollars. The currency exchange shops that had once been typical of Europe, which exercised an effective front line of control against phony money in foreign currency exchange transactions, have fallen by the wayside. The central banks are gritting their teeth and keeping mum in deference to ECB.

None of that comes as a surprise. At its 2002 international conference in Amsterdam, Interpol had approved a lengthy catalog of demands for better protection of banknotes. Expressly included were intaglio steelplate printing on both sides of the banknote, steelplate intaglio for the denominating numerals, overprint of the kinegram with steelplate intaglio, and a broader security thread. The Interpol resolution was passed with an eye on the euro. But the demands of Interpol were ignored. This was done not for the sake of saving money but because of »dominating national interests,« as the Swiss federal police declared in their »Lagebericht Falschgeld 2004« on the rising euro counterfeiting even in Switzerland. This status report, available on the Internet, revealed candidly that because of the politics involved in trying to accommodate various note printers, security standards have had to be lowered repeatedly.[12] Clearly, this is a reference to certain government note printers involved in the printing of the euro. As the director in charge of banknote printing of a central bank from outside Euroland put it diplomatically, the euro »paid the price« of its security because only the currency was aligned from its inception, but not its production. Particularly grave are the weaknesses for the first level of security composition, those features conceived especially for the consumers in their intuitive examination of authenticity. Even before the introduction of the euro, seasoned experts on banknote security said (off record) that the first level of security for the planned banknote was inadequate. »Feel, see, tilt« has no input if all the security features of the first level are counterfeited. In the summer of 2005, for example, a new bogus 200-euro note turned up, which effortlessly passed through all the testing devices of the banks, according to information from criminal investigators. On this counterfeit, designated »200P3« and suspected to have come from the Bulgarian trade-fair city of Plovdiv, even the kinegram shimmers in different colors when tilted. This category of false 200-euro notes has nearly supernote quality, it is said. With certain denominations, 40 percent of the bogus euro notes in Germany now go unrecognized and are intercepted only by the sophisticated inspection systems of the Bundesbank or its branches – a ratio never known before. In other countries the ratio is even higher. But when a phony banknote makes its way as far as the central bank, the police have no way of tracing it. Apparently, merchants as well as consumers have trouble recognizing false euro notes, or perhaps they do not want to recognize them in order to avoid incurring damage. He who turns over a phony banknote to the police, as the law requires, is actually punished for his honesty in that no one compensates him for his loss. An irreconcilable contradiction in battling counterfeiting is in play here. In the Netherlands, Germany, France, and Italy, more and more cheated grocery markets and gasoline filling stations are announcing that they no longer accept notes starting at 100 euros.

Central banks traditionally make an effort to play down existing problems with counterfeit money. Statistics offer many possibilities to cover up and even the independence of the national police authorities plays an important role. In Euroland most of the police units charged with combating counterfeiting have their offices on the premises of their national bank. This intimacy does not exactly foster a readiness to report bogus money. Moreover, the ECB counterfeit money statistics cover only notes intercepted while *in circulation*. Those confiscated *out of circulation* by police are not covered by these statistics, because, it is rationalized, this bogus money has not yet caused any economic damage. Furthermore, some central bankers believe that police undercover investigations involving simulated demand for counterfeit money actually stimulate the supply of bogus money in the first place. But false money that the police are unable to intercept today with raids and undercover work goes into circulation tomorrow, causing real damage. And the harder it is for consumers to detect euro counterfeits in daily dealings, the more important the investigative work of the police becomes.

The dispute between central banks and criminal investigators over the counterfeiting statistics has tradition. If one were to include the bogus euro notes that are intercepted before they can be circulated – a position supported by numbers from the federal German interior ministry in Berlin[13] – then ECB would have to revise its data on phony money upward by one-third. According to this data, in 2004 there were close to 900,000 counterfeit euro notes detected in Euroland, not 600,000 as reported by the

ECB statistics. And unpublished data from the police for the first nine months of 2005 show another increase of 10 percent in the number of counterfeit bills and even a rise of 22 percent in value if one considers their denomination, compared with the first nine months of the preceding year.[14] Further, when one recalls that more than 15 percent of the 9.7 billion issued euro notes are held outside Euroland, the counterfeiting gap between euro and dollar melts like ice in the sunshine. But the dollar has been around for nearly 150 years; the euro is just four years old. Even counterfeiters need time to warm up. Clearly, the security of the euro is straining under the burden of its political birth defect.

The European police authority Europol also regards the situation with counterfeit euro bills as considerably more threatening than ECB does, even if one may never say this in public. Europol, headquartered in The Hague, was founded in 1999 by all EU countries in response to the increase in border-crossing crime. The battle against bogus money received political priority there. Yet Europol initially was not granted an independent budget and was not made the clearinghouse for reports and information on counterfeiting crimes. Europol has only selective access to the Counterfeit Monitoring System (CMS), the analytical data bank of ECB and its twelve central banks. Europol may not enter data in CMS. Unlike the U.S. Secret Service, Europol's investigative powers are restricted: the mandate of the European police authority is strictly limited to the territories of the EU countries. Interpol remains the hub of coordination for worldwide crime fighting and also for combating counterfeiting outside the EU. Even within the EU, Europol is not allowed to do its own investigating; that remains the sovereign prerogative of the individual member countries. There is no European prosecutor. The creation of this important office was stopped when the European Constitution was refused by the people of France and the Netherlands. Therefore, Europol may only coordinate, and Europol agents in mutual deployment with national police forces are always unarmed. Only on television is there such a thing as a Euro cop. Nevertheless, the European police authority has now concluded what it calls »operative agreements« with Bulgaria, Rumania, and the United States. These agreements envisage an exchange of personnel and data. The Americans, however, have difficulties with this data swapping, as already described in another context.

These operating strictures on Europol weigh heavily, considering that counterfeiting gangs have little respect for the external borders of the EU.

The best counterfeits of the 50-euro note, for example, are made by the Camorra of Naples and the Mafia around Marseille. They are preferentially distributed in Euroland by Lithuanian gangs – code name: »Baltic Walker« – at least as far as the Neapolitan counterfeits are concerned. Eastern European countries play a key role not only in the distribution of counterfeit money but also in its production. Since the collapse of communism, thousands of well-trained photographers, graphic artists, and various printing specialists are standing idle in the streets. Many of them do not know how they are supposed to feed their families and are ready to accept any job. The situation is somewhat reminiscent of the collapse of London's Fleet Street, in which an army of printing tradesmen became unemployed. The British police registered a spectacular boom in bogus pound notes at that time. Nowadays Bulgaria, Lithuania, and Poland are the capitals of euro counterfeiting. Social romanticism, of course, would be out of place here. For one further legacy of communism needs to be mentioned here. Even during the era of communism the Bulgarians were regarded as *the* counterfeiting specialists among the brotherly socialist peoples. At the bidding of the Russian KGB, Bulgarian counterfeiters copied everything, from personal identification documents and college diplomas to the banknote. Their craftsmanship was awesome. Today, the Bulgarian counterfeiting scene is again controlled by these former KGB agents. They produce false euro notes – as well as dollars – of alarming quality. And they guard this turf with an iron hand. No one goes to work as a counterfeiter in Bulgaria without their permission. »Old networks« left over from communist times seem to be the main peculiarity of the eastern European counterfeiting milieu. They play a role in all of the reforming countries but are regarded as especially influential in Bulgaria, Poland, Rumania, and Hungary. These old comrades from politics, the military, and the police are always good for a surprise in the battle against the euro counterfeiters. In one case, an undercover investigation of bogus bills in Bulgaria had to be called off at the last moment because the wife of a high military officer, who worked at the telephone switchboard of the national police command, had leaked the information. Also in Bulgaria, the trail of a special machine for banknote printing suddenly went cold in a strange way – this press had been imported by the son of an influential politician. And in Poland a consignment of tons of duped banknote paper was stolen from a guarded customs warehouse. The bogus security paper was supposed to have served as a decoy. The thieves were obviously well-informed because they carefully left behind only the electronic homing device and microphone that had been hidden in the paper. The paper, by the way, turned up again later – in the form of counterfeit Russian ruble notes. A large neighboring country of Russia had paid its energy bill in Moscow with the stuff.

And the counterfeiting milieu is becoming more and more cosmopolitan. The first cases of counterfeit euro notes overseas are now being reported. In Columbia two printing plants that counterfeited euro notes have been uncovered; the Columbians actually had been regarded as specialists for counterfeit dollar notes. In South Korea and Australia, rings of distributors of false euro notes have been broken up, although this has not been widely publicized. There are even the first signs of politically motivated euro counterfeiting. In early 2005, an international gang of thirty-five counterfeiters were put out of action. Media were informed of the successful coup by Dutch police in cooperation with Europol. But the reporters were not told that plenty of »Islamic literature,« as well as arms, was found with this gang. It was the first case of this type associated with counterfeit euro money and, perhaps, a prelude of things to come. Currently, the police are especially worried about Indian and Malaysian counterfeiters, who produce bogus notes of a high caliber. If they have discovered the euro, it will be very tricky to sort them out, said a source outside the EU.

In view of such developments, the ECB does not sound very convincing when it says it has everything under control. That is more reminiscent of the attitude toward the threat of narcotics in its early years. In the interim, drug offenses have made it to first place in the Europol reporting statistics – followed in second place by crimes with counterfeit banknotes. Europol has drawn, at least, one consequence from this. In The Hague it created »Sonya,« Europol's own analytical data bank in which all euro counterfeiting data from the EU and countries that have operative agreements with it will be stored. Europol seeks to become independent of ECB data.

New euro frontiers

In light of the security problems described, the current euro series, EU A, is unlikely to have a long lease on life. It is expected to be replaced before the end of this decade by a new euro series, EU B. That replacement will transpire in stages. The word is that the citizenry is not supposed to be put upon once again with another »big bang,« a sudden conversion of all denominations. Nor are the government printing plants to suffer this either, one might add. At about the same time, the euro is supposed to be introduced in the smaller countries that are Euroland entry candidates, while the three big candidates – Hungary, Poland, and the Czech Republic – probably will not be included yet. Only these three have their own banknote printers. The preparations for EU B have been running for some time. The affected working groups are engaged. The design of the new note series will be a delicate political issue. For the euro's sake, one might hope that the planners of the second note series would commit themselves again to the European portrait tradition. Here chances are dim at best. As a security feature the portrait's value has diminished greatly with the high standard of reproduction technology. Even the Swiss national bank will do away with portraits for its new franc series, planned for 2010. Continuity in design, however, has a rising value, even for the euro. It is a matter of prestige – and a matter of trust. The citizens of Euroland are well aware that the introduction of the common currency has caused a huge erosion in real buying power, even though the central banks emphatically deny that. In order not to erode confidence any further, the appearance of the new euro notes ought not to change too much. Unfortunately, the fathers of the euro have not done themselves and the consumers a big favor with the graphic design of the current series. When asked about the image of a specific euro note, most people are unable to recall it at all. If banknotes are supposed to help establish a sense of common identity, this result of the euro design is quite a disappointment for the common currency. But it looks like the authorities want to cling to the sterile architectural themes.

Undoubtedly, the effectiveness of the security features of the first level, that which is noticed by consumers, will have to be improved in the next euro generation. In their current technical configuration, the kinegram and OVI color-shifting ink no longer offer adequate protection. Then there is the two-sided intaglio printing. It is condemned by some because of its excessive cost and technical problems with the printing, while others praise it because it nearly automatically permits authentication. Among the supporters of two-sided intaglio printing there are, needless to say, the private high-security printers thinking about the operating rates of their expensive printing presses. A feverish search for new security characteristics is therefore in progress around the world. The emphasis in this research has been placed on substances that can change their appearance quickly. The craft of the counterfeiter is made more difficult by everything that moves and changes its appearance when the viewing angle changes or because changing external conditions affect it. Only a few of the many ideas and suggestions can be covered here. The idea of putting a microchip in the banknote, for example, has attracted much attention – perhaps too much attention. It was cleverly presented by the manufacturers. These microchips, however, would be required by the billions and would be quite expensive in the long run. On top of that, every citizen would also have to run around with a device that can read them; otherwise the microchip is of no use to him. Thermochromatic inks and heat-sensitive security threads are also under discussion. These features change their appearance quickly when touched by the hand. Then, of course, the banknotes would look different in summer or winter, in warm rooms or in fresh air. The absolutely identical appearance of notes is, however, a prerequisite for the battle against counterfeiters. The thermochromatic effect also wears off with time, becoming completely lost in the end. That would perhaps be less of a problem for banknotes with a low denomination, because they are normally shredded after a few months of circulation, but it would be a problem for notes with a higher denomination. The 200- und 500-euro bills in particular would need additional protection from counterfeiting, because they live much longer. Another possibility is the use of *bacteriorhodopsin*, a substance developed by researchers from the Max Planck Institute in Munich and Philipp's University in Marburg, for optical application. This protein changes color instantly with the lighting effect and also has an unusually high capacity to store data – one megabit for every six square centimeters. Refined from rock-salt, bacteriorhodopsin, however, currently still costs around 600 dollars a gram to produce. Besides being cost efficient, a new marker substance also has to survive extremely rigorous laboratory tests. Only then is it ready for a printing test run. Not every feature preserves its initially very promising characteristics in a test run, for example, when it comes into contact with the binding agent in the ink. Only the laboratories of the central banks and the note printers can provide the definitive answer for a new security feature. Naturally, everyone is trying to steer the development in the direction that most suits him and hinders the competing product, even by resorting to litigation. After all, quite a lot of money is at stake. As stated in a Bundesbank publication, »a banknote *may* be pretty, but it *must* be secure.«[15] Neither of these conditions was actually met on the first try with the euro.

12
Quo vadis euro printing?

Creating Europe's common currency was a singular challenge, both politically and technically. Never before in history had so many countries cooperated voluntarily to introduce a new common currency. Blunders were to be expected and could partially explain the fact that the product perhaps did not entirely fulfill the lofty expectations. Yet the enemy of good is better – there is definitely room for improvement. The euro notes need qualitative improvement, and they are too expensive. That was true of the initial supply of euro notes and it is true as well of the current printing of replacement euro notes, because there continue to be political limitations on the ECB's push for more efficient production. Opinions diverge on whether the printing of banknotes is really a sovereign task. Those central banks that have already had notes produced by private printers are of the opinion that only the *issuance* of banknotes is a sovereign undertaking. On the other hand, the printing of banknotes involves cost and quality, and this is a job that can be done by private industry, on condition that the private banknote printers meet the standards set by the central banks for security in production and composition of the notes, and that they observe the obligation of strict confidentiality. If all these requirements are met, private printing promises more economical production than printing by government plants. But not all central banks have an equally strong interest in the cost of the banknotes produced by their printers, an attitude supported by powerful labor unions. There is sometimes vigorous opposition to the opening of the market for note printing. The larger the state printing plant, the greater the opposition.

The central banks, and not just those in Euroland, are very circumspect in disclosing the costs of their printers. If costs and prices of the printing works of a central bank (in technical jargon: in-house printing works) are

Moneymakers, Klaus W. Bender

ISBN: 3-527-50236-X

cited at all, what is rolled into the numbers – or better: what is left out – goes discreetly unmentioned. These are hardly calculations with full costing. The considerable expenses for the printing center, personnel, the security of the plant, and the security of the product are quietly taken over by the central bank when required. Because Bundesbank has its euro notes produced by private printers, it had less of a problem with the disclosure of the costs for the initial supply of euros. Its average price for 1,000 notes is about 100 euros, without value-added tax. For the smaller note denominations, with their more modest security composition, the average price is below that; for the larger denominations, which are bigger in size and feature a more expensive security composition, it is somewhat higher. This is more expensive than the average cost of the last Deutschmark series, although those D-mark notes were printed in smaller runs. For the Austrian central bank, which does not use a private banknote printer, the printing cost of the initial euro supply was 50 percent more than the average price calculated at full costing. And the price of Austria's euro notes was even 65 percent more than the price that the ECB paid the Austrian printing works for the very limited number of banknotes the Austrians could print for the ECB's emergency Central Reserve Stock of euro notes, according to the auditing report published in autumn 2005 by Austria's general accounting office.[1] For some other government printers the exaggeration in pricing was even greater. For Euroland, the highly unusual distribution of note printing among fifteen printers was not the only reason for the high cost in printing the initial supply of euros, but it visibly obstructed the possibilities for savings through economies of scale – the larger the volume, the smaller the cost – which play such an important role in the printing industry.

The Americans take maximum advantage of the effects of high-volume runs in their two printing plants at Washington, D.C., and Fort Worth, Texas. The Bureau of Engraving and Printing has so far produced banknotes for less than half the price of the German Bundesbank. The gigantic press runs for dollar notes of the same denomination with uniform dimensions and for a long time without a security composition accounts for this American advantage. The new 20-dollar bill issued in autumn 2003 cost 20 percent more, said a press release of the Bureau, but this increase was explained by the greatly improved security composition. Naturally, security has its price. For example, the Swiss franc notes printed exclusively by private printer Orell Füssli cost an average of 300 Swiss francs (200 euros) per 1,000 notes. This makes the Swiss notes twice as expensive as the euro notes from Bundesbank. The price is dictated by the Swiss national bank, but it is said to be a price with full costing, including depreciation of machinery. Furthermore, Switzerland prints only around 100 million replacement notes a year for its full circulation of 260 million notes, and this printing is spread over six denominations. Such small series considerably raise the printing costs, especially in a country with high wages. And the expensive security composition of the Swiss franc notes pushes up the cost. Opinions diverge on the graphic design of the Swiss banknotes, but their security composition is unanimously regarded by experts as a benchmark. When the current Swiss series is replaced by new banknotes in 2010 because this one is technically obsolete, it will have been in circulation for fifteen years. The current euro series is likely to become only half as old because of its security problems. Investment in security composition therefore pays off – assuming it is made in the right features on the right level of security checks.

Competition à la euro system

Despite the common currency, Euroland clung to the principle in banknote printing of strictly protecting national territories, which is commonly stated in the laws of any national bank. Nothing else was politically possible and this decentralization then served, as described, as justification for building up large national capacities for printing. Quantifying capacity in banknote printing is difficult. Capacity depends upon the number of shifts worked. But the high-security printing industry estimates that, in all EU countries together, a printing capacity of about 10 billion notes a year is currently being maintained. This estimate is regarded as conservative. After completing the initial supply, the euro system had assumed an annual replacement of 4 billion notes. Because the actual demand lagged far behind that, the large initial reserve of euro notes held as reserve stock by the central banks was drawn down only slowly. The need for replacements in 2004 sank to an absolute low of only 1.6 billion euro notes.

After the printing of the initial supply of euros, the member countries were no longer responsible for the printing of the euro notes required by them, but they continue to pay for them. Euro printing is now controlled by a procurement system described as »decentralized pooling.« Together with the national central banks, the ECB now first determines the required quantity of banknotes, then segregates this requirement by denomination, and finally allocates the printing orders according to the national quotas of the twelve remaining printing plants.[2] Under this arrangement, the production of each denomination of bills is supposed to be shared by two printing plants, if possible. Every central bank wants to participate in the printing, and each is allowed to do so. This solution is a political expedient, which looks somewhat like central economic planning and also probably resembles it in efficiency. Costs can be lowered only to a very limited degree in this way – certainly if one keeps in mind the exaggerated prices paid for the initial euro procurement. With a printing run of less than 100 million notes, printing costs rise steeply. Private printers also believe that they have to print 700 million notes a year on each line of machinery in order to work economically. For comparison, Austria's government printer (OeBS) produced just 203 million euro notes in 2005 with its two complete lines of printing machinery.

Given the catastrophic operating rates, some central banks have called for the introduction of 1 and 2-euro banknotes that would be issued parallel to the circulating coinage in the same denominations. This suggestion came from Italy and was taken up by Belgium, Greece, and Austria. The initiative was explained by the supposed preference of citizens in southern Europe and the ten eastern European countries that just joined the EU. In those places the income level is indeed lower than in the rest of Euroland. It is also said that notes of small denomination would heighten price awareness and suppress inflation. Such low-denomination notes would be required in huge quantities but would then have only a short life cycle, what they wanted. The United States offers an example. Nearly half of the notes printed there each year are 1 and 2-dollar bills, the smallest denominations, and the lesson for Euroland is clear: these small denominations would vastly increase the costs of the euro system for printing, processing, and destruction. On top of that would be high costs in private industry for – again – refitting all vending machines. The cost-conscious British have long since parted with the 1-pound note for this reason. Following heated internal discussions at ECB, the suggestion of the four countries was finally rejected. Had it been carried out, incidentally, it would have been associated with a large erosion of revenue of the finance ministers for their national minting privilege. This facilitated a political »no.«

The private producers of security paper and printed notes, of course, would have welcomed the idea of small euro bills. They were less enthusiastic when the highly subsidized government printers began to land orders for note printing on the world's free market. The first warning signal was the decision of Banque de France to install a KBA-Giori line for sheet-fed printing in large format at Chamalières shortly after the euro's introduction. It was exactly the installation of this type of sheet-fed printing machinery that Paris had stubbornly resisted for the initial euro printing. Printed on the new presses in Chamalières, however, are only the notes for the African partner countries in the CFA group; France's euro notes continue to be produced on the disputed web printing. The private printers drew consolation here from that fact that Banque de France had merely withdrawn its own printing allocation from a private printer, Francois Charles Oberthur Fiduciaire. More threatening is the behavior of the printers of some central banks in the smaller countries, where the national printing quotas for euro notes are too small for them to survive in the long run. The oft-mentioned OeBS, a 100 percent subsidiary of Oesterreichische Nationalbank, broke trail here with a printing order for Armenia. The order was small, and it also didn't make the Austrians very happy because there was a printing mistake that forced OeBS to print again. Private printers, therefore, did not complain about this contract. But then the Austrians bid with market dumping prices in more and more public solicitations, even in Malaysia, where Giesecke & Devrient had just begun operating a new note-printing plant. In Singapore, the Austrians finally received a contract for half a billion notes at a price of 24 dollars per thousand, as reported in the industry. Similar campaigns for export orders by the Spanish, Belgian, and Greek government printers have been reported. For Greece, this involved the printing of passports.

The private high-security printers live from the export business. They are concerned much less by the lost printing volume than by the prices with which the government printers threaten to do lasting damage to their world market. The private printers could never compete with such subsidized prices, especially not with their printing bases in Europe. Now the dispute has gone public, with calls for help even from the ECB. The activities of OeBS have had an unexpected consequence. It turned out, for one, that the government printer forgot to hedge against exchange-rate movements affecting its contract from Singapore. This major order therefore ended with a major loss, which cost the business manager of OeBS and his deputy their jobs. And then, the previously mentioned audit of the Austrian general accounting office determined that the government printer of the national bank had bid systematically below its costs in the public procurement solicitation. In other words, every additional export order only generated greater losses. No wonder the losses of the Austrian government printer were sometimes larger than its annual sales. Austria's national bank has meanwhile explained officially that the expansion policy of the purged business management has been terminated. But the problem of competitive distortion has not been resolved at all. For example, it can be learned from the auditing report that the brand new printing works worth several hundred million euro had been ceded by the Austrian central bank for the shocking amount of 0.07 euros – eight U.S. cents ! – to the government printer when it was severed from the national bank in 1998. This national bank also bequeathed to its now »independent« printer, which is still owned one hundred percent by the Austrian national bank, a large inventory of banknotes that were half printed – which it then bought back as finished notes at a record price. To top it off, this national bank kept paying the wages for those employees who were transferred from the central bank, which pays very high wages, to the less generous payroll of the printing works. The accounting office rightly fears that the Austrian government printer has only a marginal chance of ever surviving in open competition. Concealed between the lines, therefore, the official auditor recommends that the national bank simply close its banknote printing plant.

Austria is no exception here, as shown in early 2005 by the auditing report of Cour des Comptes, France's general accounting office, on the banknote printing of the Banque de France.[3] The French auditor in its lengthy report determined that the Banque de France has pursued a policy with little coherence in its note printing during the last twenty years, permitting greatly excessive capacity to accumulate. Furthermore, although wages at Chamalières are still 40 percent higher than those of Europe's private printers, productivity per worker is only half as great. This very detailed auditing report avoided recommending that the central bank close its printing plant in Chamalières, as implied in the case of Austria. That would not be politically possible. But this audit report recommended more energetic measures to overhaul the operation than it had in the past. For Banque de France, according to Cour des Comptes, the goal ought to be confronting Europe's private competitors in euro printing in open competition as quickly as possible.

Uncertain future

In the fifth year since the introduction of the euro, the situation in euro printing has relaxed somewhat. Private households are again accumulating more banknotes after depositing most of them in their cash into their accounts in order to facilitate the conversion to euros. Also, euro notes are increasingly in demand abroad. Finally, the entry into the euro zone of the first eastern European countries is casting an advancing shadow, as is the new euro series that is expected to be introduced in stages starting 2008. Therefore, seven billion euro notes will be printed in 2006, nearly twice as many as in the previous year. That is a great deal, but still not enough for the twelve printers. The ECB confirms its intention to organize the euro printing according to the principles of a free market and open competition. Resources are supposed to be used efficiently, it says. This could easily be done with open public auctions of printing contracts, and the ECB had indeed planned to do that starting 2004. But the resistance of some central banks to surrendering their protected areas proved so great that the ECB had to abandon this idea again. Thus private printers and the suppliers of supporting materials said that as a consequence of its procurement policy, the ECB might be violating EU competition law and WTO standards. The ECB now is risking a new attempt. The ECB council of governors has decided that the »single euro-system tender procedure« should take effect in 2012.[4] All printing contracts for euro notes are then supposed to be awarded on the basis of central procurement solicitations. A special procurement committee with seven members nominated by the participating central banks will supervise the implementation of the new procedures. The ECB hopes that steadily rising yearly requirements for notes will serve as an inducement for central banks to finally opt for an open market policy, because there is the prospect of snaring a larger share in an auction than any national bank and its state printing works previously had as a national quota. Smaller government printers that cannot compete and cannot live from their national quota would then be forced to close. The urgently needed reduction in capacity would be initiated less painfully.

Yet what sounds like open competition and a free market does not necessarily tend to function that way, especially not in the EU. The transition to a process of open bidding is hitched to conditions that assure that at least half of all central banks in the euro system, for at least half of the requirement for euro banknotes, opt for the single tender procedure. In a »warm-up phase« starting in 2008, the government printers are supposed to be given the option to participate in test solicitations. A condition for participation is that they will allow their books to be audited by independent certified public accountants – a condition that is supposed to avoid competitive distortions by means of cross-subsidies, as described above in the case of Austria. The government printers over the years have successfully warded off the airing of their calculations. A change in attitude cannot necessarily be expected from them, since they have probably not become more competitive, as the cases of the French and Austrian government printers indicate. The powerful labor unions in these government operations will see to that. After 2012, no central bank will be forced to join public tenders on its euro printing. Even after that deadline, a clause specifically gives them the option to keep their territories protected, as the rule was until now. Although their government printers would then be excluded from participating in the solicitations of other central banks, they would be allowed to keep printing their own national quotas of euro notes. Only a few countries – Germany, Finland, the Netherlands, and Luxembourg – have so far declared that they would solicit bids on their note requirements. France, Italy, and Spain either seem wary of the market opening or openly reject it. But, after Germany, they have the largest national printing quotas. Particularly delicate for their own private printers are the one-sided openings of procurement bidding as planned by Germany and the Netherlands. De La Rue and Francois Charles Oberthur Fiduciaire, both currently excluded from euro printing, would then have the right to participate in the auctions of Germany and the Netherlands. And those would not necessarily be linked to a reciprocal opening of the home markets of those printers.

The government printers were completely insulated from the privatization wave of the last two decades. From an economic vantage point this was not at all a given. Now, as a consequence of the common currency, a creeping »re-nationalization« threatens to overtake European banknote printing. Shortly after the introduction of the euro, therefore, the five leading European private printers banded together as the European Banknote

Printers Association (EuPBA) in Paris.[5] In a way this is a successor organization to the previously mentioned AIIF, but more restricted in its membership. As its goal, this association named »fair terms of competition« for the private printers and the industry that supplies them. One could have mixed feelings on whether precisely these providers ought to team up in a market that already suffers from multiple obstacles to competition. And regarding the internal cohesion of EuPBA, one could certainly have one's doubts. But the severe distortion of the market for banknote printing caused by the euro concern the future of the private high-security printing industry. And the world's high-security printing industry is European. The ECB rightly claims that since the launch of the common currency in 2002, it has done a lot to streamline operations, to harmonize the product quality, and even to reduce prices. Even the private printers concede that the new team at the ECB has achieved an impressive learning curve. Yet the central banks are not just cautious by nature; they are also sensitive to political pressure, especially that coming from the unions. When push comes to shove, they will vote for preserving their own printing plants and the jobs of their own employees.

For note printers and the supplier industry, there will be no market opening for many years, the director of the printing works of the Banca d'Italia warned banknote printers in a speech shortly before the introduction of the euro.[6] Why not? It is apparent that a common culture still has to take root in the management of the common European currency. In view of their historical differences, that will still take some time, probably longer than the life cycle of one or two euro series. Yet, that cannot be a justification for postponement of the market opening ad kalendas graecas, for an indefinite time. The euro central banks, in any event, cannot push convincingly for more private initiative and efficiency in all other areas of the economy, if they are doing the exact opposite in their own banknote printing. The euro is still a work in progress.

Acknowledgments

The author thanks Pericle Staderini of Rome and the late Edward D. Little of Dalton, Massachusetts, for the idea behind this book. Also deserving of thanks are Claus Jung and Rolf Westphal, both of Munich, and Arnim von Schwedler of Berlin for the author's initiation into the secret world of the printing of banknotes and other high-security products, for their thoughtful guidance in the research, and for referrals to important contacts. Many others in the high-security printing industry, central banks, the financial sector, and last but not least, European criminal police forces have contributed to this book. Since strict confidentiality was agreed upon for the conversations with the author, these persons cannot be named here. Many will recognize their role in the recounting of certain events or in the choice of words. The author thanks them all for trusting him. The author also owes a debt of gratitude to the men and women in the general and business archives of the *Frankfurter Allgemeine Zeitung* for their comprehensive research assistance. More than just a word of thanks is owed to Hartmut Gante of Wiley-VCH for his decision to have this book published in English, to Jutta Hörnlein for coordinating the editorial process, to Edward Roby for his translation of a difficult German text, and to S. Daniel Ball and Janine Micunek Fuchs for casting a careful and critical eye on the English-language manuscript. The author's greatest thanks, however, goes to his wife, Sinikka, who had to sacrifice for years while putting up with a husband who was often lost in thought and responded in monosyllables. The work that went into this book would not have been possible without her loving care and understanding encouragement.

K.W. B.

Moneymakers, Klaus W. Bender

ISBN: 3-527-50236-X

Bibliography

»Amerikanische Orte drucken ihr eigenes Geld«, in: *N.Z.Z.* vom 29.3.1999

Binswanger, Hans Christoph: *Geld und Magie. Deutung und Kritik der modernen Wirtschaft*, Edition Weitbrecht, Stuttgart 1985

Bloom, Murray Teigh: *The Brotherhood of Money. The Secret World of Bank Note Printers*, BNR Press, Port Clinton, Ohio 1983

Bloom, Murray T.: *Der Mann der Portugal stahl - der größte Schwindel aller Zeiten*, rororo Sonderausgabe für die Bundesdruckerei, Rowohlt Taschenbuch Verlag, Reinbek bei Hamburg 1973

Brion, René/Moreau, Jean-Louis: *Le billet dans tous ses Etats*, Fonds Mercator, Anvers 2001

Burger, Adolf: *Des Teufels Werkstatt. Die Geldfälscherwerkstatt im KZ Sachsenhausen*, erweiterte Auflage, Verlag Neues Leben GmbH, Berlin 1999

Cour des Comptes. La Banque de France - Rapport au Président de la République Suivi des Réponses des Administrations et des Organismes Intéressés. March 2005.

Davies, Glyn: *A History of Money from Ancient Times to the Present Day*, rev. ed., University of Wales, Cardiff 1996

Moneymakers, Klaus W. Bender

ISBN: 3-527-50236-X

»Der Stoff, aus dem die Scheine sind«, in: *Bundesbankmagazin, Zeitschrift für die Angehörigen der Bundesbank,* Nr. 1/2001, S. 12

»Der vielseitige Wertpapierdrucker«, in: *Der Schweizerdegen,* Heft XII, Art. Institut Orell Füssli AG, Zürich 1949

Deysson, Christian: »Geld. Schöner Schein«, in: *WirtschaftsWoche,* Heft 28 vom 3.7.2003

Die Bundesdruckerei, Zukunft aus Tradition. Das neue Wertdruckgebäude der Bundesdruckerei in Berlin, Sonderdruck der Bundesdruckerei, o.J.

»Die Geldmonopole wackeln«, in: *F.A.Z.* vom 3.1.2000

Elam, Shraga: *Hitlers Fälscher. Wie jüdische, amerikanische und Schweizer Agenten der SS beim Falschgeldwaschen halfen,* Verlag Carl Ueberreuter, Wien 2000

European Central Bank (ECB): *Annual Report 2004*

European Central Bank (ECB): *Review Of The International Role Of The Euro,* January 2005

European Union (EU): «Guideline of the European Central Bank of 16 September 2004 on the procurement of euro banknotes", ECB/2004/18, in: *Official Journal of the European Union,* L320/21, 21.10.2004

Gabriel, Gottfried: *Ästhetik und Rhetorik des Geldes,* frommann-holzboog Verlag, Stuttgart-Bad Cannstatt 2002

Galbraith, Kenneth John: *Money, whence it came, where it went.* Bantam Books, New York, 1975.

Giesecke & Devrient: 125 Jahre Wertpapier- und Banknotendruck im Spiegel der politischen und wirtschaftlichen Entwicklung Deutschlands. Ein Bericht aus Anlass des 125-jährigen Bestehens der Firma Giesecke & Devrient, München, am 1. Juni 1977

Gleeson, Janet: *The Moneymaker, the remarkable true story of John Law - philander, gambler, murderer and the father of modern finance*, Bantam Books, London-New York 2000

Hagen, Walter: *Unternehmen Bernhard. Ein historischer Tatsachenbericht über die größte Geldfälschungsaktion aller Zeiten*, Verlag Welsermühl, Wels und Starnberg o.J.

International Monetary Fund (IMF): *Annual Report 2005*

Janssen, Roel: *Die Euro-Fälscher*, Campus-Verlag, Frankfurt 2001

Kahnt, Helmut; Schöne, Michael H.; Walz, Karlheinz: *50 Jahre Deutsche Mark: 1948-1998; Die Geschichte der deutschen Nachkriegswährungen in Ost und West*, Heinrich Gietl Verlag, Regenstauf 1998

Karczmar, Mieczyslaw: *The U.S. balance of payments: widespread misconceptions and exaggerated worries*, Deutsche Bank Research, International Topics, Sept. 30, 2004.

Klose, Dietrich O.A.: *Ade DM! Die Geschichte der Mark von 1945 bis zum Euro*, Selbstverlag der Staatlichen Münzsammlung, München 1999

Klose, Dietrich O.A.: *Die Mark - ein deutsches Schicksal. Die Geschichte der Mark bis 1945*, Selbstverlag der Staatlichen Münzsammlung, München 1999

Koenig & Bauer: *1817 - 1992, 175 Jahre Unternehmensgruppe Koenig & Bauer-Albert*, Jubiläumsschrift, Selbstverlag der KBA

Kranister, Willibald: *Die Geldmacher. Vom Gulden zum Schilling*, 3. Auflage. Edition S, Wien 1988

Kranister, Willibald: *Die Geldmacher International.* Edition S, Wien 1989

L'Art du Billet - Billets de la Banque de France 1800-2000, Musée Carnavalet, 1er Avril - 11 Juin 2000

Löhr, Karlheinz; Holtmann, Heinz: *Unser Geld.* 3. Auflage, Steinbock Verlag, Hannover 1958

Monestier, Martin: *L´Art Du Papier Monnaie*, Editions du Pont Neuf, Paris 1982

North, Michael: *Das Geld und seine Geschichte, vom Mittelalter bis zur Gegenwart*, Verlag C.H.Beck, München 1994

Origo, Iris: *The Merchant of Prato*, Francesco di Marco Datini, The Reprint Society, London 1959

Padoa-Schioppa, Tommaso: »Der Euro und die Politik«, in: *Internationale Politik*, Heft 8/2000,

Persijn, Alexander und Jungmann-Stadler, Franziska: *Kostbarkeiten aus der HYPO-Geldscheinsammlung*, Heinrich Gietl Verlag, Regenstauf 1994

Pick, Albert: *Papiergeld-Lexikon.* 3. überarb. Aufl., Heinrich Gietl Verlag, Regenstauf 1992

Prell, Jan Hendrik; Böttge, Horst: *Giesecke & Devrient 1852 - 2002: Werte im Wandel der Zeit*, Dt. Sparkassen-Verl., Stuttgart 2002

Rebeyrolles, Jean: *La folie des Billets De Banque*, Éditions Flammarion 2003

Renesse, Rudolf L. van, editor: *Optical Document Security, second edition*, Artech House, London-Boston 1997

Report of the government accounting office. Oesterreichische Banknoten- und Sicherheitsdruckerei GmbH, Reihe Bund 2005/11.

Roesner, Charles edit.: *The World of De La Rue. The Old World And The New*, presented on the occasion of the One Hundred and Fiftieth Anniversary of The House of De La Rue 1813-1963, London 1963

Samhaber, Ernst: *Das Geld - eine Kulturgeschichte,* Keysersche Verlagsbuchhandlung, München o.J.

Solomon, Robert: *Policy Brief no. 42,* Jan. 1999, Brookings Institution.

Von der Baumwolle zum neuen Geldschein, eine neue Banknotenserie entsteht, 2. Auflage, Deutsche Bundesbank 1996

von Hayek, Friedrich A.: *Entnationalisierung des Geldes. Eine Analyse der Theorie und Praxis konkurrierender Umlaufmittel,* J.C.B. Mohr, Tübingen 1977

Walz, Karlheinz: *Falschgeld. Spannendes und Kriminalistisches, Ernstes und Amüsantes aus der Welt der Geldfälscher,* Heinrich Gietl Verlag, Regenstauf 1999

Williams, Chris H.: *European Markets for Security Printing – Strategic Forecasts and Technology Trends to 2004,* The Pira International Market Intelligence Series, Pira International Ltd. 2000

Yes! A journal of positive futures, issue no. 2 , Bainbridge Island, Spring 1997

References

Chapter 1

1 Samthaber, Ernst: *Das Geld – eine Kulturgeschichte,* Keysersche Verlagsbuchhandlung, Munich, undated.

2 An impressive account of the beginnings is offered by Origo, Iris: *The Merchant of Prato, Francesco di Marco Datini,* The Reprint Society, London, 1959.

3 Spain honored this achievement in an unusual way. When the Spanish central bank, Banco de Espana, issued the first banknote in the world with an image of an historical personality, it did not choose for this purpose a famous Spaniard, but rather Gutenberg. This choice of a foreigner remained the unique instance in the history of banknotes; see also Brion, René et Moreau, Louis; *Le billet dans tous ses États, du premier papier-monnaie à l'Euro,* Fonds Mercator, Anvers 2001, p. 49.

4 North, Michael: *Das Geld und seine Geschichte, vom Mittelalter bis zur Neuzeit,* Verlag C.H. Beck, Munich, 1994.

5 The Bank of England, the »mother of all central banks,« was not nationalized until 1946. It also experienced liquidity pinches and payment interruptions, although in the final analysis it met every repayment obligation in its history of more than three hundred years.

6 See also: Binswanger, Hans Christoph: *Geld und Magie. Deutung und Kritik der modernen Wirtschaft,* Edition Weitbrecht, Stuttgart 1985, as well as Schöne, Albrecht: *Johann Wolfgang Goethe – Faust, vol. II , Kommentare,* fifth edition, Insel Verlag, Frankfurt 2003.

7 Galbraith, Kenneth John: *Money, whence it came, where it went.* Bantam Books, New York, 1975. See also: Goodwin, Jason: *The Almighty*

Moneymakers, Klaus W. Bender

ISBN: 3-527-50236-X

Dollar and the Invention of America, Henry Holt and Company, New York, 2003.

8 Benjamin Franklin's newspaper, *Pennsylvania Gazette,* excused itself to its readers in 1736 for its irregular publishing schedule with the unusual explanation that its publisher, Franklin – and his printing press – were currently fully occupied with the printing of paper money to promote the public good, as quoted by Galbraith, loc. cit., p. 66.

9 Galbraith: *Money ...,* p. 71.

10 Von Hayek, Friedrich A.: *Entnationalisierung des Geldes. Eine Analyse der Theorie und Praxis konkurrierender Umlaufmittel,* J.C.B Mohr, Tübingen, 1977.

11 With more than 300,000 banknotes, Munich's GSS ranks among the three largest collections of banknotes in the world beside the Smithsonian Institution in Washington and the British Museum in London. Since the Bayerische Hypotheken- und Wechsel-Bank once had the privilege of issuing money, its GSS institute still automatically receives gratis from central banks today a reference specimen of every new banknote. This is done, moreover, with proprietary reservations: In the event that GSS is dissolved, all notes must be returned to the central banks that issued them. Unfortunately, the public has only limited access to this collection of monetary paper.

12 See also Gabriel, Gottfried: *Ästhetik und Rhetorik des Geldes,* frommann-holzboog Verlag, Stuttgart-Bad Cannstadt, 2002.

13 The Grand Duchy of Finland, which belonged to the czarist empire, was permitted to issue its own banknotes starting in 1860. Today's Setec OY was founded in 1885 as a banknote printer.

14 See Brion et Moreau: loc. cit., pp. 37, 41.

15 *Frankfurter Allgemeine Zeitung,* April 30, 2003.

16 *Financial Times,* Oct. 4, 1999.

17 *Süddeutsche Zeitung,* June 25, 2003.

18 Deysson, Christian: »Geld. Schöner Schein,« in: *Wirtschaftswoche,* Vol. 28 of July 3, 2003.

19 Jordan, Jerry L., presentation at the conference, The Future of Money in the Information Age, Cato Institute's 14th annual monetary conference, May 23, 1996. The British company Air Miles, for example, offered in autumn 2003 to convert accumulated gifts of air miles into »money« that would be stored on a chip card. This virtual money could then be used freely to pay for flight, hotel or car-rental bookings.

See also: *International Herald Tribune,* Nov. 21, 2003.

20 Gladisch, Erwin et al.: *Münzgeldentwicklung in Deutschland. Eine empirische Studie über den Münzgeld- und Banknotenumlauf in der Bundesrepublik Deutschland mit einer Prognose der Münzgeldnachfrage bis 2007,* Deutsche Bundesbank, 2003.

21 Deysson, loc. cit.

22 England, Catherine: *The Future of Currency Competition,* paper presented at the conference, Cato Institute, loc.cit.

23 Ferguson, Thomas A.: U.S. Currency and the Next Millennium; Currency Conference, Cape Town, May 24-27, 1998; Ferguson left the BEP after 32 years of service in January 2006.

Chapter 2

1 The professional gatherings of this branch of industry are the Banknote Conference, always held in Washington and oriented mainly toward the production of banknotes, and the Currency Conference, which concentrates more on the machinery for processing banknotes. The international police organization Interpol, which has the war against counterfeiting as one of its most important missions, also holds a conference for its 183 members every four years on this special subject. The interval between Interpol conferences was recently shortened by one year because of the mounting danger of counterfeiting.

2 *125 Jahre Wertpapier- und Banknotendruck im Spiegel der politischen und wirtschaftlichen Entwicklung Deutschlands. Ein Bericht aus Anlaß des 125-jährigen Bestehens der Firma Giesecke & Devrient,* Munich, June 1, 1977.

3 Bloom, Murray Teigh: *The Brotherhood of Money. The Secret World of Bank Note Printers,* BNR Press, Port Clinton, Ohio, 1983.

4 *Report,* the magazine of Giesecke & Devrient, 2002/03, p. 11 ff.

5 »Der vielseitige Wertpapierdrucker,« published in: *Der Schweizerdegen,* vol. XII, Art. Institut Orell Füssli AG, Zürich 1949.

6 This possibility, which had previously existed in Europe only in Switzerland and Spain, was created for the euro zone by the ECB in May 2002. See the decision of the ECB Council on a »Framework for the operation of combined electronic payment acceptance and disbursement machines (cash-recycling machines) for banks and other organizations in the euro currency zone, whereby the functions of which machines include the handling of banknotes and their disbursement to the public,« dated May 24, 2002.

Chapter 3

1 The government enterprise is now officially designated Casa Real – Moneda y Timbre.

2 In the lobby of the headquarters of Koenig & Bauer there stands a marble stele with a plaque with golden letters recalling Gualtiero Giori, a gift from Giori to his business partner.

3 The kilogram of the steelplate intaglio machine should cost 9.24 Deutschmarks and the kilogram of the simultaneous dry-offset machine 10.50 Deutschmarks.

4 The cylinder pressure can indeed scarcely be measured, and the cited value serves mainly promotional purposes. The cylinder pressure of 1,000 kilograms per centimeter of line on the paper is technically certified.

5 Engineer Ivan Orlof developed in 1886 a new technology for simultaneous, multicolor printing for the czarist banknote printing facility in St. Petersburg. It had been founded in 1819 in response to counterfeit ruble notes broadly circulated by Napoleon. The technology was also successful abroad, making Orlof rich. The first engraved printing machines using the further developed »Orlof technology,« in which the ink is transferred indirectly to the banknote paper with a rubber-coated roller, was introduced to the market by Koebau-Giori in the beginning of the 1980s and first delivered in 1986 to Gosnak.

6 Gualtiero Giori later signed over his stake holding in Koenig & Bauer to his first-born daughter, Daniela. She promptly sold the block of stock, much to the ire of her father. Part of it fell into the hands of the Italian investment bank Mediobanca S.A. De La Rue divested its Koebau stock in March 2002, a year after it withdrew from the joint venture and just days before closing its financial accounts for the business year 2001. Despite the steep decline in share prices, which also affected the Koebau share in the wake of the exchange crisis, the business report still showed that it grossed earnings of 13.7 million pounds sterling and made an extraordinary profit before tax of 9.5 million pounds sterling.

7 The Buy American Act is one of those – not really so – invisible trade barriers, which the Americans are otherwise zealously combating.

Many countries certainly use dirty tricks in their public procurement programs. The EU is now trying to clean up its act.

8 It was immediately sold by the heirs, the expensive interior appointments auctioned by an auction house in Monte Carlo.

9 One could have searched the archives in vain for a photograph of Roberto Giori – until the turn of the year 1999/2000 and a vacation trip taken by Roberto Giori, with major consequences. Since his private plane had had a technical problem, he took a commercial airliner. He was among the passengers of Indian Airline Flight 814, which was hijacked by Islamic terrorists on its return flight to New Delhi from Katmandu in Nepal and held for a week at an airport in Afghanistan. The »currency king« *(Time Asia)* probably could have paid the ransom they demanded from his pocket money. But luckily the hijackers did not learn who this passenger with the Swiss passport was.

Chapter 4

1 *Frankfurter Allgemeine Zeitung,* Nov. 10, 1997.

2 Sindh High Court, verdict of Sept. 14, 1999.

3 Special Audit Report on Joint Venture between SICPA Holding S.A., Lausanne, Switzerland, and Pakistan Security Printing Corporation, Karachi; Special Audit Report Series 18; Auditor General of Pakistan. Islamabad, October 1998.

4 Ibid., pp. 2 and 18: »SICPA ... came into a position, wherefrom it could force PSPC to roll back its advancements in developing P-5 Intaglio quick set inks.«

5 *Journal de Genève,* June 29, 1996.

6 *L'Agefi,* Lausanne, July 29, 1996.

Chapter 5

1 Exchange-listed De La Rue plc. reported for the business year ended with March 2005 a further slight decline in sales to 643.2 million pounds sterling (948 million euros), with 6,200 employees. But it said that it had more than doubled its pre-tax profit to 49 million pounds sterling (72.2 million euros) and nearly tripled its net profit to 32 million pounds sterling (47.2 million euros). With its limited disclosure requirements, Giesecke & Devrient GmbH said it had raised its group sales for 2004 by 10 percent to 1.16 billion euros, with 7,300 employees. This company succeeded at the same time in lifting its ear-

nings before interest and taxes by 40 percent to 69.7 million euros, while netting profit of 38.4 million euros, an increase of at least one-third from the previous calendar year.

2 The author thanks James C. Warren, the last living member of Ed Tenenbaum's former team, for the details of this episode, not exactly an every-day occurrence in the history of banknotes.

3 The stake holding taken in 1994 most recently had to be reduced to 20.0 percent in 2000 from the previous 26.67 percent.

4 Arjo-Wiggins, which has experienced changing fortunes on the market for banknote paper, is controlled by the Italian industrial family of Agnelli, of Fiat fame. Apart from its Brazilian paper plant Saldo, Arjo-Wiggins acquired the struggling Dutch company Van Houtum & Palm (VHP) of Ugchelen just before the start of euro printing. VHP, which had supplied the Dutch guilder paper exclusively for more than 120 years, fell victim to its own ruinous price war on the export market.

5 The rejection of all competition in its own country did not prevent Crane & Co. from taking over the state-owned Swedish paper manufacturer and banknote printer Tumba Bruk at the end of 2001. Struggling financially but well equipped with machinery, Tumba was supposed to provide access to new technology – broad security threads and production with silk screens. It was also supposed to open the market for euro paper. The U.S.-Swedish »cohabitation« has been proving onerous, however.

6 *The Berkshire Eagle,* May 22, 1997.

7 The research facilities of De La Rue and Portals were not actually combined until years later as part of austerity measures.

8 The highest zloty denominations are again printed by De La Rue, however.

9 Orrel Füssli is a high-security printer and book publisher at the same time. Thanks mainly to well-paid Swiss banknotes, the company in 2004 made estimated sales of 75 million CHF with an output of around 500 million banknotes. Orrel Füssli makes most of its money, however, with specialized application machinery for banknote printing. Joh. Enschedé gives for the »very difficult« year 2004 business year sales of around 20 million euros in banknote printing, on 500 million banknotes produced. The Dutch company, which also prints stamps and commercial products, closed the year with a loss and had to enter a drastic restructuring program.

10 Although Orell Füssli is listed on the stock exchange, Switzerland's national bank has long held a stake of one-third. This stake was exempted from a curtailment of voting rights, which otherwise applied to the share. The national bank has since sold its participation. On the other hand, France's Francois Charles Oberthur, in spite of being heavily indebted to its banks, has gone on the stock exchange only with its subsidiary, FCO Card Systems, which in turn has sold only part of its capital to the public.

Chapter 6

1 From the many publications on the background of this counterfeiting operation, see the factual report of a concentration camp inmate who was forced to work there, namely Burger, Adolf: *Des Teufels Werkstatt. Die Geldfälscherwerkstatt im KZ Sachsenhausen,* Verlag Neues Leben GmbH, expanded edition, Berlin 1999. On the foreign aspects, see Elam, Shraga: *Hitlers Fälscher. Wie jüdische, amerikanische und Schweizer Agenten der SS beim Falschgeldwaschen halfen,* Verlag Carl Ueberreuter, Vienna 2000. On the attempts to play down this crime, see Hagen, Walter: *Unternehmen Bernhard. Ein historischer Tatsachenbericht über die größte Geldfälschungsaktion aller Zeiten,* Verlag Welsermühl, Wels und Starnberg, 1955. Behind the expressively obscure pseudonym „Hagen,» according to information from the Vienna document archive of the Austrian resistance, was an SS lieutenant colonel, Dr. Wilhelm Höttl, who was personally deeply implicated in the crime.

2 Otto later had lively business contacts with the Soviet Union. In a bargaining session he once sat across from a Soviet general, who had fought on the other side at the same time on the same segment of the front line. The two men got along famously, eyewitnesses said later.

3 Information from the Berlin federal archive, Department III, letter of Feb. 20, 1996.

4 Joseph A. Schumpeter developed the idea of the »dynamic entrepreneur,« who drives the economy ahead with his passion for innovation, for the first time in his standard work: *Theorie der wirtschaftlichen Entwicklung,* 1912. Further refined in *Capitalism, Socialism and Democracy* in 1942, this proposition was celebrated particularly during his exile in the United States.

5 *Frankfurter Allgemeine Zeitung,* Sept. 23, 1952.

6 Ibid., Oct. 11, 1955.

7 This segregation of German and export notes in the printing plant of Giesecke & Devrient has long since ceased. The printing presses have to be busy. But even today every request by outsiders to tour the printing hall has to be presented to the Bundesbank for prior authorization.

8 Otto was backed here by Eckhart van Hooven, who was at that time chairman of the supervisory board of Giesecke & Devrient and a managing board member responsible for business with private customers at Deutsche Bank. Van Hooven had recognized that the Eurocheque system would force customers of his bank to keep corresponding balances in their checking accounts. The bank could work in its own favor with this money, which drew low interest. Eurocheque also cemented ties to customers.

9 The new paper factories built by Louisenthal were three each in China and Russia and one each in Iran, Korea, Spain, Uzbekistan, and Poland. Tumba Bruk of the Swedish Reichsbank and Vic-le-Comte of Banque de France were modernized by Louisenthal. Contracts with Indonesia and the Philippines were cancelled because of financing problems. The paper machinery came from Dörries, today Voith-Heidenheim. On the other hand, Giesecke & Devrient built only four banknote printing facilities abroad: in Egypt, Rhodesia, Burma, and Zaire. The printing machinery always had to be purchased for these from Koebau-Giori.

10 The Swedish company ID-Kort A.B. in Solna stumbled upon the isotope Barium 234 at about the same time in its search for a counterfeit-proof marker in the magnetic range for the evolving bank and identification cards. The Swedes had to give up this project, however, because of the population's fear of supposedly threatening radioactive contamination by this isotope. The process was later taken over by the U.S. military.

11 Bloom: *The Brotherhood of Money,* p. 75.

12 The machinery line designation ISS, international security systems, was changed at the start of the 1990s to BPS, banknote processing systems, because there was a fear that the letters »SS« in the designation might call forth a negative reaction in foreign markets.

13 In the course of their research journalists discovered, for example, that Giesecke & Devrient had not filed its financial statements with

the commercial court for a decade as is required by law. Such details contributed substantially to the bad publicity.

14 *Der Spiegel,* no. 1/1996.
15 Deutsche Bundesbank, press release of March 4, 1996.
16 *Der Spiegel,* no. 50/1995.
17 Ibid., no. 49/1995.
18 *Czerwensky Intern,* no. 101 of Dec. 12, 1995.
19 *Süddeutsche Zeitung,* June 7, 2002, and Aug. 5, 2002.
20 Giesecke & Devrient's own production of chip cards in 2004 came to 370 million cards, of which 236 million were microprocessor cards. In the cards division, which includes services as well as chip cards, Giesecke & Devrient made sales of 570 million euros. Industry leader Gemplus had sales of 865 million euros.

Chapter 8

1 *Manager Magazine,* 11/20.
2 *Die Bundesdruckerei – Zukunft aus Tradition. Das neue Wertdruckgebäude der Bundesdruckerei in Berlin.* Undated special document of Bundesdruckerei.
3 *El Nacional,* July 12, 1997; *Quinto dia,* July 25, 1997; *2001,* Sept. 19, 1997.
4 *The Guardian* (Lagos), Sept. 7, 2001.
5 *Deutsche Presse-Agentur* report of July 30, 2000.
6 Federal German finance ministry; printed minutes of the meeting of the budgetary committee on Nov. 16, 2000, on the status of the privatization of Bundesdruckerei GmbH.
7 Interview in *Sicher,* the magazine of the Bundesdruckerei group, March 2001.
8 Authentos' agenda for its task force »Groupwide restructuring and governance,« Oct. 10, 2001.
9. *FAZ,* Feb. 1, 2002.
10 *Financial Times Deutschland,* Aug. 28, 2003.
11 *FAZ,* Aug. 2, 2002.
12 *Berliner Morgenpost,* Nov. 29, 2003.
13 *Times Online,* December 08, 2005.

Chapter 9

1 *Asian Wall Street Journal,* Oct. 10, 2000.

2 See also *FAZ* of Jan. 3, March 11, and April 27, 1967.

3 The facility had been mothballed by the Mexican central bank. It was later sold to Jinchen Ciccone Beijing Security Printing Co. Ltd., a joint venture of Ciccone Calcográfica and the Chinese government for the purpose of producing passports and other travel documents.

4 These machines came from Banca d'Italia, Orell Füssli, Bundesdruckerei, and even the former VEB Wertpapierdruck of Leipzig. All four have bought new plants.

5 Argentine journalist Miguel Bonasso has taken a critical look at Yabran and his machinations. Beyond this specific link, the book is helpful for understanding Argentina's problems today. Bonasso, Miguel: *Don Alfredo,* Editorial Planeta Argentina S.A.I.C., Buenos Aires, 2000.

6 Both licenses had to be sold in 1998 in order to retire bank debts.

7 Yabran supposedly had for a time a personal financial stake in the printer because the shares of the Ciccone brothers had been signed over to him as collateral. The brothers dispute that. Economics Minister Domingo Felipe Cavallo, who had made this assertion in parliament in 1995, later had to withdraw his comment.

8 Seven denominations for Zaire, eight for Angola, two for Paraguay, one for Bahrain, two for Argentina, and one for Uruguay.

9 Although there were an estimated 21.6 million residents in 1970s, the population had risen to an estimated 52.0 million by 2000.

10 When army boss Joseph Désiré Mobutu came to power in 1967, one dollar cost only one zaire. Four million zaires had to be paid for one dollar in 1994. The self-aggrandizing Mobutu set records in not only currency devaluation but also in banknote design. Of a total of 79 types of banknotes issued during his reign over the government, his portrait adorned 71. No other tyrant, not even Saddam Hussein, managed that. See also: Rebeyrolles, Jean: *La folie des Billets De Banque,* Édition Flammarion, 2001.

11 In the 1980s Erwin Blumenthal, who came from Deutsche Bundesbank and ran the liaison office of the International Monetary Fund in Zaire in 1979 and 1982, wrote a report in which he assailed the mismanagement of the economy and »kleptocracy« in Zaire. The »Blumenthal Report« must have been devastating. It received the IMF's very

rare classification of »secret« and is among the very few IMF documents that – despite persistent efforts, even by this author – have not been released even today.

12 Casa de Moneta Argentina has never printed for Zaire, although the collectors catalog asserts this. See also: *Standard Catalog of World Paper Money,* Modern Issues 1961 – Date, Volume Three; edited by Neil Shafer & George S. Cuhaj, Krause Publications, Iola, Wisconsin, 2002.

13 Naim Khanaffer and his Egimex were later identified by a UN commission as being among the principles responsible for the looting of Congolese resources with occupation troops from Burundi, Ruanda, and Uganda. See also: DRC UN Report of the Panel of Experts on the Illegal Exploitation of Natural Resources and Other Forms of Wealth of DR Congo; UN Security Council, Dec. 4, 2001.

14 See also *Le Monde* of June 23 and July 20, 1999, as well as of Jan. 8, May 25, July 15, and Nov. 8, 2002. On the same subject see Singapore's *Strait Times* of Nov. 7, 1999.

15 For the details of this counterfeiting scandal, see Bloom, Murray T.: *Der Mann, der Portugal Stahl, Der größte Schwindel aller Zeiten,* Rororo special edition for Bundesdruckerei, Rowohlt Taschenbuch Verlag GmbH, Reinbek bei Hamburg, 1973.

16 Since there had already been frictions between Ciccone Calcográfica and De La Rue in the past, Ciccone cited these personnel links as „proof» of a plot against it by the English competitor.

17 Following several assassination attempts in Paris, the last one in late autumn 2002, the »dissident and embezzler« – »*dissident et escroc,*« as the daily *Le Monde* called him – was shot to death by hit men in August 2004 on the Spanish Costa del Sol; *Le Monde,* Aug. 18, 2004.

Chapter 10

1 Only eleven countries initially joined the currency union: Belgium, Germany, Finland, France, Netherlands, Ireland, Italy, Luxembourg, Austria, Portugal, and Spain. Greece became the twelfth member on Jan. 1, 2001.

2 Actually a river, Bonanza Creek in Canada's Yukon Territory became the scene of a real gold rush when gold was discovered in its bed in 1896.

3 Bloom, Murray T.: *Der Mann, der Portugal stahl,* loc. cit.

4 Swiss high-security printer Orell Füssli AG of Zurich obtained 76 percent of the capital of Atlantic Zeiser from an investment firm in 2002. The rest of Atlantic Zeiser's capital was held by its management. The purpose of the cooperation was the development of new security features for identifying documents. The market for numbering devices was regarded as saturated, however.

5 The 150-year-old family company, once the world market leader in machines for printing forms and stamps, had to seek insolvency protection at the end of 2000 after a long agony. Parts of the company were acquired by a Dutch investor. The company today is called Drent Goebel and continues to build its full line of machinery.

6 The Algerian state printing plant bought a new web press from Drent Goebel in 2004.

7 In the 19th century France was regarded as not only the center of engraved printing from copper and steel plates. »École francaise du billet de banque,« the French school of banknote printing, is also impressive for its graphics even today, with its imaginative and vividly colorful allegories.

8 For its last series of guilder notes before the introduction of the euro, the Netherlands did indeed choose abstract themes from architecture and geometry. But this was an exception.

9 Bruckner, Pascal, »Sommes-nous devenus suicidaires?« *Le Monde,* June 30, 2005.

10 Giesecke & Devrient counts public money dispensing machines of banks as a separate level of security inspection. Therefore it uses four categories. On this subject, see Prell, Jan Hendrik: *Giesecke & Devrient 1852-2002: Werte im Wandel der Zeit,* Deutsche Sparkassen-Verlag, Stuttgart 2002.

11 Security thread was developed by technicians of Bank of England and Portals shortly before the outbreak of the Second World War as protection against economic sabotage by Germany. It was originally made of metal.

12 See also Renesse, Rudolf L. van, editor: *Optical Document Security,* second edition, Artech House, Boston-London 1997.

13 Depending on the angle from which it is viewed, the OVI ink appears purple-red, olive green, brownish, or shimmering bronze. This color-shifting ink can be found at the bottom right in the large numerals of

the 50, 100, 200, and 500-euro denominations on the reverse side of euro notes.

14 This special ink is now employed on the reverse side of the euro notes on a precisely appointed spot so that the sensors can easily detect it.

15 *FAZ,* July 11, 2000.

16 *FAZ,* March 19, 2001.

17 The assumption was not at all unrealistic. At the end of the first quarter of 2002 only 8.1 billion of the total of 15 billion banknotes for the first installment of supply had been issued.

18 *Report,* the magazine of Giesecke & Devrient, 02/03.

19 http://wikipedia.t-st.de/data/Eurobanknoten or also www.schlaufuchs.at .

Chapter 11

1 Persijn, Alexander and Jungmann-Stadler, Franziska: *Kostbarkeiten aus der HYPO-Geldscheinsammlung,* Heinrich Gietl Verlag, Regenstauf, 1994.

2 Church, Sara E. et. al.: *Counterfeiting and Digital Technology,* lecture at Banknote 2000, Washington, D.C.

3 Press release of Bank for International Settlements, March 9, 2004.

4 Walter, Norbert and Becker, Werner: *Der Euro: Fest im Sattel als Reservewährung,* Deutsche Bank Research, EU-Monitor 28, Sept. 30, 2005.
See also: »Review of the international role of the euro.« European Central Bank (ECB), January 2005.

5 Introduction of the euro is planned by Estonia, Lithuania, and Slovenia for Jan. 1, 2007; by Latvia, Malta, and Cyprus for Jan. 1, 2008; by Slovakia for Jan. 1, 2009. Hungary and the Czech Republic want to introduce the euro in 2010. Poland and Sweden, which has a deferment, have set no date. Report of the EU Commission to the Council, the EU parliament, the EU economic and social committee, the committee of regions, and ECB, KOM (2005) 545 final on Nov. 4, 2005.

6 ECB Annual Report 2004, p. 100.

7 IMF Annual Report 2005.

8 Karczmar, Mieczyslaw: *The U.S. balance of payments: widespread misconceptions and exaggerated worries,* Deutsche Bank Research, International Topics, Sept. 30, 2004; see also Solomon, Robert: »Policy Brief no. 42,« Jan. 1999, Brookings Institution.

9 Lambert, Michael J. and Stanton, Kristine D.: »Opportunities and Challenges of the U.S. Dollar as an Increasingly Global Currency: A Federal Reserve Perspective,« in: *Federal Reserve Bulletin,* September 2001, p. 571.

10 Ibid.

11 The first case of government counterfeiting of coinage was reported in the year 524 BC: Polycrates, at that time the ruler of the isle of Samos in the Aegean Sea, is said to have bribed the Spartan army into lifting its siege of Samos with phony coins of lead. His idea found many imitators in Greece, Rome, and Europe of the late Middle Ages. The British embellished warfare with bogus money and then paper money. As described, phony notes were used as a weapon in the American Revolution. Napoleon later counterfeited the paper money of the Hapsburgs and of the czarist Russian empire. And Hungarian irredentas led by Minister Ludwig von Windischgrätz after the First World War sought to finance the struggle for the recovery of territory lost to Hungary in the peace treaty with counterfeit banknotes. The Nazis, however, undertook the most perfidious attempt at this type of economic warfare with their Operation Bernhard. The Albanian master spy Elyesa Bazna, aka »Cicero,« was paid with counterfeit pound sterling notes from a workshop in the Sachsenhausen concentration camp. Cicero served the British ambassador in Turkey. The bogus pound notes were also used to free Mussolini from captivity in the Apennines. And they were used to buy important war materials by lavishly bribing corrupt captains in Portuguese ports to sell cargoes earmarked for the Allies to Nazi Germany. In his book *Promises to Pay,* Derrick Byatt says that a total of 9 million bogus British pound notes with a combined face value of 134.5 million were printed in Sachsenhausen. This was a huge amount of money in those days. After the end of the war, the Bank of England sought to quantify the damage to the British economy in the *Reeves Report,* named for a member of the investigating commission from its own banknote printing plant. This secret report with its alarming conclusion is today officially said to have disappeared. The concentration camp's excellent counterfeit notes forced the central bank to declare as invalid a complete series of white pound notes printed on one side.

12 See www.fedpol.ch.

13 According to the German Ministry of the Interior, ECB in 2004 registered 887,085 instances of bogus euro cash, an increase of 38 percent from 2003. Internet press release of the Ministry of the Interior, July 12, 2005.

14 In the period January to September 2005, 629,000 counterfeit euro banknotes with a total face value of 42.7 million euros were registered. Of these, 243,000 bogus bills with a total face value of 20.3 million euros were confiscated by the police. In the period January to September 2004, 574,000 counterfeit euro banknotes with a total face value of 35.0 million euros were registered. Of these, 142,000 notes with a total face value of 9.4 million euros were confiscated by the police. Of the 629,000 bogus notes mentioned for the period January to September 2005, 220,000 were found in Italy; 110,000 in France; and 80,000 in Spain. Apart from the rising number of counterfeit notes, the sharp rise in the face value is particularly conspicuous. More and more excellent counterfeit euros with high denominations are finding their way to Euroland from eastern Europe especially.

15 *Von der Baumwolle zum Geldschein, eine neue Banknotenserie entsteht,* 2d edition, Deutsche Bundesbank, Frankfurt, 1996.

Chapter 12

1 Report of the government accounting office. Oesterreichische Banknoten- und Sicherheitsdruckerei GmbH, Reihe Bund 2005/11.

2 De La Rue and Francois Charles Oberthur Fiduciaire no longer participate in euro note printing. Giesecke & Devrient prints its share only at its Munich printing plant.

3 Cour des Comptes. La Banque de France – Rapport au président de la République suivi des réponses des administrations et des organismes intéressés, March 2005.

4 Guidelines of the European Central Bank of Sept. 16, 2004, on the procurement of euro banknotes, ECB/2004/18.

5 The EuPBA has its seat in Brussels. The five founding members are Bundesdruckerei (Germany), De La Rue (UK), Joh. Enschedé (Netherlands), Francois Charles Oberthur Fiduciaire (France), and Giesecke & Devrient (Germany).

6 Ardizzone, Vittorio Emanuele: „Dalle banconote nazionali ad una banconota unica per un sistema – nuovi fattori di successo tra cooperazione e competizione« (paper presented at the 18th International Security Printers Conference, Sept. 26-28, 2001, Sorrento, Italy).

Index

Moneymakers, Klaus W. Bender

ISBN: 3-527-50236-X